Anonymous

The One Hundred and Fiftieth Anniversary, 1748-1898

Of the Congregational Church of East Hampton, (Chatham,) Conn

Anonymous

The One Hundred and Fiftieth Anniversary, 1748-1898
Of the Congregational Church of East Hampton, (Chatham,) Conn

ISBN/EAN: 9783337007591

Printed in Europe, USA, Canada, Australia, Japan

Cover: Foto ©Lupo / pixelio.de

More available books at **www.hansebooks.com**

THE

ONE HUNDRED AND FIFTIETH

ANNIVERSARY

1748–1898

OF

The Congregational Church of East Hampton, (Chatham,) Conn.

———✠———

November 30, 1898.

PRESENT CHURCH EDIFICE.

PROGRAMME.

MORNING SERVICE BEGINNING AT 10 O'CLOCK.

Organ Voluntary, - - - - - - - Miss Lola Barton.
Anthem—"Send out Thy Light," - - - - - - Gounod.
Scripture Reading and Prayer, - - - - Rev. C. W. Collier.
Solo—"He shall feed His flock," - - - - - - Handel.
            Miss Lois J. Barton.
Welcome by the Pastor, - - - - - Rev. William Slade.
Duett—"Love Divine," - - - - - - - Stainer.
      Miss May Boutelle and Mr. Newton Curtis.
Historical Address, - - - - - - Rev. Joel S. Ives.
Hymn 651—"How firm a foundation."
A Sketch of the Life of Rev. John Norton,
    first Pastor of the Church, - - - - Mr. Martin L. Roberts.
Hymn 781—"For all thy saints who from their labors rest."
                Benediction.
                  Postlude.

Collation at Siebert's Hall at 12:30 o'clock.

AFTERNOON SERVICE AT 2:30 O'CLOCK.

                Organ Voluntary.
Anthem—"Praise ye the Father," - - - - - - Gounod.
Reading of Letters from former Pastors.
Solo—"Come unto Him," - - - - - - Handel.
           Miss Boutelle.
Address, - - - - - - - - Rev. H. E. Hart.
Hymn 770—"Blest be the tie."
Address, - - - - - - - - Rev. C. W. Collier.
Solo—"Fear not ye, O Israel," - - - - - - Buck.
           Mr. Curtis.
Words of Congratulation and Reminiscence, - *Rev. E. E. Lewis.
                                    *Rev. A. W. Hazen, D. D.
Prayer, - - - - - - - - - By the Pastor.
Hymn, written for the occasion by - - - Rev. Joel S. Ives.
                Benediction.
                Postlude.

* Not present. Account of the Inside of the Old Church introduced.

ANNIVERSARY HYMN.

Tune: Stockwell.

Bells are ringing! Bells are ringing!
  Everywhere the world around,
Calls to duty, calls to danger,
  Peals of praise, or sadder sound.

Toil and skill have wrought the music,
  Willing hands and earnest thought;
Year to year has told the secret
  Closely kept and dearly bought.

Hearken! What is now the message?
  "Holiness unto the Lord!"
Hear, Our Father, while we praise Thee,
  With Thy blessing speed The Word.

As the Lake pours out its treasure,
  Failing not from year to year,
So Thy saints have brought their worship,
  Sire and son, in holy fear.

Witnesses are 'round about us;
  Holy mem'ries stir within.
Comforter, Divine Redeemer,
  Cheer our hearts, forgive our sin.

Heavenly blessings, never lacking,
  Thou hast given in the Past:
Blessings more abundant ever
  Grant us, even to the last!

REV. WILLIAM SLADE,
Acting Pastor, 1897.

INTRODUCTION.

IN SENDING out this record of our Anniversary, it seems fitting that there should be a word of introduction. For several years the people of the church had been looking forward to their one hundred and fiftieth birthday, hoping to celebrate it in some becoming manner. At the annual church meeting on January 13, 1898, the following resolution was proposed by Deacon H. D. Chapman, and passed:

Resolved, That this church observe the one hundred and fiftieth anniversary of its organization with services appropriate to the occasion, and that a committee be appointed to act with a committee of the society, to make all suitable arrangements and provisions for the proper carrying out of this resolution.

The committees were appointed, whose names will be found in this volume. They all worked with enthusiasm and fidelity. These committees together formed a general committee, which appointed sub-committees. A. A. Bevin was chosen chairman of the general committee; S. Mills Bevin served as clerk, and H. D. Chapman as treasurer. If one were to single out a committee for special praise among all who did so well, it would be the collation committee. They prepared in Siebert's Hall a repast most abundant and attractive for a multitude of friends who could not come, and then these hard working women did outwit the weather, carrying through the feast without financial loss.

It was at first proposed to have the celebration on the 28th of September, before the boisterous weather of late fall. It was found, however, that our historians wished more time for their work, and especially desired the Anniversary to occur on the actual date, November 30th, when the church would complete its century and a half. This date was therefore chosen, and more time given for preparation and investigation. Indeed, the thorough work represented in this book could hardly have been done by busy people except by extending the time.

At last the day came, and what a day! The Sabbath before had warned us of what might be, for as the pastor looked from his study window he could not see the beautiful church spire till near 12 o'clock, so thick was the air with drifting snow. Even the sexton staid at home from church that day. There was a little pleasant weather, then came Wednesday, the 30th, with another blizzard. The streets were filled with drifts. The trains were blocked and several hours late. Some brave descendants of brave John Norton reached us from Willimantic and Portland. These, with those who had come to town the night before, represented the outside world of all the friends who had planned to rejoice with us. The people were disappointed, but decided to go on with the exercises. We shall not forget the generosity of those who with their horses and sleighs brought the stranded ones to the church. Nor will some forget the ride on an ox sled from Barton Hill to the church. But all regretted especially the disappointment of those whose health or years prevented a ride over the drifts and in the storm to a service they had been looking forward to with so much pleasure. This day was probably an "old-fashioned winter," come back to make more vivid the days of long ago, a specimen of the environment in which our fathers struggled for existence, but a day in which we had a service of inspiring memories, music, and devotion.

The exercises proceeded as the programme indicates, with the exception of the words of reminiscence and congratulation. These were omitted, Rev. A. W. Hazen, of the North Church, Middletown, being ill, and Rev. E. E. Lewis, of Haddam, being kept at home by the storm. In place of these addresses the pastor introduced an interesting description of the inside of the old church, given him by Miss Julia A. West, granddaughter of Rev. Joel West. It would be quite impossible to reproduce the impromptu speeches at the table. They were made by the Rev. F. W. Coleman, of the Methodist Church; Rev. C. W. Collier, a former pastor; David Strong, a former resident of the town, and Rev. Joel S. Ives, pastor from 1874 to 1883, and were a fine combination of laughable and sober thoughts, with some very remarkable stories effectively told.

There was in the vestry a fine collection of relics and mementoes, of which a full catalogue was made, and a sermon by the Rev. John Norton was printed from an ancient manuscript and served as a souvenir of the day.

There is an appendix added to the record of the Anniversary which we trust will be especially valuable, since it gathers as far as possible the names of those whose lives and devotion have made the spiritual substance of this venerable church. It gathers, too, the petitions and old papers that record the beginnings of church and town life, and there are short sketches of deacons whose faithful lives have kept the faith steady and strong. But it remains for some future chronicler to write more fully the story of this church and town, for church and town grew on together. The business meetings of the church were the business meetings of the town. In those meetings they provided for the first public schools as well as for the preaching of the gospel. This volume is therefore only a beginning towards a fuller knowledge of those days of first things, of hard work, and faith in God, of which the present town of Chatham reaps the fruits.

Special appreciation and thanks should here be extended to Martin L. Roberts and S. Mills Bevin for their continuous and faithful work in gathering the materials that make the appendix such a valuable store of history for those who have this town as their home or their birthplace.

EAST HAMPTON, August 1, 1899.

Prayer.

Lord, thou hast been our dwelling-place in all generations; before the mountains were brought forth or ever thou hadst formed the earth or the world, even from everlasting to everlasting, thou art God. We feel like crying with thy servant of old: What is man that thou art mindful of him, or the son of man that thou visitest him! We are but of yesterday, but thou dost endure throughout all generations. Our little systems have their day; they have their day and cease to be, and thou, O Lord, art more than they! Into this refuge of thy power, thy care, thy love, at this time we would retreat.

For we remember at this time that the kingdom is thine; not ours, but thine; for thine is the kingdom, the power, and the glory, forever and ever. The church is thine; it was born not of blood, nor of the will of the flesh, nor of the will of man, but of God. Thou didst redeem it with the precious blood of Christ. And we would thank thee, not only that thou didst bring thy church to pass, but that thou hast preserved it also through the tempests of the ages, that thou hast brought to naught the wrath of man that stormed against it, and hast prevailed, too, over the weakness and frailty of thy people. As thou didst feed thine ancient people with manna, and as thou didst open fountains for them in the wilderness, so hast thou nourished thy people unto this day with manna from on high that has sustained their souls.

We thank thee for the unspeakable heritage that has come to us through thy church; for apostles, prophets, martyrs; for holy men of old who spoke as they were moved by the Holy Ghost, for the revelation of thyself made to men through them; we thank thee for the services of thy house, for the place of worship, that our faith is not of yesterday, but has been hallowed by holy men through ages; we thank thee that we, too, can join therein, can unite our voice with that of thy church universal in its unbroken anthem of gratitude and praise.

We thank thee for this particular church, that thou didst call it to take its place in thy great church universal. Through it thou hast greatly blessed this community; thou hast ministered to it the water of life, thou hast greatly enriched it with the river of God; thou hast blessed all these homes through it; thou hast blessed the bridal hour and made it sacred; thou hast comforted thy people in the hour of death. We thank thee for all thou hast done in this very house. Wert thou to make these walls to speak they would tell of rich ministrations of thy grace: for here thou hast again and again met with men far from thee; thou hast melted the stony heart, thou hast wrought penitence, thou hast forgiven sin, thou hast broken the bonds of sin, thou hast sent them away with a new song in their mouth. O that men would praise the Lord for all his wonderful works! How often, O thou comforter of thy people, hast thou comforted thy people here! They have come to thy house with strength exhausted, with courage almost gone, but thou didst renew their strength, thou didst make them to run and not be weary and to walk and not faint, thou didst make their hearts to mount up like eagles, thou didst restore their souls. Thou hast hallowed this place, not with holy oil as of old, but through the abundant ministration of thy grace, through which thou hast endeared it to thy people as no stranger could tell.

And now we pray for the continuance of thy blessing. Thou dost call us to-day to thanksgiving and praise for what thou hast wrought in the past, yet thou wilt hear our petitions. Thou hast carried this thy church lo these many years, carry thou it for the days to come! Let there be underneath the everlasting arms! Manifest thyself here that thou hast not changed, that thine arm is not shortened that it can not save! Repeat the days of old, and show that thy blessings are indeed new every evening and fresh every morning! Fulfill in the days to come that which thou hast begun, those intimations thou hast given in what thou hast already done, and may this church be as a field which the Lord has blessed, like a tree planted by the rivers of water, like a branch of the true vine of which thou thyself art the husbandman!

In particular we pray that sound wisdom and the Spirit of God may ever dwell with thy people. May the love of God continually be shed abroad in their hearts by the Holy Ghost. Guide thou its pastor; may he live, move, and have his being in God and in the love and confidence of his people. Working together in the fellowship of thy Gospel, may they bring forth much fruit. May there be born into thy kingdom continually such as shall be saved, reclaim to thyself those who fall, fill all this thy church with the spirit of Christian service, and may they count it their chief privilege to walk with Christ and serve thee. So through the years to come, as thou dost perfect the lives of thy servants and minister to them of thy grace, may they in turn minister to thy church of such as thou hast given them, that through thy church there may flow here rivers of living water, of which men shall drink unto eternal life. Hear thou our prayer: yet not according to our words alone, but according to thy church's needs. We ask in faith. For thy church is dearer to thee than to thy servants, dear as the apple of thine eye and graven on thy hands. In Christ's name we pray. *Amen.*

REV. JOEL S. IVES,
Pastor, 1874-1883.

HISTORICAL ADDRESS.

The One Hundred and Fiftieth Anniversary of the First Congregational Church, East Hampton, Conn., November 30, 1898.

"HE who does not take an interest in his ancestors does not deserve to be remembered by his posterity."
Every Christian takes an added interest in recounting the mercies of a covenant keeping God during the days of old. And while clouds of witnesses are around about us, we will listen to the story—the trials and the triumphs of this century and a half, while this church has maintained among these hills and valleys the ordinances of the Gospel in accordance with the Pilgrim faith and form. We are fortunate in being able to celebrate this anniversary upon the very date when this church was organized one hundred and fifty years ago.

It was then the Town of Middletown and the County of Hartford. On this east side of the Connecticut river there was already a church, called East Middletown Parish—now Portland—the church having been organized October 25, 1721. But the excellence of the water privilege caused by the overflow of our beautiful Pocotopaug pond, with its deep and never failing springs, attracted settlers hither, who built a forge for the smelting of iron ore brought from West Point, N. Y., and as iron was in much demand for ship building a considerable business was done. In 1825 a new forge was built, and also a scythe factory.

A petition, dated "Midleton, April 29th, 1743," signed by twenty-five names, states that the "nearest of us" were "five mile distent" and "most of us seven mile" from the "place of publick worship," and that they had hired "by the approbation of the society's committee" a person "approved to preach amongst us for more than six months the last year," and therefore ask relief from one-half the taxes imposed by the society. The twenty-five names are as follows:

John Clark,	Thomas Lewis,	Hezekiah Russ,
Samuel Wadsworth,	Stephen Griffith,	David Bailey,
John Bevin, Junr.,	Jonathan Baley,	Ebenezer Clark,
Jabez Clark,	Joseph Parke,	Shubal Lewis,
Josiah Cook,	William Clark,	William Norket,
William Norket, Junr.,	Isaac Smith,	Ezra Andrews,
James Johnson,	Daniel Young,	William Bevin,
Seth Knowles,	Caleb Johnson,	John Markham.
	Isaac Williams,	

A second petition was sent to "the Honourable Assembly of his Majestyes Colony of Connecticut to be held in New Haven," signed by thirty-six names, and dated October 8, 1744. This states that the former petition was granted, and that some of the petitioners are ten miles distant from a place of worship, "and the Rhoads we are to travel in are very Rough and Bad to Travel in," and while mindful of their "poor circumstances" they are still hopeful of being able to support a minister, and therefore petition that they be set off as a society—the definite bounds being stated—with all the powers of such ecclesiastical societies. The following names appear on the second petition, but not on the first:

John Clark, Junr.,	Aaron Clark,	Samuel Eggleston,
Zaccheus Cooke,	David Cerby (?),	Elisha Cornwell,
Solomon ——— (?),	James Cady,	David Anderson,
Giles Hall,	Hamlin John Hall,	George Hubbard,
Isaac Thompson,	Mary Johnson,	Hezekiah Russ, Junr.

A third petition, presented by Benjamin Stillman as agent, dated April 29, 1746, declares that certain rights were given in answer to the petition of 1744, that they had employed a minister for eleven months each year, that they had increased in strength, and that as "the Society" was about to build a new meeting house, and their taxes would be increased, they "humbly request" that they may be "sett off from said society and be a distinct ecclesiastical society," and to this end that a committee be appointed to view the circumstances and report to the assembly.

At the October session the right was given to lay a tax of fourpence an acre on all laid-out lands for the next three years for the settlement of a minister and the building of a meeting house, full rights of a society having been given and the name East Hampton having been decided upon, probably because some of the settlers were from Eastham, Barnstable County, Massachusetts. At the October session of 1748, on petition of the society "now about to settle the Rev. Mr. Norton in the work of the ministry among them, and asking liberty of this assembly to embody into church estate," it was "Resolved, that they have liberty, and are hereby granted liberty to embody into church estate with the approbation of the neighboring churches." The 30th of November, 1748, marks the date of the consummation of that purpose, which had thus been ripening since the spring of 1743; and even earlier, for the first petition shows that there had been regular preaching here in the year 1742.

This was then the Third* Society of East Middletown, the second being the Middle Haddam Society, organized September 24, 1740. In 1767 this part of Middletown, east of the river, was incorporated as a separate town and named Chatham, from Chatham, England, because of the importance of the shipbuilding. In 1842 the town of Portland was incorporated. It would have been a great improvement if at that time East Hampton had appropriated the name Chatham. I wonder if it is too late for that improvement now!

While the building of the forge at the outlet of the lake was the reason for a settlement in this part of the then town of Middletown, it is the bell business which has given distinction to the place and has been the cause of its prosperity, although every one must regret that the skill and toil of many years have not brought larger wealth to the community.

It appears from the records that William Barton was in Colonel Flower's regiment of Artillery Artificers during the War of the Revolution, with the rank of Captain, and also that his son William served as an assistant to his father. The son later worked in the Springfield Armory, and in 1808 moved to East Hampton and commenced the manufacture of hand and sleigh bells. He first conceived the idea of hollow castings, which enters now so largely into many branches of trade; but it was never patented, although there were "millions in it." It is a remarkable fact that for many years all the cast sleigh

* Middletown sixth.

bells of North America were made in East Hampton or by East Hampton men. The trade seems to be indigenous.

William Barton, son of Capt. William and Sarah (Sage) Barton, was born November 26, 1763, in Kensington, Conn. He married, February 14, 1790, Clarissa, daughter of Ezekiel and Betsy (Penoyer) Betts, born in Sharon, Conn., February 10, 1768. He was probably the first manufacturer of sleigh bells, making them then in two parts and soldering them together. It is said he would make a small quantity and take them to the markets, carrying them on his person, jingling through the streets, and dispose of them. He died July 15, 1849, universally respected and lamented. She died October 4, 1858.

Coffin trimmings were manufactured here in considerable quantities for several years, and for the last twenty years the thread and silk industries have been important. The railroad, although a necessity, has laid a heavy burden of taxation, and doubtless retarded growth, which in spite of hindrances has been considerable.

As a special paper is to be given upon the life and work of the first pastor, the Rev. John Norton, I pass at once to the history of the second pastorate.

After the death of Mr. Norton a committee, consisting of Deacon Isaac Smith, Deacon John Clark, and Captain Silas Dunham, were instructed at a society meeting held "Sept. ye 24th, A. D. 1778," to apply to Mr. Parsons "to preach with us on probation;" and a receipt is on record, signed "Received in full of ye above account, Lemuel Parsons," of seventy-six pounds, fifteen shillings, for preaching thirteen "Sabbaths and one Thanksgiving day." On January 5th, 1779, the society voted to call Mr. Parsons to "settle with them in the Gospel Ministry," upon a "settlement" of two hundred pounds to be paid in four years, by equal installments; his salary during these four years to be seventy pounds, and after the payment of the settlement, eighty pounds a year. This salary and settlement were to be paid in country produce at prices defined in the call; as, for example, rye at three shillings and sixpence per bushel, cheese at fourpence per pound, sheep's wool at one shilling and fourpence per pound, flax at eightpence per pound. There was also added to the salary twenty cords of wood annually.

This was the unsettled and most trying period of the Revolution, and Mr. Parsons, with commendable foresight, being himself a Connecticut Yankee, replied as follows:

"BELOVED:—I have taken into serious consideration your call and invitation to settle with you in the work of the ministry, and take this method to gratefully acknowledge your kind and generous offer, and whereas in the proposals of the society no method of ascertaining what shall from time to time be esteemed an equivalency in current money respecting either settlement or salary, to prevent all difficulty in that respect it is proposed that this shall be fixed by agreement between me and a committee of the society for that purpose chosen from year to year." [The method of choosing this committee here follows:]

"Provided the parish should consent hereto and nothing discouraging should hereafter arise, I hereby signify my consent to settle with you and take the pastoral charge of you. That grace, mercy and peace may be multiplied unto you and yours, through the knowledge of God and Jesus Christ, is the desire and hearty prayer of, gentlemen,

Your humble servant, LEMUEL PARSONS."

These terms were accepted, for his marriage took place the same month and his ordination the following month. The house in which he lived was near the site of the present parsonage. After a pastorate of twelve years he died in office, and was buried in Lakeview Cemetery, where, near the northern entrance, may be found two red sandstone slabs with winged heads, upon one of which may be read this inscription:

In memory of
THE REV. MR. LEMUEL PARSONS,
PASTOR OF THIS CHURCH.

His temper was cheerful, manners kind, and heart benevolent. He lived beloved by relatives, dear to his people, in friendship and esteem with his brethren, and respected by his acquaintance.
He was born in Durham, May 2d, 1753; educated at Yale College, 1773; ordained over this flock Feb. 10th, 1779, and after a short but useful course, he departed in the hope of Christian Salvation, Feb. 14th, 1791, in the 38th year of his age.

Upon the other stone may be read, doubtless in Mr. Parsons' own words:

The memory of an amiable and virtuous consort,
MRS. KATHERINE PARSONS,
who died April 9th, A. D. 1780, in the 26th year of her age,
By an affectionate husband,
THE REVEREND LEMUEL PARSONS,
God adoring and in flesh mourning his own and new born son's
AFFECTING LOSS ON THIS MONUMENT IS INSCRIBED.

Virtuous bands of Hymen's yoke,
By death's rough hands can ne'er be broke,
Each kindred mind by grief refined,
With Angels joined, its mate shall find.

In connection with this passionate and poetical burst of affection must be recorded the cold fact that the disconsolate widower married before the Christmas season of the same year, viz., December 12th, 1780, Faith, the daughter of the Rev. Ephraim and Elizabeth (Woodbridge) Little, of Colchester, who survived him and married John Partridge, of Dalton, Mass., April 18, 1796. The first wife was the daughter of John and Ann Coe, of Durham. Mr. Parsons was fifth in descent from Cornet Joseph and Mary (Bliss) Parsons, of Springfield, Mass.*

It should be remembered to the credit of the parish and of the ministerial brethren of the neighborhood, that just one month from Mr. Parsons' death the following vote was passed: "That the widow of the Rev. Mr. Parsons shall have the liberty to supply the pulpit six months from the first of January last, and will pay her according to our covenant with the Reverend Mr. Parsons during his life, for such proportion of the time as she does supply the pulpit." At the same meeting Deacon Isaac Smith, Deacon John Clark, Captain James Bill, Bryan Parmelee, Esq., and Ensign Gideon Arnold were chosen a committee "to use their discretion in hiring a candidate." But their labors were not immediately successful. The church was pastorless for a year and eight months. During this time the Rev. David Porter, D. D., a native of Hebron and a graduate of Dartmouth College, and who died at Catskill, N. Y., at the age of eighty-nine, after a long and successful ministry, preached for several weeks near the end of 1791.

April 30, 1792, the society voted that the committee "apply to Mr. West to preach with us upon probation for four Sabbaths;" and May 21st they were directed to "apply to Mr. West to preach with us till the first of September next." August 8th, a committee of nine men from different parts of the parish were chosen to bring in proposals as to Mr. West's

---

* Rev. Samuel Parsons, son of Lieut. Samuel and Elizabeth (Chipman) Parsons, was born in Durham, Conn., May 2, 1753. He married first, January 28, 1779, Catharine, daughter of John Coe, of Durham, who died April 9, 1780; he married second, December 12, 1780, Faith, daughter of the Rev. Ephraim and Elizabeth (Woodbridge) Little, of Colchester, who survived him and married, April 18, 1796, John Partridge, of Dalton, Mass.

Children by first wife: John, born March, 1780, married Abigail Faxon, Attica, N. Y.

Children by second wife: Samuel, born November, 1781; Catharine, born 1784, married Dr. Charles Stewart; Nancy Woodbridge, born 1786, married Quartus Knight.

settlement. They were George Cummings, Moses Cook, Lemuel West, Timothy Rogers, Isaac Smith, Jr., Nehemiah Gates, Bryan Parmelee, Samuel Sexton, and Selah Jackson. On the 20th of the same month the proposal of the eastern committee (Rogers, Smith, and Gates) was accepted, and at an adjourned meeting, September 3, 1792, it was voted to offer two hundred pounds for a settlement, with salary of seventy pounds for four years, and eighty pounds after the settlement was paid. Possibly Mr. Parsons' health had put the parish to some expense, for a proviso is added that if it became needful to hire assistance the salary should be cut down one-half.

The Rev. Joel West was the oldest child of Captain Samuel and Sarah (Hunt) West, and was born March 12, 1766, in that part of Lebanon then known as "The Crank," and which was in 1800 incorporated as the town of Columbia. He graduated from Dartmouth College in 1789, and studied divinity under Rev. David McClure, of South Windsor, where he united with the church on confession of faith in 1790. He was licensed to preach November 18, 1790, and was ordained the third pastor of this church October 17, 1792. His emigrant ancestor was Francis West, born in 1606, in Salisbury, Eng., and was in the line of John and Priscilla Alden of the "Mayflower" company. March 11, 1794, he married Elizabeth, the daughter of the Rev. Thomas and Eunice (Lathrop) Brockway, who was born November 28, 1774, and died September 28, 1853. It is related that he brought his bride home in a carriage, the first that had been seen in the place, and this with the fact that she had the first carpet, awakened both curiosity and envy. Eleven children were born to them; descendants of whom are still members of this church, and proofs of the vitality of the "Mayflower" blood, than which no one can boast a nobler heraldry.

Mr. West was a man of sunny and hopeful disposition, and was greatly beloved by this people. Especially during the first part of the pastorate religion was at a low ebb. For years there was not a member of the church upon whom he could call for a public prayer. There were a few faithful women. Many withdrew from the society by certificate. The half-way covenant was working out its inevitable results. But the faithful pastor labored on and better days came. "The Great

18   CONGREGATIONAL CHURCH OF EAST HAMPTON.

Revival" as it was called of 1818 and 1819 followed, and it was indeed a "New Way" throughout New England. Taxation for the support of the church was gradually done away with. The flood of infidelity which had swept over the country was stayed. The standard of church membership was raised. Fifty-two were admitted to the church, among them strong men, pillars in the church, of mighty influence in the whole community. I may mention in this list Sparrow Smith, Eleazur Veazey, David Buell, Lazarus Watrous, Nathaniel C. Smith, Willard Sears, Horace Clark, and Diodate D. West.

As indicative of the feeling of church union then prevalent the following vote of March, 1819, is interesting: "That the several brethren might be at liberty to invite to our communion a friend belonging to another denomination of Christians, if he had a desire for it."

After a pastorate of thirty-four years, the Rev. Joel West died suddenly, October 26, 1826, in the sixtieth year of his age. He was buried in Lakeview Cemetery, only a short distance from his residence, the house in which his son, Diodate B. West, always lived, and now occupied by his granddaughters, the Misses Mary A. and Julia A. West.

CHILDREN OF REV. JOEL WEST.

Nancy Brockway, born Oct. 28, 1795; died Nov. 15, 1795.
Brackett, born Feb. 21, 1797; died March 4, 1797.
Diodate Brockway, born July 20, 1798.
Eveline Orvilla, born May 19, 1800.
Delia Elliott, born April 21, 1804; married J. W. B. Smith.
Betsey Emeline, born Sept. 11, 1806; married Justin Dickinson.
Brackett Mortimer, born Sept. 4, 1808.
Alice Amanda, born April 13, 1810; died October 29, 1841.
Maranda Matilda, born Oct. 31, 1812; married Erastus Day, of Colchester.
Chittenden Griswold, born 1814; died Nov. 5, 1814.
Samuel Wales, born Dec. 3, 1815; died Jan. 22, 1846.
Stiles Davenport, born Oct., 1818; died Dec. 4, 1818.

Deacon D. B. West united with the church July 4, 1819, and was elected deacon December 11, 1823. He died June 14, 1881, being eighty-three years old, having been a member of the church sixty-two years and an officer fifty-eight years—a very remarkable record.

The first deacons of the church were Ebenezer Clark, John Clark, and Isaac Smith. (See appendix.)

The members of the association supplied the pulpit for some time in aid of Mrs. West. But church affairs were evidently less prosperous, for help was received during the next year from the Missionary Society of Connecticut, and Rev. William Case, of Chester, writing to Dr. Leonard Bacon, at that time the secretary, says: "Aid from your society will probably be the means of saving them from an entire deprivation of the privilege of the gospel." The grand list of the community was then $6,481, viz., Baptists $546, Methodists $570, Congregationalists $2,468, with no society $2,895. The population was about 1,000.

March 14, 1828, it was voted that "the members of this meeting feel a willingness to settle the Reverend Timothy Stone in the work of the ministry if they can obtain the sum of ninety-six dollars from the domestick Missionary Society, and raise a sufficient sum by subscription to pay him his salary." Deacon Warren A. Skinner was appointed a committee to secure this aid, and his letter to Dr. Bacon says: "By the utmost exertions we shall raise two hundred and ten or twenty dollars. With this and the aid of $96 a year for five years we shall be able to settle the Rev. Timothy Stone." Mr. Stone's salary was fixed at three hundred dollars.

The Rev. Timothy Stone was born in Goshen, in the town of Lebanon, May 29, 1774, where his father, of the same name, was pastor from 1766 till his death in 1797. His mother was Eunice, daughter of the Rev. Solomon Williams. At the age of thirteen, while preparing for college, he suffered a stroke of paralysis from which his organs of speech never fully recovered. For this reason he studied for some time the art of painting with the celebrated John Trumbull, also a native of Lebanon. Afterward, becoming a subject of Divine Grace, he resolved to enter the ministry, and placed himself under the instruction of President Dwight and lived in his family. November 20, 1803, he was ordained pastor of the church in South Cornwall. In 1804 Yale conferred upon him the degree of M. A. After a pastorate of nearly twenty-five years he was dismissed, and installed pastor here June 4, 1828.

Mr. Stone's letters to the Missionary Society give various facts of interest. It would appear that the first Sabbath School was begun during 1828, and that in the same year a temperance society was formed. During a revival in 1829, "more than sixty, including all classes and denominations, are now indulging a hope of regeneration." In 1830 he writes it is "becoming more and more manifest" that the "church could not prosper on union principles." In 1831, that "fifteen years ago the Baptists threatened to swallow up the Congregational Church." In the same letter: "my good members and my deacons have been too fond of mingling with the Methodists in their meetings, allured by the cheering sound of Christian union." Also he saw that he "damped their devotion" by discountenancing women taking part in prayer meetings and by insisting upon the direction of the meetings. The "ardent brethren" evidently made it somewhat uncomfortable for the pastor, and he was dismissed February 7, 1832, being "cordially recommended as a faithful and worthy minister of Christ to confidence and employment."

Mr. Stone was a man of great simplicity of character and singleness of purpose. Owing to the ill-health of his wife she did not remove from South Cornwall, and after his dismission he returned there, where he died April 14, 1852, being held in high respect by all. The Rev. Timothy Dwight Porter Stone, late of Springfield, was his son.

It is very interesting to remember that we have two living representatives of Mr. Stone's pastorate—Mr. John William Burke Smith and Mrs. Alice S. (Bevin) Child, who united with the church in 1833—sixty-five years ago! Mr. David Watson Watrous and Mrs. Laura A. (Markham) Skinner are next in age, having united with the church in 1842 during the pastorate of Mr. Smith. Mrs. Amanda M. Clarke, Mrs. Belinda Bevin Veazey, and Mrs. Amelia A. Watrous have also been members for more than fifty years, having united with the church in 1846, while the Rev. William Russell was pastor.

Questions of Old School and New School—East Windsor or New Haven—began about this time to agitate the theologians. Samuel Ives Curtis was employed to supply the vacant church. Middlesex Consociation was Old School and Mr. Curtis had graduated from New Haven. Mr. Parsons, of East Haddam, and Dr. Harvey, of Westchester, were champions of the "faith once delivered to the saints" on East Windsor Hill, but not to

REV. SAMUEL I. CURTIS.
Pastor, 1832-1837.

Dr. Taylor at New Haven! Middlesex Consociation was true to its convictions and refused ordination; the church was true to its purpose and called a council, which ordained Mr. Curtis, the fifth pastor.

Samuel Ives Curtis, the son of Ivah and Hannah (Ives) Curtis, was born in Meriden, March 5, 1803; Yale Seminary, 1829-32; approbated to preach by New Haven East Association, 1831, and ordained here November 1, 1832. He was dismissed November 21, 1837. Served the church at North Woodstock about two years, when he was called to the church in Union in April, 1839, and was installed there April 12, 1843, remaining as pastor till his death, March 26, 1880.

October 2, 1832, he married Rebecca T. Hough, of Wallingford, who with her daughter Ann was killed by lightning in her home in Union, Fast Day, March 25, 1842. Her son, Rev. George Curtis, is pastor at Mayville, North Dakota. His second wife was Eliza, the daughter of the Rev. Jesse Ives, one of the first pastors of the Congregational Church in Monson, Mass. Their only child was Samuel Ives Curtis, Jr., born February 5, 1844; Amherst, 1867; and now Professor of Biblical Literature in Chicago Theological Seminary. His third wife was the granddaughter of the Rev. Daniel Grosvenor.

It was during this pastorate that the square pews were removed from the church. There was a marked revival during 1833.

After an interim of six months the Rev. Rufus Smith began to supply, June 10, 1838, and "an ecclesiastical council was convened at the house of Mr. Harvey Arnold, September 18, 1838," and after "a thorough examination" it was voted to proceed with the ordination exercises on the following day. He was the son of Matthew and Anna (Strickland) Smith, of Chaplin, Conn., and was born April 26, 1795. He was for a time a physician in Griswold, afterward studied theology at Yale, and was approbated to preach by the New London Association, May 30, 1836.

He was a strict disciplinarian and had high views of the powers of a pastor. His formula for the prayer meeting was: "Brother West, will you pray? Brother Skinner, will you remark?" Deacon West told me that upon returning from a meeting at Wethersfield he kneeled down to pray in a prayer meeting without being called upon by Mr. Smith, but was at once stopped with the decided remark, "I must have order in my meetings." I have been also told that Mr. Smith asked the brethren to meet him at the Arnold house where he lived, a certain Sunday noontime, with the remark, "I want to consult with you, but I shall do as I choose in the matter!" He was greatly troubled by Abby Kelly and "her followers." And no doubt he had just cause. In closing his report to the Missionary Society he says, "This will be a good society: when, the Lord only knows!" Two years later he writes, "In degree, the susceptibilities of this people to novelty and ultraism are certainly unusual. The wisdom of Solomon and the strength of Samson would not hold them with bit and bridle." Poor man, how little he understood human nature! In 1842 he reports that they had almost succeeded in raising funds to build a new church. In 1844 he is more hopeful, and believes the society will be able to get along without aid and also build a church. Ill health and the evident friction between himself and certain members of the church induced him to ask for a dismission, which was granted June 24, 1845. He had no other pastorate, and died in East Hartford, June 1, 1854.

Although there are these recollections and records which cause us to smile, his seven years' pastorate was evidently productive of blessing and helpfulness. There was need doubtless of a strong hand and a firm loyalty to Congregational principles and methods. And it should be remembered that the church has never after this needed aid from the Missionary Society. The whole amount granted between 1827 and 1844 was $1,339. The offerings to Home Missions from this church have been more than twice the amount of aid rendered, while the total charities are more than nine times that amount.

Early in October, 1845, the Rev. William Russell, son of Alden and Sarah (Andrews) Russell, and great-great-grandson of the Rev. John Norton,* the first pastor, began his work

---
* Rev. John Norton married Eunice Hitchcock.
Son, John Norton, Jr., married Ede Clark.
Daughter, Sarah Norton, married Elizur Andrews.
Daughter, Sarah Andrews, married Alden Russell.
Son, William Russell, married, May 10, 1842, Sarah Elizabeth Brown, of New Haven. Children: Hattie Hamlin, born March 1, 1844; Sarah Norton, born July 6, 1847; Minnie Williams, born November 22, 1851.

REV. LEUMAS H. PEASE,
Acting Pastor, 1856-1858.

here and was installed the seventh pastor, October 14, 1846. He was born in Stratford, Conn., February 15, 1815; Yale, 1837; Yale Divinity School, 1841; and was ordained pastor at Wakeman, Ohio, December 1, 1842. Difficulties arose regarding the location of the new church, and at his request he was dismissed October 11, 1855. He was pastor at New Ipswich, N. H., for three years, and preached at Sherman, Conn., from 1860 to 1862. Because of a severe asthmatic trouble, he relinquished further ministerial service and obtained a clerkship in the Treasury Department at Washington, where he remained till 1886, and died in Washington, March 17, 1889.

The Rev. Leumas Hoyt Pease, born in Colebrook, Conn., January 20, 1811, supplied about a year and a third between 1856 and 1858. During the war (1861-1865) he was chaplain of Ellsworth's Avengers (a New York regiment), and was also in the Christian Commission. From 1865 till his death, May 20, 1887, he was seamen's chaplain at New Orleans, and made frequent visits here, at which time it was often the custom of the Sunday School to present him with a National flag for his Bethel. His strong individuality and kindly disposition will make him long remembered.

Many candidates were heard and several calls were extended before November 24, 1859, when a unanimous call was extended to the Rev. Henry Alanson Russell, who was installed the eighth pastor, December 14, 1859. He was born in Prospect, Conn., August 14, 1826; Yale Divinity School, 1853; ordained pastor of the First Church, Winsted, April 19, 1854, and was dismissed from that church August 25, 1858. After a pastorate of four and one-half years he was dismissed June 28, 1865, and served the churches in Centerbrook and Colebrook, Conn.; Moers, N. Y.; and Cabot, Vt., and is now residing in Winsted in honored old age.

Another marked figure in the pulpit of this church was the Rev. Gustavus Dorman Pike, who was here about two years, but made many visits to the place during his employment by the American Missionary Association. He was born in Topsfield, Mass., August 6, 1831; Dartmouth, 1858; Andover, 1861; ordained pastor of the Olivet Street Church, Nashua, N. H., April 23, 1862. He traveled extensively with the Fisk Jubilee Singers in their campaigns which secured over $70,000. He died in Hartford, January 29, 1885. His quaint and racy words will not soon be forgotten.

The ninth pastor was the Rev. George Whitefield Andrews, born in Wayne, Ohio, February 4, 1833; Oberlin, 1858; Andover, 1867; ordained pastor of this church, November 13, 1867. At his request he was released from pastoral duties, November 14, 1870, that he might go south for his health. He was afterward formally dismissed by the Consociation, and remained in the employ of the American Missionary Association. He is now Professor of Theology in Talladega College, greatly honored and beloved. It was during this pastorate, in 1866, that the parsonage was built (at a cost of $3,000).

Rev. Burritt Augustus Smith, born in Oxford, Conn., August 4, 1820; Yale, 1843; preached for three years and a half till April, 1874. After teaching in Middletown from 1875 to 1883, he removed to Worcester, Mass., and died there June 16, 1899.

The tenth pastor, Rev. Joel Stone Ives, began May 17, 1874, and was ordained September 29, 1874. He was born in Colebrook, Conn., December 5, 1847, the son of Rev. Alfred E. and Harriet (Stone) Ives; Amherst, 1870; Yale Divinity School, 1874. After being dismissed October 31, 1883, he was installed at Stratford, Conn., November 20, 1883, and was dismissed October 31, 1899, to accept the office of Secretary of the Missionary Society of Connecticut.

Rev. Edward Payson Root, born in Montague, Mass., August 4, 1844; Amherst, 1871; Yale Divinity School, 1875; ordained pastor at Hampden, Mass., June 1, 1876; dismissed December 28, 1883; was installed the eleventh pastor, February 7, 1884. Being dismissed in 1891 because of ill health, he has since supplied churches in Colorado. October 19, 1887, the Young People's Society of Christian Endeavor was formed with Mr. Root as president.

From June, 1891, to May, 1893, Rev. Henry Holmes, born in St. Paul, Minn., June 30, 1861, studied at Carlton College three years, and graduated at Hartford Seminary, 1892, served the church and was ordained June 7, 1892. He has been pastor at Wauwatosa, Wis., since 1893.

Rev. Christopher W. Collier, born at Westbury, Wiltshire, England, February 23, 1866; Williams, 1892; Harvard, 1893; Yale Divinity School, 1896, was ordained at North Adams,

REV. BURRITT A. SMITH,
Acting Pastor, 1870-1874.

Mass., January 3, 1894. Acting pastor of this church from November, 1893, to October, 1897, when he was dismissed for the purpose of further study in Germany, and we are glad to have him with us to-day.

The church is now acceptably supplied by the Rev. William Slade, who was born in Thetford, Vt., December 13, 1856; Dartmouth, 1884; Andover, 1887; ordained pastor at West Newbury, Mass., September 18, 1888; pastor at Williamstown, Mass., six years; beginning service here in October, 1897.

It would be impossible to give a complete record of the church membership. In 1792, there were 45 males and 59 females, total 104; in 1818, the number had fallen to 55; but 52 were added in 1819; in 1833, the number was 74; in 1856, there were 68 members. During the last 64 years there have been 419 additions—just 100 were received to the church in 1874-83; the number last January is 262, and during the 150 years the grand total is probably above 700.

A few Baptist families moved here in 1775, a church was organized September 10, 1784, and a building was erected on the corner southwest of this church, but it has long since been removed.

Rev. Joel McKee began to hold Methodist services about the year 1817. In 1830 a meeting house was built on Miller's Hill; in 1850 the building now standing near the railroad was erected, and the edifice now in use was built in 1875.

The Catholics have held services for more than thirty years, and have recently built a commodious place of worship on Bevin Hill.

The Swedes within a few months have come into possession of the building formerly owned by the Union Congregational Church, where the Lutheran forms of service will be observed.

The location of the present church building was the result of much discussion, and even after its completion there was not satisfaction with the result, so that, together with other causes which obtained in the community, the Union Church was organized in 1856, twenty-five members being dismissed from this church September 5th, and for more than twenty years maintained a vigorous life, and not a few of the useful workers in this and the Methodist churches were once members of the Union Church.

It is an interesting record that up to the close of the last century the ecclesiastical society had charge of the schools. In 1754, it was voted to lay a tax and "Sargeant" Cook, Joseph Parke, and William Bevin were appointed a committee. In 1758, the school was kept in the house of Joseph Parke on Bevin Hill. In 1796, a separate school organization seems to have been formed.

December 20, 1750, Captain Ebenezer Clark being moderator, the society voted "to build a meeting house for divine worship, two-thirds of the qualified voters being present," of the following dimensions, "46 feet long, 36 feet in width, and 22 feet between joints." The question of location was not easily solved. Petitions to "affix a place for a meeting house for divine worship" were sent up in 1751 and in 1752. The location agreed upon was near the present site, but it is uncertain when the building was first occupied. The last vote on record, for payment for the use of a private house "to meet in on the Sabbath," is December 15, 1755; when it was also voted to make a rate of twelve hundred pounds to pay the charges already laid out on the meeting house and to provide pulpit, doors, sashes, and glass, "and set said glass." The first vote to seat the meeting house is July 8, 1762. And any men who would assume such a delicate duty should have their names on record. They were Isaac Smith, Deacon John Clark, Lieutenant Stephen Olmstead, Captain Abijah Hall, and Ensign Silas Dunham.

There were at first the square pews, galleries on the east, south, and west sides, with the pulpit and its sounding board on the north, under which were the seats for the deacons. The young men from twenty years and upward and the young women from eighteen years and upward—when would they cease to be young women?—were assigned to the galleries.

This building became dilapidated during its century of use, and was injured by fire on the night of January 9, 1854. Seven years previously a special meeting, of which Lazarus Watrous was moderator, voted to build a new church, if sufficient funds could be obtained. Samuel Skinner, Timothy R. Markham, Amos Clark, and Amiel Abell were appointed a committee thereto. Again the difficulty of location arose, nor is it hard to see why there should have been decided differences of opinion. In October, 1849, the question was left to a committee. The fire settled the matter that something must be done, and March 4, 1854, the majority decided to build on the old location, appointing Hiram Veazey, Amiel Abell, Timothy R. Markham, Stephen G. Sears, Alfred Williams, Abner G. Bevin, Amos Clark, Alexander N. Niles, and Henry Skinner the building committee. January 2, 1855, it was voted "that the meeting house be now received into the hands of the society." During 1874 the pulpit was replaced by a desk and platform, the prayer meeting room was improved, and in 1881 nearly $1,500 were expended in extensive repairs and improvements. Funds are in hand toward the building of a chapel, which has always been an especial need of the church. It is worthy of note that electric lights were placed in the church last spring.

Early action was taken in reference to music. May 15, 1760, it was voted, "Captain Jonathan Alvord—chosen to sett the psalm." Also, "Seth Alvord chosen quorister." "November ye 27th, 1762, voted to sing Watts' Varshon the whole of the time." Robert Shattock, Titus Carrier, and Bryan Parmelee are also chosen "quoristers." In 1791 eighteen were thus chosen. A pitch pipe furnished the key. This was a small wooden instrument, in shape something like a long narrow book, with a mouthpiece at one corner and on the opposite edge slides marked for the different keys. After the hymn was announced, the chorister gave out the tune, sounded the pitch pipe and raised the tune. The audience would then join in various degrees of harmony. Sometimes the pitch pipe would make its journey quite around the meeting house from one chorister to another. After this came the tuning fork. Still later Silas Hills played a single bass viol, and about 1839 William F. Clark when only twelve years of age began playing the violin in the church services. After this a reed instrument was used, and the present pipe organ was obtained in 1866. For some time previous to 1854 Dr. Nettleton's Hymns were used, and in October of that year "Psalms and Hymns," recommended by the General Association in 1845, was adopted. Sunday, May 9, 1875, "Hymns and Songs of Praise," edited by Drs. Hitchcock, Eddy, and Schaff, was used for the first time. This has now given place to the "Church Hymnal."

The organization of this church was just as the country was emerging from the War of King George II. Mr. Norton had suffered a year's imprisonment in Canada. Many, doubtless, of the members in those early years took part in the colonial wars, but they left no record except the military titles here and there. In the French and Indian wars, from 1755 to 1759, the following names deserve mention, being more than one-third of the members known to have served from East Middletown:

Benjamin Goff,	Samuel Goff,	James Webb,
Josiah Caswell,	Elkanah Sears,	James Bill,
Joshua Bailey,	William White,	Recompense Bailey,
Bryan Parmelee,	Stephen Knowlton,	Daniel Hills,
Stephen Ackley,	Titus Carrier,	Simeon Young,
Joseph Smith,	John Norton,	Marcus Cole,
James Bailey,	Moses Freeman,	Simeon Freeman.
Michael Smith,	John Hailing,	

And, also, as serving under Captain Savage in 1755: John Bevin, Josiah Cook, Amos Dewey, Thomas Shepard; and Lemuel Shurtleff, Samuel Mott, and Abner Norket, under Captain Champion.

During Mr. Norton's pastorate the Revolutionary War began, and only age prevented him from participating in it. The train-band under Captain Silas Dunham started at once to relieve the beleaguered citizens of Boston, but returned after five days' absence. The second officer in this company was Lieutenant Timothy Percival, who lived within the borders of Middle Haddam parish, but in 1767 was set off to this parish for his convenience in attending church. Benjamin Kneeland was ensign and Marcus Cole clerk or orderly sergeant. Other names in this roll of honor are:

Stephen Olmsted,	Benjamin Kneeland,	Lazarus Watrous,
Ralph Smith,	Thomas Hill,	Nathaniel Markham,
Samuel Kilbourn,	Daniel Clark,	Elisha Cornwell,
Samuel Hill,	Amos Clark,	John Norton,
Daniel Hill,	Elijah Clark,	Ezra Ackley,
Caleb Cook,	Samuel Freeman,	David Cornwell,
John Johnson,	Hezekiah Goff,	Ezra Purple,
Nehemiah Day,	William Bevin,	Joshua Bailey,
Sylvanus Freeman,	Daniel Park,	James Johnson, Jr.,
William White,	Elijah Bailey,	Nathaniel Garnsey,
Samuel Sexton,	Daniel Mackall,	Ithamar Pelton.

To this roll the following names are added of persons who saw more or less active service during that trying period, but it is not pretended that it is a complete list:

Stephen Ackley,	Samuel Cowdrey,	Sylvanus Norcott,
Stephen Ackley, Jr.,	Benjamin Cobb,	John Park,
Hewitt Alvord,	Joshua Frank, colored,	Peter Parker,
Seth Alvord,	John Fuller,	Rowland Percival,
Ruel Alvord,	Stephen Gates,	Randall Shattuck,
Soloman Bailey,	Josiah Goff,	David Sears,
William Barton,	Samuel Goff,	William Stoddard,
Samuel Brown,	Jabez Hall,	Sparrow Smith,
Titus Carrier, Ensign,	Isaac Johnson,	Michael Smith,
Aaron Clark,	Daniel Judd, Jr.,	Lemuel West,
Abner Clark, died,	Ichabod Lucas,	Hopkins West,
Stephen Clark,	John Markham,	John West,
David Clark,	Jacob Norton, died,	John Welsh,
Abner Cole, Lieut.,	Elias Norton, Surg. Mate,	Joel Wood,
Hendrick Cole,	Reuben Norcott,	Philip White,
Moses Cole,	William Norcott,	Thomas White, died.

In the war of 1812, the only member of this church known to have been in the service was Warren West.

The Civil War, while it called for a less sacrifice in numbers, revealed no less patriotism and valor. The names of this Grand Army of the Republic who have been members of this church are the following:

Abner A. Bevin, 1st Lieut.,	Alexander E. Ingraham,
William H. Bevin, 1st Lieut.,	Osmer C. Hills,
David Strong, 1st Lieut.,	Henry Snow,
James M. Moore, 2d Lieut.,	Gwinnett Carpenter,
Clark Strong, Adjutant,	Nelson Flood,
Lumas H. Pease, Chaplain,	Lorenzo D. Rich,
John W. Skinner, Drum Major,	Henry T. Sellew,
Samuel T. Rodman,	Horatio D. Chapman,
Stephen R. Demay,	D. Carlos Carpenter,
Hubert E. Carpenter.	

In all these trials of faith the women were no less patriotic and self-sacrificing than the men, and to record their names would be to make a record of the membership of the church. And while we pray for the triumph of the Prince of Peace, we can see that in this world of partial things even the sword may be the minister of righteousness and war the hastener forward of His coming.

East Hampton may rejoice not only that it has the Gospel preached to it, but that it has preached the Gospel, not only in the lives of holy men and holy women, whose faith and alms come up as a memorial before God, but also by those, whose names we mention, who have given themselves distinctively to the heralding of the Good News. The Rev. Howard Norton Smith,* great-great-great-grandson of the Rev. John Norton, born December 16, 1858—how well I remember the day he united with this church, July 12, 1874; studied at Oberlin, 1896; ordained at Berea, Ohio, June 6, 1889; pastor at Saratoga Church, Omaha, Nebraska, 1889-91; at Rock Springs, Wyoming, 1891-97; and at San Luis Obispo, California.

Amasa West, born August 15, 1775; united with the church in 1803; studied at Williams; studied divinity; taught and preached at Jamestown, N. Y.; approbated to preach in 1815; preached in Ohio and Michigan; died in Wisconsin in 1850.

Benjamin Sears, born Feb. 10, 1771, married Ann Bigelow, and removed to Delaware, Ohio. Changing his views of the Christian religion, he joined the Baptist Church and devoted himself to the ministry. After serving the church in Delaware for some years he received an appointment as missionary, and with his two sons, John and Benjamin, went to Fort Wayne, Ind., where he aided in constructing a church, the first church established in Indiana.

Stephen Olmsted, Jr., the son of Captain Olmsted, who was buried on Miller's Hill in the same plot with the Rev. John Norton, was born in this parish, and for forty years was a Baptist clergyman in Schodack, N. Y. Another son, Jonathan, liberally endowed Hamilton College.

John Watson Alvord, born in East Hampton, April 18, 1807; Oberlin, 1836; for a long time was secretary of the American Tract Society.

Time would fail me to tell the whole story. Indeed, I suppose if all were told the world could not contain the books. I have tried to choose the most important facts. But it is always

---
* Rev. John Norton married Eunice Hitchcock.
Daughter, Elizabeth Norton, married Nathaniel Clark.
Daughter, Eunice Clark, married Sparrow Smith.
Son, Nathaniel C. Smith, married Charlotte Strong.
Son, Henry S. Smith, married Helen M. Niles.
Son, Howard N. Smith.

sad, as Dr. S. Weir Mitchell says, that "the siftings of memory let so much of thought and feeling escape" that we keep little more than the barren facts; and yet, as he says again, some things live for us "the life of eternal remembrance." And there is an encouragement in the words of Bacon: "Industrious persons, by an exact and scrupulous diligence and observation, out of monuments, names, words, proverbs, traditions, private records and evidences, fragments of stories, passages of books that concern not story, and the like, do save and recover somewhat from the deluge of time."

Have I heard someone say "the former days were better than these"? Surely such an one cannot have read of those former days. All honor to the faith, fidelity, self-sacrifice, courage, endurance, accomplishment, of those who have gone before us. We are their debtors. But they without us are not made perfect. Ours is a better heritage—as much better as the fulfillment is better than the promise—the fruition than the flowering. They laid the foundations in the far-off past—those noble men and women, who had such "bad rhoades to travel in" that they were ready to endure hardness for the having of a church and a minister of their own. But the temple is better than the foundations. And in the larger view of the Kingdom of God, He who died for our sins sits now at the right hand of God, "from henceforth expecting until he makes his enemies the footstool of his feet." The Expectant Christ is upon the Throne.

We look across the landscape and only the tops of the hills attract our vision. In the backward glance of history it is the prominent events which hold our attention. Fortunately we try to find the best things in the past to remember. But if we study the landscape the valleys are as important as the mountains, and as surely as the universe is slowly moving towards its great center, so the lives of men, for the Cosmos is made up of particulars, are moving toward "the far-off, divine event"—the perfected Kingdom of God.

In this accomplishment the faithful life of an individual is of uncounted worth, by how much more the one hundred and fifty years of a Christian Church!

A Sketch of the Life of the Rev. John Norton.

To the Members of the Congregational Church in East Hampton and their friends assembled upon the One Hundred and Fiftieth Anniversary of its Organization, GREETING:—

Your anniversary committee during the past summer extended me an invitation to prepare and read upon this occasion a paper relative to the life and labors of the first settled pastor of your church and parish, the Rev. Mr. John Norton, and his family. Though the preparation and reading of such papers was somewhat out of my line of business, I accepted the invitation and endeavored to obtain from reliable sources all the information respecting them that was available. That this paper is deficient in many important particulars, will be apparent to you all, but the deficiency is entirely due to the loss of important records upon those points, as every possible clue that gave any promise of throwing any light upon the subject has been closely followed, either by myself or some of his descendants, who have generously given me the benefit of their investigations, and to whom let me here express my sincere and heartfelt thanks for the kindly interest they have taken in the matter.

Mr. Norton was born in the parish of Kensington, in the present town of Berlin, but which was at the time of his birth a part of the town of Farmington, Conn., November. 16, 1715. He was the fourth son and child of John and Anna (Thompson) Norton, of Kensington, grandson of John and Ruth (Moore) Norton, of Farmington, and great-grandson of John and Elizabeth (———) Norton, whose name appears upon the first page of the first book of records of the town of Branford, Conn., in connection with the sale of land, and who was one of the eighty-four original proprietors of that township. The family is of Norman descent, and the first of the name, La Seur de Norville (afterward changed to Norton), came into England

ALONZO CLARK,
1822-1876.
Sexton of the Church for nearly 30 years.

MARTIN L. ROBERTS,
1839.

HIRAM BARTON,
1799-1878.
For many years a member of the church choir. Son of Wm. Barton, founder of the Bell business, East Hampton's principal industry.

FRANCIS GRISWOLD EDGERTON, M. D.,
1797-1870.
The beloved physician who for more than 40 years practiced medicine in East Hampton Parish and vicinity.

from Normandy in 1066 in the celebrated filibustering crew of William the Conqueror as his constable, at that time an office of high military rank. The place to which the family traces its planting after crossing the English Channel is at Sharpenhow, a hamlet of Bedfordshire. Mr. Norton was of the sixteenth generation that have been definitely traced in this country and England, but their pedigree has been questioned so far as it relates to some of the early families in England, but of its correctness in relation to the family since they settled in America, there can be no doubt. His father was a well-to-do farmer and resided on the main road leading from Middletown to Farmington, near what is known as Mill River crossing. He is sometimes mentioned in the Farmington records as John Norton, 3d, and also as Sergeant John Norton, which fact shows that he held that rank in the train-band, as the militia was at that time designated. The ancestors of his mother were prominent among the early settlers of Hartford and Farmington. No materials from which any particulars or incidents relating to his early life could be gathered have been found, and it is fair to presume that his early years were passed amid such scenes as were common to the youth and young men of that period, nearly all of whom were compelled by the mere force of circumstances to toil early and late upon the farm, which was the main dependence of the people of that time.

He graduated at Yale College in the class of 1737, being at that time in the twenty-second year of his age. It is not definitely known, but the probabilities are that he was prepared to enter that institution by the Rev. William Burnham, who at that time was the pastor of his native parish. He studied theology probably at Springfield, Mass., as the records of that place show that he was a resident there soon after his graduation, but the name of his tutor has not been ascertained. He was ordained at Deerfield, Mass., on the 25th day of November, 1741, as the pastor of a church that day organized for the parish of Fall Town, then a part of the town of Deerfield, but since then incorporated as a separate town by the name of Bernardston.

Bernards-town or Bernardston at the time Mr. Norton was ordained was, as has just been mentioned, called Fall Town. It was thus designated because it was granted to the soldiers or the descendants of those soldiers who were in the fight with the Indians at the Great Falls in the Connecticut River, May 18, 1676. The first meeting of the proprietors of this township was held on the 23d of September, 1741, at the house of Lieut. Sheldon, when it was voted to invite the Rev. John Norton to settle in the ministry, and he have £200 as a settlement, half in money, half in work, and a salary of £130 for the first five years, afterward to be increased £5 a year until it should amount to £170. Mr. Norton accepted this invitation, and as before stated was ordained on the 25th of November, 1741.

The Rev. Jonathan Ashley, of Deerfield, preached the ordination sermon from the fifteenth chapter of Romans and the thirtieth verse: "Now I beseech you, brethren, for the Lord Jesus Christ's sake and for the love of the spirit, that ye strive together with me in your prayers to God for me." This sermon was printed under the following title, which was taken from a fine copy in the possession of the Connecticut Historical Society at Hartford:

> The United Endeavors and Earnest Prayers of
> Ministers and People to promote the great Design of the Ministry
> Recommended in a
> SERMON
> Preached at Deerfield Nov. 25, 1741
> Upon the gathering a Church for Fall-Town and the Ordination of
> MR. JOHN NORTON
> as Pastor to the Church there
> BY JOHNATHAN ASHLEY A. M.
> and Pastor of the Church in Deerfield
> to which is added
> The charge given by the Reverend Mr. Benjamin Doolittle
> and a Right Hand of Fellowship by the Reverend Mr. Joseph Ashley
> Boston Printed by S. Kneeland and T. Green
> in Queenstreet 1742

"Owing to the unsettled state of the times" and the fact that his parish was situated in the angle between the military line of the Connecticut and that of the Deerfield, and consequently his parishioners had as much as they could do to maintain their families in a war already commenced, and raging to that extent that in some cases the women were necessitated to bear arms in defence of their dwellings, Mr. Norton labored among them but about four years, when he was dismissed, and appointed chaplain to the line of forts that had been recently built for the protection of the inhabitants living upon the western frontier of Massachusetts from the ravages of the French and their savage Indian allies.

This line of forts consisted of "Northfield," "Fall Town," "Colerain," "Fort Shirley in the Town of Heath," "Fort Pelham in the Town of Rowe," "Fort Massachusets in the town of Adams," and the soldiers posted at the "Collars," "Shattuck's Fort," "Rhodetown," and "New Hampton," all under the command of Capt. Ephraim Williams, the illustrious founder of Williams College at Williamstown, Mass.

He entered upon the service of chaplain in the month of February, 1746, and passed his time in one or the other of the forts just mentioned, as his sense of duty to each garrison might prompt or circumstances permit. His wife and three small children resided in Fort Shirley, which he seems to have made his headquarters.

He was at Fort Massachusetts when it was besieged and captured by a large body of French and Indians, in August, 1746, and was taken captive with the rest of the garrison and carried to Quebec, where he remained about a year, when he was exchanged and returned to Boston. He wrote an account of the siege and of his journey to Quebec, his captivity and return, which he entitled "The Redeemed Captive," possibly after a memorable precedent. The full title of this little book is as follows:

THE REDEEMED CAPTIVE
being a Narrative of the taking and carrying into captivity
THE REVEREND MR. JOHN NORTON.

When Fort Massachusetts surrendered to a large body of French and Indians, Aug. 20, 1746, with a particular account of the defence made before the surrender of that Fort and the Articles of Capitulation etc Together with an account both entertaining and affecting of what Mr. Norton met with and took notice of in his traveling to and while in captivity at Canada and till his arrival at Boston, on Aug. 16, 1747.
Written by himself.

Jer. 21-4. Thus saith the Lord: Behold I will turn back the weapons of war that are in your hand wherewith ye fight against the King of Babylon and against the Chaldeaus, which besiege you without the walls I will assemble them into this city.
Chap. 50-33. The Children of Israel and the Children of Judah were oppressed together and all that took them captives held them fast, they refused to let them go.
Lam. 1-3. Judah is gone into captivity because of affliction.
Neh. 7-6. These are the children of the Province that went up out of the captivity of those that had been carried away.
Boston Printed and Sold opposite the Prison 1748.

There are but few copies of the original edition of this plain, unattractive, but highly interesting narrative of the daily details of his captivity in existence, and they are in the possession of public and historical libraries. The only copy of this edition that I have heard of being for sale was held at the sum of $650. A limited edition of one hundred copies was reprinted by the late Samuel G. Drake, of Boston, in 1870, to which he added copious notes, and that edition has now become so scarce as to readily bring $5 per copy. A part of this work was also printed in the appendix of Drake's Particular History of the French and Indian War, 1744–1749, published in Albany, N. Y., in 1870. The greater portion of it was also reprinted, interspersed with interesting notes and comments, in Prof. Perry's "Origins in Williamstown," published in 1894. The first edition of this little work, that consisted of only forty duodecimo pages, was from necessity comparatively small, arising from the fact that only his immediate friends and the friends of those who were in captivity with him would be interested in its publication, which fact would limit its circulation to a great extent and in some measure account for its scarcity. From this narrative we learn that Mr. Norton left Fort Shirley on Thursday, August 14, 1746, in company with Dr. Thomas Williams and fourteen of the soldiers, and went to Fort Pelham, and from thence to Captain Rice's, where he lodged that night. On Friday, the 15th, he proceeded to Fort Massachusetts, where he states that he designed to tarry about a month. This fort at that time was garrisoned by some twenty soldiers, about half of whom were sick, under the command of Sergeant John Hawks. On the 19th, he states that there were in the fort twenty-two men, three women and five children, and that between eight and nine o'clock of the forenoon they were attacked by a party of eight or nine hundred French and Indians under the command of Monsieur Regaud de Vaudril, who having surrounded the fort on every side began with hideous acclamations to rush towards it, firing incessantly. This mode of warfare they kept up during the day and evening and also upon the forenoon of the 20th, suffering but little damage from the defenders of the fort, who were short of ammunition. About twelve o'clock of the 20th the enemy desired to parley, which was agreed to by Sergeant Hawks, who was given two hours to consider the matter of surrendering. Although the little garrison had held out bravely and only lost one of their number thus far during the engagement, the fact that they were surrounded by a vastly superior force, while only eight of their number were in a condition to resist an attack, and they short of ammunition, induced them, after praying to God for his guidance and a careful consideration of their circumstances, to surrender upon the best terms they could obtain. The general tenor of these terms were, that they should all be prisoners to the French and that the savages should have nothing to do with them; that the children should live with their parents during the term of their captivity, and that all should have the privilege of being exchanged at the first opportunity. Contrary, however, to the expressed stipulations of the articles of capitulation, a part of the garrison were turned over to the Indian allies in order to pacify them, as they were complaining bitterly because they had not been allowed a share in the spoil. Mr. Norton strongly protested against this action upon the part of the French, but without avail, and he writes that his heart was filled with sorrow and that he trembled with fear, expecting that many of those who were weak and feeble would fall by the merciless hand of the savages. It seems, however, that contrary to his expectations, the captives who fell into the hands of the Indians were well treated and kindly cared for during the long and distressing march to Canada, which they took up on the morning of the 21st of August, the next day after the surrender. During this march Mr. Norton was in charge of Lieutenant Dumuy, a French officer who had been in much active service. The route by which they proceeded lay through an unbroken wilderness to East Creek, one of the tributaries of Lake Champlain, now known as Pawlet River, thence north by Lake Champlain and the Sorelle and St. Lawrence Rivers to Montreal, and from thence to Quebec, where they arrived on the 15th of September, having traveled the greater part of the way after leaving East Creek in canoes. During this long and distressing journey, and after their arrival at Quebec, Mr. Norton ministered to the spiritual needs of his fellow-prisoners and improved every opportunity that presented itself to advise and cheer them as best he could under the unfavorable circumstances in which they were placed. On the 20th of May, 1747, he was taken severely ill and was, he writes, given over to die by all who saw him, that during this period his reason departed from him and returned not again until the 14th of June, when he began to recover and speedily regained his health, so that on the 27th of July he set sail for Boston under a flag of truce, where he arrived on the 16th day of August, which was he writes a day of great joy and gladness to him, he having been in captivity a year lacking four days.

Shortly after his release from captivity he presented a petition to the General Assembly of Connecticut at its October session in 1747, showing that he was taken and carried into captivity, and had suffered great loss and damage, and at present was much deprived of the means of living. In consideration of this petition the Assembly voted him the sum of £100 in bills of credit, old tenor, worth at the current rates of the time perhaps £20 in silver. In January, 1748, he appears to be living in Springfield, Mass., as he presented a memorial to the General Court of Massachusetts at that time, dating from that place, "showing that he entered into the service of that province as a chaplain to the line of forts on the western frontier, was captivated and carried into Canada by the enemy, where he was detained a prisoner for the space of twelve months, during which time he constantly officiated as a chaplain among his fellow-prisoners, in the manner he was able under the great difficulties and suffering of his imprisonment, and besides the great difficulties and hardships that he endured, his family were reduced to great straight and difficulties at home." He prayed that they would take his distressed circumstances in consideration and grant him such help and relief as they should deem meet. In consideration of this petition the General Court of Massachusetts ordered that the sum of £37 10s. be allowed him for services as chaplain to the prisoners whilst in captivity at Canada.

The records of the church and society of North Guilford, in this State, show that on the 1st of December, 1747, they voted to treat with him as a probationer, and on the 1st of March, 1748, gave him a call to settle with them in the work of the ministry, but for some reason not recorded he did not accept the call. In June, 1748, a committee from this parish applied to the Hartford South Association of Ministers to recommend them a suitable candidate to supply their pulpit, and that body advised an application to Mr. Norton. At the October session of the General Assembly following, a committee consisting of Ebenezer Clark and Ezra Andrews represented that the inhabitants of this parish being now about to settle him, asked and obtained liberty to be embodied into church estate, which was granted provided they obtained consent of the neighboring churches. It seems that there was no difficulty in obtaining this consent, as upon the 30th day of November, 1748, one hundred and fifty years ago to-day, this church was organized and Mr. Norton duly installed as its first pastor. The names of those who officiated at his installation here have not been recovered, but without doubt they were the regular settled pastors of the neighboring churches. His salary voted at a society meeting held on the 9th of August, 1748, was one hundred ounces of silver, or public bills of credit equivalent thereto, for the three years next after his settlement, and after that to add to his salary annually in the same proportion as we shall advance in our lists until it shall amount to one hundred and thirty ounces of silver, and that to be his standing salary. This salary, one hundred and thirty ounces in silver, was equivalent to forty-three pounds, six shillings and eight pence in 1759, and in the present currency $166.66⅔. It was also voted to the Rev. Mr. Norton his firewood, to be brought to his house. The amount given him as a settlement, as it was called, is stated in Fields' Statistical Account of Middlesex County, published in 1819, as equivalent to $666.66⅔, but there are no votes upon record that tell how or when it was to be paid. The last mention made of it upon the records is at an adjourned annual meeting of the society held December 18, "Anno Domini" 1752, when it was voted "to the Rev'd. Mr. Norton fifty pounds old tenor, which is in full of his settlement."

After being installed, Mr. Norton took up his residence among this people and ministered unto them in spiritual things until his death, with the exception of a few months in 1755–56, during which time he was chaplain of the government forces raised by the colony to go to Crown Point. During his absence the members of the Hartford South Association supplied his pulpit, the appointments according to their records covering the time from October 12, 1755, to February 2, 1756. In 1760 he served as chaplain of the third regiment raised for the expedition against Canada, taking the place of the Rev. James Beebee of that parish in Stratford, which is now the town of Trumbull, who received the appointment, but for some reason failed to serve. The length of this term of service is unknown, but was probably only for a short period. Mr. Norton died March 24, 1778, of the small-pox, and was buried in the field east of the present residence of Mr. Charles H. Strong, doubtless as was the custom of the time in such cases, at the solemn hour of midnight. Seven persons victims of the same dread disease are interred in the same locality. The terror inspired by the presence of that disease in a community at that period can hardly be realized or understood at the present time when vaccination has been substituted for the original disease. Then its subjects were banished as far as possible from the abodes of men while living and from the public burial places when dead. Mr. Norton it is believed contracted this disease while returning from a business trip to Middletown from some parties who made inquiries of him respecting the locality, one of the number being in the first stages of the disease at the time. The records of the First Church in Chatham (now Portland) also show that a number of persons of that parish died about that time of the same dread disease.

A red sandstone slab, ornamented after the manner of the times, marked his grave at the place of his interment for one hundred and twenty years, when it was removed to the Lakeview Cemetery and set up by the side of that of his wife. It bears the following inscription:

In Memory of
THE REV. JOHN NORTON,
Pastor of the 3d Church in Chatham,
who died with the Small Pox, March 24, A. D. 1778,
In the 63d year of his age.

His remains are still at their original resting place, it not being thought best at this time to have them disinterred, but it is much to be regretted that his dust could not be permitted to mingle with that of his kindred and the parishioners among whom he mingled in the daily walks of life and to whom he ministered in holy things for nearly thirty years. But while in the course of events his last resting place may be forgotten by men, and the hallowed spot where his remains lie be desecrated and given over to other purposes, it cannot be forgotten by Him whose watchful eye never slumbers, and in due time his being shall hear the voice of the "Son of Man" and come forth to everlasting life. Until then, may the wild flowers ever shed their sweetest perfume and the birds of the air carol their sweetest songs above the hallowed place where they rest undisturbed by the din and turmoil of the busy world.

The inventory of his estate amounted to £494 and included a library of twenty-nine volumes and ninety-six pamphlets.

Mr. Norton's residence was on Miller's Hill, his house standing near the present residence of William I. Brooks. This property containing twenty-two acres, three roods and four rods of land, with houses and barns standing thereon, he purchased in 1752 of Elisha Cornwell and Ann, his wife, for £800, old tenor. This was a part of lot No. 147 in what was known as the three-mile division, a tract of land granted to the proprietors of Middletown in 1683 by the General Assembly. He married Eunice, daughter of Luke and Elizabeth (Walker) Hitchcock, of Springfield, Mass., who was born March 2, 1712–13. She died May 27, 1796, in the eighty-fourth year of her age, and was interred in Lakeview Cemetery by the side of a son who died in infancy. She is said to have been a woman "that looked well to the ways of her household," and in every sense of the word was a helpmeet for her husband.

They were the parents of nine children, the oldest a daughter, Asenath, who was born in Springfield, October 13, 1738, and who married, July 13, 1758, James, son of Lieut. James and Kesiah (French) Bill, who was born in Lebanon, Conn., February 20, 1736. He settled on some land near the northwest corner of the lake, given him by his father in 1763. He was very prominently associated with the affairs of the town and society, and held many offices of profit and trust in the gift of his townsmen. He was elected representative to the General Assembly in the years 1782, '83, '84, '87, '89, '90, '92, '95, and '98. He was one of the deacons of this church, having been appointed to that office February 5, 1795, and for several years was a Justice of the Peace. He served as a soldier in the French and Indian war, and during the Revolution served the town upon committees to enlist soldiers for the Continental service and furnish supplies for soldiers' families during that trying period. She died January 2, 1810, and he July 25, 1823. Their family consisted of five sons and six daughters, all but one of whom reached the years of maturity and their descendants settled in various parts of the Union.

James Bill, Jr., their eldest son, settled in the State of New York, and at one time represented Albany in the State Legislature, and later was a judge in the County of Oswego. Norton Bill, their third son, studied medicine with Dr. John Richmond, and is said to have been a physician of great promise, but fell a victim to consumption in the twenty-eighth year of his age.*

Elizabeth, the second child and daughter of the Rev. John Norton, was born in Springfield, December 19, 1740, and married November 6, 1766, Nathaniel, son of Jabez and Sarah (Judd) Clark, born August 7, 1743. She died May 18, 1770, aged twenty-nine years and five months, leaving a daughter, Eunice, who married May 3, 1787, Sparrow, son of Deacon Isaac and Mary (Sparrow) Smith, whose son, John W. B. Smith, is the oldest living member of this church.

John Norton, Jr., third child and first son, was born in 1743, probably in Fall Town. He married September 19, 1765, Ede, daughter of Jabez and Sarah (Judd) Clark, born August 29, 1745, sister of Nathaniel Clark, Elizabeth Norton's husband. He resided near the Samuel B. Child place on Bevin Hill, and for many years was the teacher of the public school and is reported to have been a very strict disciplinarian. In 1771 he was appointed by the General Assembly a surveyor of land for the County of Hartford. He was also a member of Captain

---

* *Family Record of Deacon James and Asenath (Norton) Bill:*

Asenath, born Nov. 18, 1759; married Oct. 18, 1781, Jonathan Bill.
Lucy, born Dec. 31, 1761; married April 12, 1784, Apollas Arnold.
James, born Feb. 4, 1764; married Aug. 31, 1783, Hannah Goodrich.
Elvira, born Feb. 22, 1766; married Jan. 17, 1793, Elizur Skinner, of Cambridge, N. Y.
Erastus, born July 6, 1768; married Nov. 27, 1788, Sarah Hall.
Norton, born July 14, 1770; married May 1, 1791, Sally Buell.
Clarissa, born Aug. 18, 1772; married Nov. 16, 1797, Oliver Bill.
Achsah, born Nov. 1, 1774; died July 8, 1775.
Achsah, born ———, 1777; died May 3, 1812.
Amos, born June 9, 1779.
Abner, born Aug. 11, 1781.

Silas Dunham's company that responded to the Lexington Alarm, as it was called in 1775. He died May 11, 1808, of the gout, aged sixty-five years, and his widow married April 11, 1809, Deacon Moses Cook, whom she also survived, dying February 18, 1827, in the eighty-second year of her age.

His family consisted of nine children, three sons and six daughters. John, the eldest son, died in infancy, and a second son of that name, born April 7, 1775, married March 7, 1798, Lucy, daughter of John and Lois (Brainerd) Johnson, born May 13, 1775, and removed to Otsego County, N. Y., where they resided together for more than seventy years before death did them part, he dying in 1868 in his ninety-fourth year, she dying in 1873 in her ninety-ninth year.

Jabez Clark Norton, third son of John, Jr., and Ede Norton, followed the sea, and was swept from the deck of the vessel of which he was in command during the September gale of 1819, and was never seen again. His grandsons, Jabez Clark Norton, of Willimantic, Lieut.-Commanding U. S. Ship Pompey, and James Phillips Norton, commercial traveler for the Whitney Paper Co., are the only living male representatives of the Rev. John's family that bear the family name.*

Sarah Norton, the fourth child and third daughter of John, Jr., and Ede Norton, married Elizur Andrews, of Glastonbury, and removed to Stratford and was the grandmother of the Rev. William Russell, who was pastor of this church from 1846 to 1855. Mr. Russell graduated from Yale College in the celebrated class of 1837, just one hundred years later than his illustrious predecessor and ancestor.

Anna Norton, the third daughter and fourth child of the Rev. John, was born at Fall Town, September 22, 1745, and died in Fort Shirley, August 26, 1747. A rough stone upon

---

* *Family Record of John Norton, Jr., and Ede (Clark) Norton:*
 Dorinda, born Nov. 19, 1766; married (1) May 17, 1795, Jesse Penfield, (2) Andrew Shepard.
 Lucinda, born Feb. 11, 1769; died it is said with yellow fever.
 John, born March 3, 1771; died Mar. 17, 1771.
 Sarah, born Feb. 2, 1773; married ———, 1793, Elizur Andrews.
 John, born April 7, 1775; married Mar. 7, 1798, Lucy Johnson.
 Belinda, born April 12, 1779; married (1) Nov. 1, 1797, Hezekiah Smith, (2) Thomas Child.
 Jabez Clark, born June 26, 1781; married Oct. 24, 1804, Sarah Pelton.
 Celinda, born July 18, 1785; married Nov. 25, 1807, Erastus Carrier, of Colchester.
 Florinda, born Jan. 3, 1789; married (1) Mar. 28, 1808, Jesse Hubbard, (2) —— Isham.

which was chiseled, probably by some soldier of the garrison, the following inscription:

> Hear lys ye body of Anna
> D. of ye Rev
> Mr. John Norton. She died
> Aug ye   aged   1747

was set up at the head of her grave, and for one hundred and thirty-seven years withstood the wars of the elements until the day in August on which she died and the number of years that she had lived became entirely obliterated. In 1884 this stone was placed in the museum of Williams College, where with other relics of the old fort it still remains. Professor Perry, of Williams College, writes that the tradition is still lively in Heath that there used to come up from Connecticut on an occasional pilgrimage to the site of Fort Shirley, and particularly to the grave of Anna Norton, some of her relatives, probably her mother. This, he says, is very likely and may well pass into an historical fact.

Jacob Norton, the second son and fifth child of the Rev. John, was born December 15, 1748, and died in a prison ship in New York during the Revolution.

Elias Norton, the third son and sixth child of the Rev. John, was born October 21, 1750, and died November 5, of the same year.

Anne, the fourth daughter and seventh child of the Rev. John, was born March 29, 1752, but of her we have no further record, unless she is the person of that name who was received into full communion in this church August 12, 1769.

Eunice, the fifth daughter and eighth child of the Rev. John, was born October 23, 1754, and died unmarried October 12, 1845, leaving her property, which amounted to about $100, to this ecclesiastical society. After the death of her mother Aunt Eunice, as she was usually called, resided alone in a house that formerly stood near the residence of the late Matthew Haling, and which with its contents was destroyed by fire during her temporary absence. It was this fire that is supposed to have destroyed the early records of the church and also important papers that belonged to the family, which would be valuable and interesting had they been preserved until to-day. A new house was erected for her by subscription upon the site where now stands the house of Thomas O'Connell, in which she lived until it was deemed imprudent for her to remain alone any longer and she was removed to the house of the late Amos Clark, where she died.

Elias Norton, ninth child and fourth son of the Rev. John Norton, was born October 23, 1754, twin brother to Eunice. He studied medicine with Dr. Thomas Mosely, of East Haddam, and January 29, 1776, was appointed surgeon's mate to Dr. Robert Usher, surgeon to Colonel Wadsworth's Regiment of the Connecticut Line. He eventually, however, cast in his lot with the Loyalist party, and before the close of the war sought refuge in the provinces. Soon after the beginning of the present century he returned to Addison, Me., where he married an English lady and was granted a pension of ninety-six dollars a year by the government. The granting of this pension was considered an unjust proceeding at that time by many persons, but it is evident that the government considered the service that he rendered to his country more than offset his disloyalty. He died in Addison, Me., about 1846, leaving a widow who died shortly afterward. I have not learned that he left any family.

There are but few records extant from which any opinion of Mr. Norton's literary ability can be formed. His published narrative, though a work full of valuable and interesting facts, is written in the dryest manner possible. The few manuscript sermons from his pen that have been preserved show that he was well versed in the doctrinal views of the church of his time and compare well in a literary point of view with the average preacher of those days. The few records of the church kept by him, that are known to be in existence, show him to be a careful, painstaking and methodical man, giving as they do the dates of births, baptisms, marriages, and deaths that occurred in the parish. It is a source of profound regret that the greater portion of them are irrecoverably lost, as their aid would be of inestimable value at this time, when there are so many searching among the records of the past for the story of their ancestry. Upon the records of Yale College his name appears as the nineteenth in a class of twenty-four, but prior to the year 1767 the names of the scholars in that institution are entered upon the catalogue in the order of their family rank and give no indication of their rank in scholarship. The few traditions that have been handed down to us relating to his pastorate here, show that he allowed no seeming lapse from duty on the part of any of his parishioners to pass unnoticed. The absence of any of the heads of families from the regular Sabbath services were investigated at the earliest possible moment, and the offender was sure to be severely reprimanded unless a valid excuse could be found for his neglect of duty. The impression is that he was a man of sterling, substantial qualities, and that he considered himself as settled over this parish in every sense of the word.

Thus briefly have we summarized the principal incidents and events that we have been able to collect, that relate to the life and labors of him who was the first to "tend these few sheep in the wilderness," and by whom doubtless he was looked upon as a man "sent from God." Lapse of time and the destruction of early records of both the church and family have rendered the task extremely difficult, but with the material that has been at my command I can only say that I have done what I could, the best that I could, and certainly there can be no person who regrets more than myself that in some important details it is so unsatisfactory and incomplete.

And now, in closing, let me again express my sincere and heartfelt thanks to all who have kindly aided me in the preparation of this paper, and also to fervently hope that the efforts of some future historian may be crowned with success in searching for "the hidden things that remain."

REV. CHRISTOPHER W. COLLIER,
Acting Pastor, 1893-1897.

Address Representing the Former Pastors.

DEAR FRIENDS:—I do not see how I am to keep out the personal in what I am expected to say to-day, for, as I understand it, I am to represent the former pastors of this church. Of course, if one is to represent them one must be like them, in some respects at least; in more than one sense he must be one of them. Now I am going to assume not so much that I think and feel as they do, but that they think and feel as I do. So I shall speak pretty freely the feelings of my own heart and from my own experience.

Speaking in that way, I am sure it will have to be largely in the vein of congratulation; it will consist in telling you of some things that have greatly cheered and helped your former pastors.

For one thing: they have taken great satisfaction in the *substantial character* of this church. That is the reputation this church has in all the surrounding country. I used to hear it at the Ministers' Association; at the confereuces, and when talking with individuals. Let us keep in mind that by the "church" I mean the membership, not the building in which we worship. Unless we keep this point clear we shall run into difficulties, as did one of my friends from whom I heard the other day. He had just been called to become pastor of a church in this State, and he was describing the church in some detail; at one point he overlooked this distinction between the church building and the membership of the church, and went on to say that there were 168 members in his church, built of granite! That must be a very substantial church! But I am glad to say that the membership of this church, though substantial, is not built of granite. This church is substantial in the character of the men and women who constitute it; in the number of its membership; in the general stability of its character, and in the steadiness of its financial concerns. And this last is no mean thing. I myself can testify, so far as the minister's salary is concerned, that during my pastorate with you it was ready when it was due, and sometimes it was paid before. Now that is as it should be, though it is not so common as it should be. The community has a right to expect the minister to be an example as regards money matters, and it has the right to expect as much of the church. There should be no institution in town more jealous of its good reputation for promptness and reliability in financial affairs than the church. Often the minister finds it impossible to do as he would like in such affairs because of the dilatoriness of the church; but I am glad to say such is not the case here, and I trust this church will always be found at the farthest remove therefrom.

This substantial character of the church has been supplemented by the fine quality of its spirituality, and this too has been a great comfort to its pastors. There are as earnest Christians here as anywhere. I shall never forget some of the prayer meetings we have held together in the basement of this church. Yet the spirituality of this church has come out in other ways than in the prayer meeting, as goes without saying, for a spirituality that shows itself there, but only there, is not worthy of the name. I felt all this the first Sabbath I was with you, and it drew me to you.

Yet this spirituality has existed along with a broad and generous tolerance. I do not see how a preacher has the right to expect or indeed needs a greater freedom of utterance than you have granted here. Personally I do not know how many heresies I may have broached here, but you listened and waited with a patience and kindliness that as much as said, "Oh, it is all right; we know what he is driving at, and he will come out all right by and by!" Certainly I have said some things that I would not say now. Yet I believe still in the freedom you grant. The Kingdom of God is not much hurt by mistakes conscientiously, reverently made, no more than the oak is hurt by some unusual blast. The minister is to be trusted in the realm of spiritual things; if in the main he cannot be trusted, then by that very fact he is shown to be unfit for the Christian ministry. To be sure he will make mistakes in theology and religious matters, but if in the main he is the right kind of a man, *trust* him, give him liberty, and he will work out all right in the end. Now this is what this church has done; it has not dictated to its ministers. Neither has it been cursed by any one man taking the reins and trying to "run" things. You have been careful in choosing your pastor, then you have trusted him.

And you have done all this in a most kind-spirited and appreciative way. Some churches let their minister alone, to be sure, but they let him too severely alone. There is too little sympathy exchanged, yet the best preaching and the best pastoral work is dependent on the best of feeling existing between pastor and people. Now, personally, I do not see how you could have treated a minister more kindly than you treated me. Away at Yale as I was a good half of the time! And my own feeling in the matter is fully shared by my wife! I hope only that wherever my lot may be cast, the people to whom I minister may be as kindly as the East Hampton people have been.

Yet in this, too, I believe I voice the feeling of the other pastors. For instance, only yesterday I was talking with Brother Ives about a certain church, and he said: "Why, I know that church; I have preached there several times. It is a good church. I have often thought it was a second East Hampton on a larger scale!" Let me say I shall consider that church carefully.

But this church has been appreciative as well as kindly. When a good piece of work has been done, you have not gone away content with saying that you pay the salary promptly and that this squares off that. You have not done that, but by your words of appreciation you have shown your pastor that his work has told, that he has accomplished what he set out to do, and he has taken great satisfaction in it. Was that pride on the pastor's part? Possibly; but more likely it was the satisfaction of an earnest man whose heart is in his work, who longs to see some fruit of his work, to be assured that his work is not in vain; for no man can do his best work and keep it up constantly save in the spirit of hopefulness, and probably that is nowhere truer than in the Christian ministry. Now you, by your appreciation of good work, when good work was done, have aroused in your pastors fresh hopefulness and power. That is the way to get the most and the best work out of a pastor, and I trust this church will never lose sight of it.

My word to-day, then, is a word of congratulation, of congratulation on what the past has been. It is a good past. This should be a day of joy, therefore, because of much work well done. That is our feeling as we look back. And as we look forward it is with hope. For this church in its latent powers and possibilities was never stronger than it is to-day, and the success of the past should be but the prelude of a success greater still in the days to come, as the dawn is the prelude of the coming day. God looks to you for such a future. As a church *determine that it shall be so*, and lay hold of Him for help. God bless you. He will bless you. You can and will succeed.

C. W. COLLIER,
Pastor, 1893-97.

ADDRESS BY REV. HENRY E. HART.

MY RETURN to this place and anniversary was trying in many respects. After receiving the invitation, it came to me often and with a peculiar heartache, How shall I sing the Lord's song in a strange land? A friendly letter came to my relief and lifted me to the duty. I come as if to speak of a dear and honored friend who had passed away. Your pastor introduced me happily to this occasion by his letter of invitation, in which he says: "Please write me that you will come with your message to help us, or your memories to cheer us."

My memories of the North Church are delightful. The organization of that church may be likened to a river that in time of high water overflowed its banks and made for itself a new channel, and later, further down the stream, united itself again to the original river.

The Union or North Church was organized in September, 1856. Public worship was continued there until May, 1880, a period of twenty-four years. Twenty-five members from the First Church constituted the nucleus of the new church. During the twenty-four years of its existence, ninety members were added on profession of faith, and nineteen by letter from other churches, in all one hundred and thirty-four members; of these, fifty-two have died, twenty-one joined the South or First Church at one time, and twenty-eight were dismissed and recommended to other churches.

Of money contributed, there were $73.50 in 1868, $88.10 in 1869, with $90 given the same year for the Sunday School library. In 1870, $77.97 were given for various objects, and $17 for the Home of the Friendless; $94.97 in all for 1870.

What about the pastor? He came, a young man of 32 with a wife ten years younger. He had preached three years to a church in Litchfield County, and so had a little experience and entered zealously on the work. The people cordially supported and encouraged him in every proper way.

Of the deacons, one may say, they were plain men, eminently faithful in their office, never troublesome or in the way. Deacon Sears and Deacon Markham were good men and true; they did their whole duty. And the young people! How many were there! Young people of the ages from 12 to 25 years and a little over, a large, faithful and sincere company of Christian youth. They were well behaved and orderly. It is a pleasure to think of them even now and recall their religious experience, their fidelity, their close and loyal attachment to the church of their choice. As Miss Ella Buell once said, "We were all young together."

As to the doctrines we held, they were the old-fashioned orthodox kind, and we were not disturbed by new theories. There was no Revised Version then. I was not critical, but practical. We worked for results. I lived and labored together with them from July 29, 1866, to November, 1871.

What, now, were the justifying principles or motives in organizing and supporting the North Church?

First: A regard for independent and manly action. The South Church would not yield an inch in regard to the location of the new church. They would not make *any* concession to the wish of the North people. The company that went off were somewhat numerous. Twenty-five people formed the nucleus of the new church, and these with their families probably made the congregation of about one hundred persons. Business had begun to prosper, the village was growing, and altogether they felt justified in forming a new church.

Second: The separate organization of the North Church led the people there to bestir themselves to a degree of activity that would not have been possible had they continued with the South Church. The independent organization called out their best activity. They worked and gave, they lived, prayed in secret, worshiped publicly, and put forth their best energies for their church. They came to love their church more deeply for the toil and sacrifice they gave.

Revivals: One in 1860, when Rev. J. J. Bell was pastor; again during the winter of 1866–67 in the first year of my own pastorate, resulting in the addition of thirteen young people to the church the first Sunday in July, 1867, and many at various times afterward.

Rev. Fred W. Chapman did excellent work for the church during two years before I came, and prepared the way for my period of service.

Good men were reared in the North Church, and they are a power for good with you to-day. There are Deacon John Watrous, too well known among you to need any recommendation from me; Elijah C. Barton, my ever dear and faithful friend; Edwin Barton, with a wife every way as good and excellent as he; Robert Hall, true and good, and a host of other names might be added, but especially should be mentioned those faithful helpers on Clark's Hill, Mr. Lyman H. Clark and his brother Francis, who with their families gave and maintained excellent and efficient choir service.

F. J. Stedman, ever memorable for his heroic attempt to keep sober at a critical time, and last and noblest of all, that most true and loyal brother, George H. White, now several years in glory. Brother White was pure gold. He was a diamond which the Master polished for his own most holy service. He came out on the Lord's side, February 19, 1867, the first one to thus declare himself, and ever remained one on whom all the church might depend. His rest is glorious.

THE INSIDE OF THE OLD CHURCH.
An Interview with Miss Julia A. West.

THE OLD CHURCH was put up a good while before it was finished. Rough boards served for seats. There was no entry. The doors opened directly into the church, much to the embarrassment of those who came late. There were three aisles—a main aisle up the center and two side aisles. A row of box pews was on the sides of the church and two rows of box pews between each aisle. In these old-fashioned pews part of the people faced the preacher and part of them turned their backs to him, and some of them were sidewise to the preacher as they sat around the inside of those box pews. The top of the pew was of ornamental open work, and these pieces of wood could be made to squeak as you turned them around in their sockets. This was a delight to the children, but the special privilege of the children came when they stood during the long prayer and looked out over the railing.

In the old days there was one stove. It was in the middle aisle. It was hard to tell just where the pipe went to, perhaps out of the window. It was very cold in the old church. There were great cracks in the uneven floor, and one who sang long ago in the choir used to tell how her breath froze upon her veil as she sang.

The pulpit was longer than broad. It was reached by a stairway on the west side of it. Three steps brought you to a broad stair, from which you turned and passed to the pulpit, which was paneled and painted white, and had turned yellow. A red cushion projected out over the front of the pulpit. Under the pulpit was a place called the "dungeon," of which the children were much afraid. Over the pulpit was the sounding board, shaped like an umbrella without a handle. It had no visible means of support and was a great mystery to the little folks, but it was probably supported in some way

PARSONAGE—Erected 1868.

FIRST MEETING HOUSE—Erected 1755.
(From a drawing made from memory by Mrs. E. E. Marcy, Evanston, Illinois.)

from the back. This sounding board was white, and had at each corner of its many sides a big carved blossom painted bright red, which looked like a peony.

In the old church a stairway led from each side of the south doors to the gallery. The galleries were on three sides, and the choir sat in the front seats. Hannah Sears, who lived one hundred and twenty years ago, is said to have remarked: "There were no tunes. We took the Psalms and sung them along like a chant." Some of the old singers were Betsy Smith and Nabby Smith, sisters of Uncle John Smith. There was Dolly Parmalee and Dempsey Parmalee, too. They got a piece of music and pricked off the notes for extra copies, which they called "patent note." They often sang "Judgment Anthem" and "Easter Anthem." When Mr. Curtis was here they say he used to give out "How Firm a Foundation" every Sunday. They had only a pitch-pipe to help them in singing.

In the southeast and southwest corners of the gallery, a few steps higher than the other pews, were the "nigger pews." Here sat old Phyllis, a colored woman, whom tradition says was quite disturbed because she was black. She had short curly hair, and to remedy the defect she raveled worsted stockings and hung the yarn down the sides of her face. Later the "nigger pews" were put down stairs on the west side. Then it was only a plain seat with a back and near the wood room.

The church was lighted with tallow candles. The posts under the galleries were dark blue. To these the candles were hung. They were set in sockets with a rim to keep the melted tallow from dripping down. For extra lights they brought their brass candlesticks with candles in them. The tithing man rapped on the floor with his stick when there was any mischief or disorder, and sometimes pointed at the offender, which was considered a great disgrace.

By and by things were changed inside the old church. This made a great deal of talk. They partitioned off an entry from the main part. Two windows were put into the partition, so one could look in upon the audience. They took the box pews from the body of the church, leaving pews only on the sides. They put in two stoves, one by the east door, the other by the west door. Long pipes from the stoves met in a drum above the center of the church; then from the drum a pipe went up into a very small chimney. These stove pipes leaked. Square pans were wired under the joints to catch the drops, but many a hat and cloak were spoiled. But, most wonderful of all, they put in a whale-oil chandelier. By and by some people began to carpet their pews and put in cushions. They commenced to dress better and think more of themselves.

Rev. Joel West was ordained in the old church, October 17, 1792. To his ordination the people came from all the country round. One woman came before sunrise in order to get a seat. Rev. Thomas Brockway rode over from Lebanon, now Columbia. His beautiful daughter came, too, and as she passed the house soon after purchased by the young preacher ordained that day, she was so much pleased with it that she said in jest to her companions, "See, that is my house." Indeed, the young preacher soon brought this girl of eighteen or nineteen home as his bride. The house by the lake was improved till it became the pride of the town, and her house at last; and there is the cradle still in which her twelve children were rocked to sleep. Perhaps no minister's wife ever made such a stir as this young bride made when she came to church in her wedding costume. Her dress was of changeable silk of bright colors and very beautiful. Over her shoulders was a red broadcloth cloak with a large hood, the whole trimmed with white swansdown. And she had a white satin bonnet trimmed with white swansdown. Her hair was "banged" across her forehead and hung in a long braid down her back. This woman, Mrs. Joel West, of a hundred years ago, had the first carpet that was ever owned in town, and what an extravagance for a minister's wife! When Deacon Bill came to the parsonage he did not dare step on the beautiful covering of the floor, but carefully walked around the edges, thinking that carpets were never made for boots. These are memories of the old church and days gone by.

REV. GEORGE W. ANDREWS, D. D.,
Pastor, 1867-1870.

LETTERS FROM FORMER PASTORS.

TALLADEGA, ALA., September 24, 1898.
To the South Congregational Church, East Hampton, Conn.:

DEAR FRIENDS:—I am glad to send you a word of greeting on this one hundred and fiftieth anniversary. As the ancient church of Phillipi was Paul's first love in Europe, so you were my first love among the churches of New England, and as Paul's faith and interest in that church never faltered, so my interest and faith in you have ever remained steadfast.

It is always a joy for me to visit you and to know of your prosperity, spiritual and material. I am with you in spirit on this interesting occasion, though far separated in body. Except for the Macedonian call, "Come down into the south land and help us," which we heard, I believe our relation as pastor and people might have been long.

It is twenty-eight years in November since we came into our present mission field fresh from our good-byes and farewells with you. These have been short years, full of work and full of joy in the Lord. We cannot doubt that our mission here was from Him who ever guides His church and His disciples.

During all these years my faith in God and His word has grown stronger and stronger. I am as certain that the Bible in its spirit and teachings is the Book of God, as I am that the world I live in is the work of God. Let me exhort you to be diligent students of the Bible. I like often to repeat Isaiah, 50th chapter, 7th verse, and to make its experience and its spirit and its faith mine.

My dear friends of the South Church, my heart goes out to you afresh upon this anniversary occasion. May the dear Father bless and keep you all to His praise and glory, both the living and the dead, alive for evermore.

Affectionately yours, G. W. ANDREWS.

Rev. Mr. Slade:
DEAR SIR:—My father wishes me to acknowledge the receipt of your letter, inviting him to be present at your one hundred and fiftieth anniversary next September, also an invitation received from Mr. Mills Bevin.

It would give him great pleasure to be with you, but his very feeble state of health makes it impossible. He is not even well enough to write you a letter to be read at the anniversary.

He hopes that it will be a very interesting and memorable occasion, and regrets very much that he is unable to be with you and enjoy it with you.

Yours truly, ANNA COLBURN BARNARD.
For REV. B. A. SMITH.

WORCESTER, MASS., 69 Lincoln St., July 29, 1898.

BUENA VISTA, Colo., October 7, 1898.

To the Church at East Hampton, Conn.:

DEAR BRETHREN:—It would give me great pleasure to join in your celebration, but that seems impossible. Of course it will be an occasion full of interest. You still have a warm place in my heart, and my desire and prayer to God is "that all may be richly blessed."

The last few years have wrought great changes. Many familiar faces will be seen no more. One by one those who have loved the church have passed to the church triumphant, and who knows but what in the glorified presence they have as much interest and joy in this celebration as the earthly participants. Be assured of my deep interest in the church. Trusting that the celebration will be pleasant and profitable,

I am most cordially, EDWARD P. ROOT.

ىك ىك ىك

To the Members of the First Congregational Church of East Hampton, Conn.:

DEAR BRETHREN:—From this new parish in the finest city in the northwest, Mrs. Holmes and myself send greetings to a beloved church in one of the most beautiful nooks of all New England. We may find other people with whom to labor will be a delight, but none with whom it can be a greater delight than to have labored with you. It is safe to say that no other church will ever be to us dearer than was and is the East Hampton Church.

May you be blessed abundantly in this one hundred and fiftieth anniversary of your organization. To have completed such a term of usefulness may well be a matter of congratulation on the part of any church. God grant that the younger portion of the congregation, just entering upon their work in and through the church, may appreciate the history lying back of the church into which they come, and appreciating it, may be true to it, worthy of those who have gone before.

We shall ever consider it one of the privileges of our lives to have labored for even two years among you, to have stood in such a close relation to the church whose history reaches back so far into the life of this nation; the church whose influence has been felt in all parts of the world. And if it shall be found in the day when all things shall be made plain by the Spirit of God, that we added ever so little to the measure of the influence exerted by the church, we shall be more than satisfied.

I need not tell you that it would be an unspeakable pleasure to be with you on the day of your anniversary. But the distance between us is so great that however mighty the desire to be with you, and to enjoy the exercises of the day, it is impossible. But we shall be with you in spirit, and the day will be marked by us in this our distant home.

The dear Father command his richest blessings upon you as a church, not only upon this day of deep interest historically, but upon all the days which lie down the years yet to come.

Now the God of peace, that brought again from the dead our Lord Jesus, that great Shepherd of the sheep, through the blood of the everlasting covenant, make you perfect in every good work, to do His will, working in you that which is well pleasing in his sight, through Jesus Christ, to whom be glory forever and ever.

Very sincerely yours, HENRY HOLMES.

MINNEAPOLIS, MINN., Sept. 23, 1898.

COMMITTEES OF ARRANGEMENTS.

CHURCH.
REV. WILLIAM SLADE,   DEA. E. C. BARTON,
    DEA. H. D. CHAPMAN,   DEA. H. W. PORTER,
                    J. W. SMITH.

SOCIETY.
A. AVERY BEVIN,   S. MILLS BEVIN,   A. H. CONKLIN,
       HALSEY MEAD,   ROBERT H. HALL.

SPECIAL COMMITTEES.
COLLATION.
MRS. ROBERT H. HALL,   MRS. A. H. CONKLIN,
    MRS. WILLIAM H. BEVIN,   MRS. PHILO BEVIN,
         MRS. H. E. CARPENTER.

INVITATION AND PRINTING.
REV. WILLIAM SLADE,   S. MILLS BEVIN.

RECEPTION.
HALSEY MEAD,   MRS. PHILO BEVIN.

ENTERTAINMENT AND FINANCE.
H. D. CHAPMAN,   HERBERT CLARK.

DECORATION.
WALTER C. CLARK,   HERBERT CLARK,   MRS. HAYDEN CLARK,
    MRS. JAMES FORBES,   MRS. ROBERT A. BECKWITH,
          ROBERT A. BECKWITH.

MUSIC.
A. W. SEXTON,   MRS. WILLIAM SLADE,   MISS LOIS J. BARTON.

RELICS.
CLARK M. WATROUS,   E. D. BARTON.

USHERS.
ROBERT A. BECKWITH,   D. CLIFFORD BARTON.

APPENDIX.

Deacons.

THE first deacons of this church were Ebenezer Clark and Isaac Smith, who were probably chosen to that office at or not far from the time of its organization. Ebenezer Clark was the son of John and Sarah (Goodwin) Clark, and was born in Middletown, probably in that part that is now Cromwell, July 11, 1711. He married first, June 21, 1733, Abigail, daughter of Joseph and Hannah Whitmore, who died April 9, 1738, and was interred in the old quarry cemetery in Portland. He married second, September 20, 1739, Ann, daughter of Captain John and Ann (Ward) Warner, of Middletown. In 1743 he was appointed by the General Assembly ensign of the first company or train-band on the east side of the Connecticut river, and afterwards had the title "Captain." He was one of the leading petitioners for the incorporation of this society in 1744, and prominent in the administration of its early affairs. He removed from this parish about the year 1755 to the parish of Judea, then that part of the town of Woodbury since set off as a separate town by the name of Washington. His second wife died there March 3, 1795, aged 79. He died April 5, 1800, at the age of 89. His gravestone, now standing in the cemetery at Washington, states that he was a deacon of the church there for forty-four years.

CHILDREN OF DEACON EBENEZER CLARK.
(By his first wife.)
Abigail, born April 1, 1734.
Jedediah, born Jan. 16, 1736.
(By his second wife.)
Tabitha, born June 18, 1740; baptized June 22, 1740.
Ebenezer, born Feb. 28, 1742; baptized April 4, 1742.
Ann, born March 1, 1744; baptized April 8, 1744.

CONGREGATIONAL CHURCH OF EAST HAMPTON.   61

Rebecca, born Dec. 28, 1745; baptized Jan. 13, 1746; died Nov. 11,
  1755.
Susannah, born April 23. 1748; baptized May 1, 1748.
Joseph, born May 30, 1750.
Jerusha, born April 24, 1752.
Sarah, born March 3, 1755; died June 30, 1776.
Moses, born March 4, 1757; died March 4, 1757.

Isaac Smith, chosen with Ebenezer Clark as one of the first deacons of this church, was a son of Ralph and Mary (Mayo) Smith, and was born in Eastham, Mass., November 17, 1716. He married at Eastham, March 9, 1738, Mary Sparrow, born March 10, 1718. She died April 17, 1785, and he married, second, Lydia ———, who died March 24, 1799, aged 75. He removed with his father and brothers to Middle Haddam about 1740, and he and his wife Mary united with the church there April 5, 1741. His residence in East Hampton was near the present residence of Henry Hutchins on Walnut avenue. He died July 29, 1802, full of years and full of honors.

CHILDREN OF DEACON ISAAC SMITH.

Azubah, born Dec. 7, 1738, in Eastham, Mass.; married Jan. 10,
  1760, John Hinckley.
Ralph, born March 15, 1742, in Middletown, Conn.; baptized April
  25, 1742; married Dec. 2, 1767, Hannah Hollister.
Isaac, born Nov. 18, 1745, in Middletown, Conn.
Mary, born Feb. 6, 1747, in Middletown, Conn.; baptized March 22,
  1748; married Dec. 3, 1767, Nathaniel Bosworth.
Sarah, born Jan. 27, 1750-1, in Middletown; married ——— Sage.
Phebe, born April 22, 1753, in Middletown, Conn.; married Oct. 25,
  1775, Ezekiel Wright.
Asenath, born March 20, 1756, in Middletown, Conn.; married Jan.
  11, 1781, John Markham.
Sparrow, born August 14, 1760, in Middletown, Conn.; married May
  3, 1787, Eunice Clark.

John Clark, Jr., son of John and Sarah (Goodwin) Clark, born December 9, 1715, was chosen deacon to fill the vacancy occasioned by the removal of his brother Ebenezer from the parish. He resided upon Clark's Hill, in the first frame house erected in the parish, and kept an ordinary or public house in addition to carrying on a large farm. This house was erected in 1744, and was situated on the main thoroughfare leading from Middletown to the northeastern part of the colony. As the mode of traveling at that time was principally upon foot or horseback, there is no doubt but that many a weary traveler has partaken of the good cheer of this famous hostelry. This house was destroyed by fire October 28, 1887, but a fine photograph of it was exhibited at the anniversary by Mr. Clark M. Watrous, as was also the unique sign that swung before its door, which was kindly loaned by Mrs. Stewart D. Parmelee. Deacon Clark held for many years the office of Justice of the Peace, an office of far greater powers and jurisdiction at that time than the present, and his court records show that a large number of cases were brought before him for adjudication and settlement, and that many offenders against the peace and order of the community learned from him in a practical manner that "the law was a terror to evil-doers." He married, February 1, 1744, Sarah, daughter of Captain Nathaniel and Mehitable (Hurlbut) White, born October 24, 1724, who died January 26, 1780. He died August 8, 1809, aged ninety-four years.

CHILDREN OF DEACON JOHN CLARK.

John, born March 15, 1745; married Feb. 15, 1767, Deborah Mosely.
Mehitable, born Nov. 14, 1746; died Nov. 1, 1747.
Sarah, born Feb. 20, 1747-8; married first, Nov. 18, 1767, James Johnson, Jr.; second, Jan. 18, 1781, Capt. Silas Dunham.
Mehitable, born April 8, 1750; married November 13, 1771, Daniel Judd, Jr.
Daniel, born Oct. 13, 1752; married June 30, 1780, Lydia Davison. A Revolutionary soldier, Pomfret, Conn.
Esther, born Oct. 2, 1754; married Peter Parker.
Elijah, born Nov. 1, 1756; died Nov., 1776, in the army in New York State.
Desire, born June 12, 1759; died June 12, 1759.
David, born May 23, 1760.
Lydia, born April 13, 1763; married Nov. 21, 1784, Joseph Davison, of Pomfret, Conn.
Moses, born Nov. 23, 1766; baptized Nov. 30, 1766; married June 3, 1788, Millicent Blish.

Deacons Smith and Clark, having become incapacitated from performing the duties of the office by reason of the infirmities of age, it was deemed best by the church to appoint their successors, and on the fifth day of February, 1795, James Bill, Esq., and Gideon Arnold were selected for that purpose. An account of Deacon Bill will be found in connection with the family of the Rev. John Norton, whose daughter he married.

Gideon Arnold, who was chosen as the colleague of James Bill, was the son of Deacon Gideon and Abigail (Brainerd) Arnold, and was born in Haddam in 1735. He married, September 2, 1761, Lucy, daughter of Gershom and Mary (Buell) Hinckley, of Lebanon, born March 19, 1738. He resided in a house now standing near the silk mill and was licensed as a tavern keeper and carried on a small farm. His wife died March 1, 1801, in the sixty-third year of her age, after a long and painful illness, which she endured with exemplary patience and resignation in the hopes of Christian salvation. He died February 17, 1807, in the seventy-second year of his age, and his tombstone, standing in Lakeview Cemetery, tells the passer-by who pauses for a moment to read, that being highly respected in life, his death was universally lamented.

> " In veracity he was strict,
> In his profession sincere;
> In his friendship he was close,
> In his manner meek,
> In religion exemplary."

CHILDREN OF DEACON GIDEON ARNOLD.

Apollos, born March 23, 1763; married August 12, 1784, Lucy Bill.
Mary, born Sept. 5, 1765; baptized Sept. 15, 1765; died Jan. 10, 1768.
Dan, born June 11, 1767; baptized July 26, 1767; married Arethusa Gillett, and lived in Hebron, Conn.
A son, born June 6, 1769; died June 8, 1769.
* Mary, born Sept. 14, 1772; died April 18, 1793.
Charles, born Nov. 16, 1776; married first, Deborah Thomas; second, Lucy Thomas, of Lebanon, Conn.
Lucy, born Jan. 12, 1779; married April 7, 1803, Capt. David Buell.

---

* Copy of inscription on tombstone in Lakeview Cemetery:

> Sacred to the Memory of
> MISS POLLY ARNOLD
> daughter of Mr Gideon & Mrs Lucy Arnold
> who after a short illness departed this life ye 18th of April AD 1793
> in ye 21st year of her age.

She was a person unaffected in her mien, mild and sedate in her temper, benevolent in her nature, sincere in her profession, exemplary in her life, engaging in her manners, pleasant, calm and resigned in death.

> Let weeping virtue mourn around thy tomb
> And meek eyed pity vail thy early doom
> Yet worth like thine sustains no wide decay
> Tho. time should sweep these sculptured lines away
> In realms of bliss beyond the verge of time
> Thy name shall flourish in immortal prime
> Tho. here alas thy lifes short circuit ends
> Thou best of daughters, sisters and of friends

On the 16th of May, 1805, a little more than ten years after the election of Deacons Bill and Arnold, Moses Cook and Isaac Smith were elected as their successors. Moses Cook was the son of Josiah and Hannah (Sparrow) Cook, and was baptized in the church at Middle Haddam, September 26, 1742. He resided north of the lake, and in company with his younger brother, Richard, carried on a grist mill that formerly stood where the East Hampton Bell Company's manufactory now stands. He married, December 18, 1765, Elizabeth Cone, and they were admitted to full communion in this church April 23, 1769. She died October 8, 1808, aged sixty-four years, and he married second, April 11, 1809, Ede, daughter of Jabez and Sarah (Judd) Clark and widow of John Norton, Jr. He died May 15, 1818, aged seventy-five years, and his second wife died February 18, 1827. His children were by his first wife, and were, as far as can be ascertained, as follows:

    Lydia, born Sept. 23, 1766; baptized May 18, 1769; married Comfort Beebee.
    Selden, born Mar. 17, 1768; baptized May 18, 1769; died Nov. 16, 1769.
    Selden, born Jan. 4, 1770; baptized Jan. 14, 1770.
    Moses, born Jan. 7, 1772; baptized April 3, 1772.
    Elizabeth, born 1774; married Sept. 11, 1794, Adonijah Strong, Jr.
    Josiah, born ——; died June 4, 1778.
    Susanna, born 1776; died May 8, 1778.
    Josiah, born ——; baptized May 9, 1779.
    Susanna, born ——; baptized September 6, 1779; married first, April 25, 1798, Daniel Butler Newton; second, Sept. 17, 1801, Henry Strong.
    Hannah, born ——; baptized June 6, 1782.
    Livia, born ——; baptized July 18, 1784; married Nov. 3, 1803, Wix Watrous.
    Selden, born ——; baptized June 25, 1786.
    Orrin, born ——; baptized Nov. 16, 1788; married June 22, 1813, Polly Parmelee.

Isaac Smith, colleague of Deacon Cook, was the son of Deacon Isaac and Mary (Sparrow) Smith, and was born November 18, 1745. He married, January 9, 1772, Jerusha Brooks. He was a farmer and resided in a house now standing near the eastern terminus of Walnut avenue. He died October 28, 1815, aged seventy years. She died July 11, 1836, aged ninety-one years and six months.

CHILDREN OF DEACON ISAAC SMITH.

Isaac, born Oct. 11, 1772; married Sept. 12, 1796, Hannah Brown, and was a successful physician in Portland, Conn.
Amasa, born July 22, 1774; married Mary Williams; was a school-teacher.
Jerusha, born June 29, 1776; died May 13, 1860.
Mary, born June 5, 1778.
Brooks, born June 8, 1780; baptized July 23, 1780; married Mar. 7, 1811, Elizabeth Brooks.
Infant son, born May 29, 1782, still-born.
Azubah, born Oct. 15, 1783; baptized Nov. 30, 1783; married Benjamin Cobb.
Infant daughter, born Jan. 8, 1785, still-born.
Porter, born April 8, 1788; baptized Nov. 16, 1788; married Statira Brainerd, Nov. 3, 1811.
Washington, born Jan. 28, 1791; married first, Cynthia Barstow; second, Mary J. Davis.

Joseph Sage was elected a deacon July 24, 1815, and was the son of Ebenezer and Abiah (Southmayd) Sage, and was born in Middletown in 1757. He kept the toll gate on the turnpike road near the Griffith place, where the railroad now crosses. He died February 20, 1818, aged sixty years, and was interred in the cemetery at Middle Haddam. He had no children.

David Clark, elected deacon of this church July 10, 1816, was the son of Deacon John and Sarah (White) Clark, and was born May 23, 1760. He was a farmer and tavern keeper, and for many years a Justice of the Peace. He was the first Worshipful Master of Warren Lodge, No. 51, F. and A. M., instituted August 1, 1811, and which for many years met in the house of Orrin Alvord, near the meeting house. He served a short term during the latter part of the Revolutionary War as a private, and in 1831 was granted a pension of $26.66 per annum. He died January 8, 1839, aged seventy-nine years. He resided at the old homestead on Clark's Hill, and was thrice married. His first wife was Jerusha, daughter of Captain Abijah and Margaret (Dewey) Hall, who was born May 21, 1760, and to whom he was married September 19, 1782. She died August 24, 1800, and he married second, November 15, 1801, Eunice, daughter of Joshua and Ruth (Mayo) Griffith, born April 16, 1780. She died July 27, 1811, and he married third, May 28, 1813, Mehitable, daughter of George and Mehitable (Miller) Hubbard, born June 12, 1782. She died November 26, 1854.

CHILDREN OF DEACON DAVID CLARK.
(By first wife.)
Elijah, born Jan. 28, 1784; baptized Oct. 3, 1784.
Chauncey, born Jan. 19, 1789; baptized April 26, 1789; married Zilpah Griffith.
Jerusha Hall, born August, 1800; baptized Aug. 25, 1800; died Oct. 23, 1800.
(By second wife.)
Deborah Griffith, born Nov. 3, 1802; baptized May 15, 1803; married Hubbard Barton.
Emilia Adeline, born Jan. 1, 1805; baptized April 28, 1805; married Minories Watrous.
Jerusha Hall, born Dec. 1, 1807; baptized Dec. 1, 1807; married Lewis Utley.
(By third wife.)
Mary Esther, born July 27, 1814, town record; baptized July 10, 1814, church record; married William Bailey.

Warren Ackley Skinner, who was elected deacon May 1, 1818, was the son of Samuel and Ruth (Ackley) Skinner, and was born in the parish of Westchester, in the town of Colchester, March 7, 1789. He was a farmer, and resided on Miller's Hill in the house occupied by Mrs. Sarah A. Skinner. He died January 4, 1862, and after the record of his death upon the church books is written the following quotation from the twelfth Psalm, first verse: "Help, Lord! for the godly man ceaseth!" He and his wife united with this church by letter from Westchester in 1816. He was ever zealous for the work of the Lord, and in the Lord's hand was an important factor in the building up of the church, both in spiritual and temporal things, during the forty-five years that he was a faithful watchman upon the walls of Zion. He married, November 28, 1810, Anna, daughter of Asa and Anna (Marvin) Day, born January 28, 1791, who died September 18, 1879.

CHILDREN OF DEACON WARREN ACKLEY SKINNER.
Diantha, born Sept. 19, 1811; baptized July 28, 1816; married Feb. 15, 1832, Anson Carpenter.
Samuel, born May 14, 1814; baptized July 28, 1816; married Oct. 6, 1841, Laura A. Markham.
Ruth Ann, born Nov. 24, 1816; baptized May 11, 1817; married Oct. 6, 1841, Ambrose N. Markham.
Emily, born Feb. 21, 1819; baptized June 20, 1819; married Nov. 8, 1843, John B. Hungerford.
Mary Octavo, born July 27, 1821; baptized July 27, 1821; married Sept. 23, 1844, Daniel N. Markham.

DEA. WARREN A. SKINNER,
1789-1862.

MRS. ANNA SKINNER,
1791-1879.

RESIDENCE OF DEA. WARREN A. SKINNER.
(MILLER'S HILL.)

DEA. SAMUEL SKINNER,
1814-1895.

MRS. LAURA SKINNER.

Henry L., born May 30, 1823; baptized Aug. 24, 1823; married Oct. 7, 1849, Clarine A. Markham.
John Williams, born Feb. 26, 1825; baptized Sept. 11, 1825; married Oct. 3, 1847, Amelia Stranahan.
Warren, born June 17, 1828; baptized Sept. 28, 1828; married April 29, 1855, Sarah M. Ackley.
Lyman Francis, born Sept. 18, 1830; baptized July 3, 1831; married first, Dec. 31, 1855, Nancy M. Clark; second, April 25, 1865, Grace E. Brown.
Rosannah, born Oct. 5, 1832; baptized Aug. 25, 1833; married Nov. 26, 1852, Horatio D. Chapman.

Diodate Brockway West was chosen deacon December 11, 1823. He was the son of Rev. Joel and Elizabeth (Brockway) West, and was born July 20, 1798, and was admitted to communion July 4, 1819. He was a farmer and commercial traveler, and resided at the old homestead near the outlet of the lake. He represented the town in the General Assembly in 1870. He married, May 1, 1822, Nancy, daughter of Capt. Timothy and Hannah (Sears) Rogers. She died July 5, 1855. He died June 13, 1881.

CHILDREN OF DEACON DIODATE BROCKWAY WEST.
Child, still-born, Jan. 20, 1823.
Marianne Rogers, born Sept. 26, 1824.
Julia Brockway, born Sept. 10, 1828.
Herbert Rogers, born March 16, 1831; died Jan. 26, 1855.

December 30, 1857, Samuel Skinner and Allen Cushman Clark were chosen, and continued to exercise the duties of that office until December 18, 1888, when they were relieved from active service, and a new method of choosing incumbents of that office came into vogue.

Samuel Skinner was the son of Deacon Warren A. and Anna (Day) Skinner, and was born May 14, 1814. He resided near Skinner's Mills and carried on the manufacture of paper boxes to a considerable extent. He united with the church on profession of faith, in 1833, and ever after was a faithful, earnest worker in the service of the Master. He was rarely absent from any service of the church, and for years was the acknowledged leader of the prayer meetings. He married, October 6, 1841, Laura Ann, daughter of John and Anna (Estabrook) (Niles) Markham, born October 25, 1813, and died without issue.

Allen C. Clark was the son of Amos and Betsey M. S. (Smith) Clark, and was born August 9, 1817. He married, April 2, 1845, Frances M. Ackley, who died April 5, 1897. He was a farmer and stonecutter, and is still living on Miller's Hill at the age of eighty-one years. They had one child, who died in infancy.

Beginning with December 18, 1888, the deacons were chosen biennially to serve four years. After four years' service they are ineligible for election to this office for the space of two years. Under this new method the following persons have served the church in the office of deacon: Hubert E. Carpenter, Chauncey B. West, Elijah C. Barton, Walter C. Clark, Edwin D. Barton, Horatio D. Chapman, John Watrous, Horace W. Porter.

Of this number only one has passed away—Chauncey B. West, who died August 28, 1893. He was an earnest Christian man and ever faithful to the church.

Dea. Elijah C. Barton.

Dea. Hubert E. Carpenter.

Dea. Horatio D. Chapman.

Dea. Walter C. Clark.

Dea. Chauncey B. West.

Dea. John Watrous.

Dea. Edwin D. Barton.

Dea. H. Welton Porter.

OLD DOCUMENTS.

ROLL OF COMPANY that responded to the Lexington Alarm from Chatham in 1775, and their term of service, copied from "Connecticut Soldiers in the Revolution." The entire Company were residents at the time of East Hampton parish.

Silas Dunham, *Captain*,	-	5 days.	Amos Clark, -	-	- 5 days.
Timothy Percival, *Lieutenant*,	5	"	Elijah Clark, -	-	- 5 "
Isaac Kneeland, *Clerk*,	-	5 "	Samuel Freeman,	-	- 5 "
Marcus Cole, *Sergeant*,	-	5 "	Hezekiah Goff, -	-	- 5 "
Privates.			William Bevin, -	-	- 5 "
			Daniel Park,	-	- 5 "
Stephen Olmsted,	-	5 "	Elijah Bailey, -	-	- 5 "
Ralph Smith, -	-	5 "	Daniel MacKall,	-	- 5 "
Samuel Kilbourn,	-	3 "	Lazarus Watrous,	-	- 5 "
Samuel Hill, -	-	5 "	Nathaniel Markham, -		- 5 "
Daniel Hill, -	-	5 "	Elisha Cornwell, -	-	- 5 "
Caleb Cook, ·	-	2 "	John Norton, Jr.,	-	- 2 "
John Johnson, -	-	5 "	Ezra Ackley,	-	- 3 "
Nehemiah Day, -	-	5 "	David Caswell, -	-	- 2 "
Sylvanus Freeman,	-	5 "	Ezra Purple, -	-	- 3 "
William White, -	-	5 "	Joshua Bailey, -	-	- 3 "
Samuel Sexton, -	-	5 "	James Johnson, Jr.,	-	- 3 "
Benjamin Kneeland, -	-	5 "	Nathaniel Garnsey,	-	- 3 "
Thomas Hill, -	-	5 "	Ithamer Pelton, -	-	- 5 "
Daniel Clark, -	-	5 "			

✺ ✺ ✺

Upon the Memorial of John Clark, Stephen Griffith, Hez. Russ, Samuel Wadsworth, Jonathan Bayley, David Bayley, John Bevin junior, Joseph Parke, Ebenezer Clark, Jabez Clark, William Clark, Shubal Lewis, Josiah Cook, Isaac Smith, William Norket, William Norket junior, Daniel Young, Ezra Andrews, James Johnson, Caleb Johnson, William Bevin, Seth Knowles, Isaac Williams, John Markham and Thomas Lewis, all of Middletown, in Hartford County, showing to this Assembly that they live very remote from the place of publick worship in the third society in Middletown whereunto they belong, praying that upon their hiring an approved minister to preach to them six months in a year they should be released from paying towards the minister's salary of said society one-half of their rates or taxes that shall be taxed against them on that account.

Resolved by the Assembly, That the said John Clark, &c., for this current year and annually on their procuring an orthodox minister to preach to them six months in a year, they be released and are hereby released from paying to said society one-half of what might otherwise be taxed against them by said society for their minister's salary.

May, 1743.   Past in ye Lower House.
                              Test: JNO FOWLER, *Clerk.*
               Concurred in the Upper House.
                              Test: GEO. WYLLYS, *Secy.*

            ᴕ ᴕ ᴕ

To the Honourable General Assembly to be held at Hartford In the County of Hartford on the Second Thursday of may 1743

We the under written all Inhabatants In middleton in said County in the third society in Middleton afsd to this Honourable assembly Humbly sheweth that the several Habetations wherein we dwell are more than five mile distent the nearest of us and most of us seven mile & some more from the place of publick worship whereto we Belong and the Roads are very dificult to Travel & especially the winter & spring season; and by the approbation of the Society's Committee we have hired app person approved to preach amongst us for more than six months the Last year & we being under such circumstances Humbly pray that this Assembly wold—Grant that on our hireing a minister to Preach six months In ayear yearly we may be Released from paying Taxes to the Society whereto we Belong six months in ayear, or that we may Receive of the Society's Committee one half of what shall be colected from us for the Seport of our ministers yearly Salary.—or some other way Grant Relief as your Honours in your Great wisdom shall think fitt and your memorialists as In duty Bond shall ever Pray.

Middleton April 29th 1743.
                              Signed by JOHN CLARK and twenty-four others.
Ecclesiastical Records,
Vol. 9, p. 40.

To the Honourable General assembly of his Majestyes Colony of Connecticutt to Be held at Newhaven In the County of Newhaven on the Second Thursday of October A.D. 1744

the Humble memoral of us under written all of the third Society In Middleton In Hartford County to this Honourable assembly Humbly sheweth that your memorelist all of us Living In said Society and are agreat way distance from the Publick worship the Nearest of us more than five miles and some Ten miles and the Rhoads we are to Travel in are very Rough and Bad to Travel in and upon our memorials to this Honourable assembly In May 1743 this assembly Released us from paying to the Support of our minister one half of our ministeral charges on our hireing preaching amongst our Selves.part of the year—and your memorilst have ever Since hired a minister among our Selves and we are Sensible of our poor Circumstances & Inability to be asociety but wold hope that we are and shall be able to Hire a preacher among our Selves if we were not obliged to pay to the Seports of our minister in the Society and the Circumstances of the Rest of the Society are able to Seport our minister without us wold therefore Humbly pray that this Assembly would Release us and all others within the Bounds following (viz South on Middle Hadam Society. East on Colchester Bounds & to Extend west by said Society to a Highway that Runs North & South the west side of the Greate Hill so coled to Run by said North & South Highway from Middle Hadam Souciety to the South end of the Great Hill then to Run Northeasterly by the west side of the said Hill to the three mile division so caled then to Glausenberry Bounds then East by Glausenberry to Colchester) from paying any ministeral charges to said Society on our Hireing an orthodox minister among ourselves and that we may be enabled to Raise a Tax on our poles and Ratable Estate to pay the minister or ministers we shall so hire or In some other way Grant Relief to your poor memorelist and we as In duty Bound shall ever pray.

Middleton October 8th 1744

Signed by EBEN'R CLARK and thirty-five others.

Ecclesiastical Records,
Vol. 9, p. 43.

The first petition, dated April 29, 1743, has the following names attached:

John Clark,	Jabez Clark,	James Johnson,
Stephen Griffith,	William Clark,	Caleb Johnson,
Hezekiah Russ,	Shubal Lewis,	William Bevin,
Saml. Wadsworth,	Josiah Cook,	Thos. Smith (erased),
Jonathan Baley,	Isaac Smith,	Seth Knowles,
David Bailey,	*his*	*his*
John Bevin, Junr.,	William X Norket, *mark*	Isaac X Williams, *mark*
Joseph Parke,	William Norket, Jr.,	John Markham,
Ebenezer Clark,	Daniel Young,	Thomas Lewis.
	Ezra Andrews,	

The second petition is dated October 8, 1744, and is signed by thirty-six petitioners, as follows:

Ebenezer Clark,	Hezekiah Russ,	James Cady,
John Clark, Jr.,	Hezekiah Russ, Jr.,	David Anderson,
Aaron Clark,	Seth Knowles,	John Bevin,
William Clark,	Isaac Smith,	Giles Hall,
John Markham,	David Cerby (?),	Hamlin John Hall,
John Clark,	Isaac Williams,	Samuel Wadsworth
Joseph Parke,	William Norket, Sr.,	George Hubbard,
Jabez Clark,	Jonathan Bayley,	Isaac Thompson,
Samuel Egelston,	Ezra Andrews,	Caleb Johnson,
William Norket, Jr.,	Elisha Cornwell,	Mary Johnson (?),
Zaccheus Cooke,	William Bevin,	Daniel Young,
James Johnson,	Soloman —— (?),	Josiah Cook.

	£	s.		£	s.
Jabez Clark,	39	9	James Johnson,	86	
Nathan Harding,	27		Seth Knowles,	58	10
Samuel Wadsworth,	40		Stephen Griffith,	45	
Eben'r Clark,	42	13	John Bosworth,	18	
John Clark,	143	10	Daniel Young,	22	
John Markham,	21		Josiah Cook,	32	6
Hez'h Russ,	100	16	Azariah Andrews,	30	
Daniel Hills,	31		John Stephens,	26	
Jon'an Bailey,	48	16	Isaac Williams,	18	
John Bevin, Junr.,	34	6	Isaac Smith,	30	
Will'm Bevin,	20		Widow Johnson,	9	
Joseph Parke,	26		William Norket, '	41	
David Bailey,	27		William Norket, Junr.,	20	
Sam'l Eggleston,	30				
George Hubbard,	33			1100	6

The foregoing is a true copy of the Lists of Sundry of the Eastern Inhabitants of the East Society in Middletown taken in ye year 1743 and I certify that the total sum for the whole of Sd Society in Sd year including the above lists is £5653 1.

Per WILLM ROCKWELL, T. Clerk.

State Archives Ecclesiastical,
Vol. 9, pp. 41, 42.

⁂ ⁂ ⁂

To the Honourable General Assembly of the Colony of Connecticut to be held at Hartford the Second Thursday of May A.D. 1746

the Humble memorial of John Clark Ebenezer Clark and others some of the Inhabitants of the Third Society in Middleton Living at the Eastern part of said Society In ye County of Hartford by there agent Benjamin Stilman Humbly sheweth that this assembly at there sessions at Newhaven in October 1744, upon the petition of your memorelest to the Number of about forty persons this assembly Granted that all the Inhabitants that dwelt within the following Bounds shold have power meet together and choose a clerk to vote and agree to hire aminister and Grant Rates & Taxes to defray the Charge of hiring aminister &c, and the bounds to Districts to begin at the No. East Corner of Middle Hadam Bounds and from thense Running west to a highway Running Northerly and Sotherly on the west side of a hill coled the great hill and from Said Highway northerly by the Same to the South end of the Said Hill then Northerly by the west Side of Said Hill until it Comes to the three mile Division So caled thense by said Division to Glassenbery bounds then East by Glassenbery bounds to Colchester bounds then Southerly by Colchester bounds to the first mentioned place—and thereupon your memorilest have eversince hired a minister eleven months in a year and sence that Time We have Increased so that we are Now on the publick List about Seventeen hundred pounds and we Live very farr distant from the place of public worship None Less than five miles—and if we shold longer continue with Said third Society it is Likely our Taxes wold be Great there for that said Society are about to Build a new meeting house we wold therefore Humbly Request that those that Live within Said Bounds may be sett off from said Society and be a Distinct Ecleastical Society with such preveliges as allowed by Law for Societys or that a Committe be appointed to view our circumstances and make Report to this assemble—and your memorests as In Duty Bound shall ever pray.

BENJAMIN STILMAN *agent*.

Middletown April 29th 1746.

Ecclesiastical Records,
Vol. 9, p. 45.

※ ※ ※

To Honourable General Assembly of the Colony of Connecticute in America Now setting att Hartford in the County of Hartford and Colony aforsd,

the memoriall of us the Subscribers Inhabitants of the Parish of East hamton in Middletown in the County of Hartford together With Some of the Inhabitants of Middle hadam Society Humbly Sheweth to this Assembly that a question Ariseth Concerning the bounds of this our Parish as we lye Adjoining upon the Society of Middle haddam by Reason of an Alteration In the Length of a tear of Lots Colled the great Lotts now middle haddam grant Saith beginning att the great highway near the great River and running East on the north side of thomas Hatch Lot to the End of the great Lots to another highway then Turning and Runing Southerly in sd highway untill it Intersects a west Line—Drawn from the northwest corner of West Chester Society as it Lyeth in middletown which Grant was given out before that any allteration was made on the rear of sd Lots

East Hampton grant Saith beginning att the North East Corner of middletown bounds next to Pine Swamp alias West Chester Society and from thence Runing West to the Rear of the Long Lots then runing northerly by the Rear of Sd Lots to the great highway which give eth to Easthampton Society a Tract of Land about one hundred rods in Wedth which was Esteemed to belong to middle haddam Society

now there was taken out of the South East Cornar of Middletown next to Haddam bounds and added to the West Chester Society (before either of middle haddam or East hampton Societeys was made) a certain Tract of Land as by there grant Appears in these Words viz. and that part of Middletown be that tear of lots or so many of sd Lots as butte on Colchester bounds East between Sd Haddam bounds and Salmon River which Lots Lye on Length one mile East and West Viz so much out of Middletown

Here With us Lyeth a Question whether or no this Includes only the Land South of Salmon river or the Whole of the Lots mentioned part of the West-End of Which lott are on the north side of the River So that we know not where to find pine Swamp Corner by Reason of the Rivers varying so much to the South Which Leavs a Tract of Land in Dispute of Considerable value and with Inhabitants upon it &c

And for Relefe on this Case We your Honours Humble memorialists bring this Address and pray to have it taken into your Honours Consideration and to Afford us your gracious Assistance that So we may Know our bonds Either

by sending us a Cmttee to Determine the matter or Provide some other way for us as you in your great Wisdom Shall Think best.
So prays your Honours Humble memorialists att Comand and as in Duty bound Shall Ever pray

    Dated in middletown may ye 14 A.D. 1751
                 Signed by SAML WADSWORTH
                 and nine others for East Hamton.

} Easthamton

Saml Wadsworth	Ebener Darte	} of Middlehaddam
John Clark jun	Theodor Higgins	} midle Hadam
Jabez Clark		
Ebenezer Clark		
Wm Norket		
James Cole		
Moses Cole		
Abijah Hall		
James Johnson		
Samuel Egelston		

Ecclesiastical Records,
  Vol. 9, p. 52.

                 ♣ ♣ ♣

To the Honourable General Assembly of the Colony of Connecticut to be Holden at Hartford in said Colony the Second Thursday of May 1752

    The Honourable Memoriall of John Clark Thomas Alvord & Isaac Smith all of East Hampton Parish in Middletown in Hartford County and the Rest of the Inhabitants of said Parish by Ebenezer Clark there Agent Humbly Sheweth That about Twenty years last past This Honourable Assembly did Grant that the Western part of the Bounds of Colchester with those Lands in Middletown In the first Tear of Lots in the Three mile Division Lying between Salmon River and East Haddam should be one Eclesiastical Society and some years afterward did Grant and make a Society now called Middle Haddam which North Extention & part of East Extention of said Society is said (viz the north part to begin on the South side of a certain forty Rod highway called the Great highWay that is in the Division of Land in Middletown called the great Lots which high Way is Two miles and half in Length—East and West and the North Bounds of said Society to Run East by the South Side of said high Way to the End of said Great Lots to another high-Way than Southerly by the orther high Way untill said line shall Intersect a West Line drawn from the North-West Corner of Westchester Parish as it lyes in Middletown to said high-Way running Southerly and than to Turn and Run East by said West line to Salmon River than Southerly by said River to the South Extention of Middletown &c
and that about six years since on Petition of your Memorialists This Honourable Assembly did Grant and make us a distinct Society by our Selves beginning

CONGREGATIONAL CHURCH OF EAST HAMPTON.   75

the Bounds thereof at the North West Corner of Westchester Parish in Middletown and from thence to Run West to the East End of said Tear of great Lots Than to Turn and Run North by the East end of said great Lots so far North as said great high Way Than to Turn and Run West by the South Side of said great high Way about one mile & half to a high way that runs North than turning and running north by said high Way &c and wheras since our Grant wee have settled a minister among us to our good Satisfaction and have voted to Build a meeting House for Divine worship and have Petitioned the Honourable County Court in the County of Hartford for a Committee to State the Places to Build on which was granted and a Committee sent to affix the Place and wheras there has a Dispute now lately arisen where the North West Corner of West Chester Parish was Intended to be by your Honours your memorialist soposing it to be where Salmon River cut across the West End of the first Tear of Lots in Middletown next Colchester which is about a mile from Colchester Bounds. But West Chester Parish and Middle Haddam Parish would have the North West Corner farther Northward: Continuing the north Line of West Chester Parish from Colchester where it Runs West into Middletown Bounds through the whole first Tear of Lots about a mile which croses said & River & brings that Corner on the West of said River more Northward than where said River crosses said Tear of Lots at West End and Wheras we suppose the said River was Intended by this Honourable Assembly to be the West Extention of West Chester Parish in every Place therof as that is a dificult River to pass and your Honours have taken off all those Lands Westward of West Chester Parish South of said River to East Haddam, and wheras there is another Tear of Lots in said Three mile Division West of Salmon River southward of East Hampton Parish that contains about five hundred acres of Land which as yet has no Inhabitants settled on it but is now about to be Settled and the owners of said Land or the most of them are desirious to be Included in East Hampton Parish and as said Parish at present is Poor and is likly to be poorer and less able to Support Parish charges than Middle Haddam Parish We would therfore Humbly Pray this Honourable Assembly would now Enact and declare to End said Dispute between said Parishes that the north West corner of West Chester Parish in Middletown be where said Salmon River Intercepts and cuts across the East Tear of Lots in sd division of Land at the West End of said Tear of Lots and that the aforsd Land in the Second Tear of Lots in sd Division on the West Side of Salmon River in said Middletown might be annexed to East Hampton Parish and taken from Middle Haddam and that the Bounds of said East Hampton Parish on the South part may be declared to be To begin where said River cuts across sd first Tear of Lots in Middletown at the West End therof and from thence to run Southerly by said River untill said River runs West of said Second Tear of Lots to a high Way that runs North about 17 Degrees West Than to turn & run by said Way so far north as shall Intersect a West Line drawn from said Place where said River cuts across said first Tear of Lots at West End and then to run a Due West Line by the needle of the Surveyors Instrument untill the Line come to the aforsd Tear of said great Lots then to turn and Run by the East End of said great Lots northerly to said great high Way than to continue as first Granted to said Parish until it comes to ye aforsd north West Corner of West Chester Parish or Send a

Committee to Enquire and affix the Bounds of said Parish or In some orther way Grant Relief as your Honours in your great Wisdom see good and your memorialist as In Duty Bound shall Ever Pray Dated in Middletown April 30th Anno Domini 1752

EBENR CLARK *agent.*

Ecclesiastical Records,
 Vol. 9, leaf 55.

NOTE.

The foregoing records have been copied line for line from the original documents on file in the State Library. I have attempted to preserve the spelling and capitals of the papers copied.

GEO. S. GODARD.

AMOS CLARK,
1794-1885.

DEA. DIODATE B. WEST,
1798-1881.

DEA. ALLEN C. CLARK,
1817.

JOHN W. B. SMITH,
1806.

RECORDS OF REV. JOHN NORTON.

NOTE.—The numerals enclosed in parenthesis thus (1) refer to the pages of the original record of the Diary of Mr. Norton.

COPY of the Record or Diary kept by the Rev. Mr. John Norton, Pastor of the East Hampton Congregational Church from 1748 to 1778. Made by Martin L. Roberts from the original manuscript now in possession of Edward E. Cornwell, M. D., 146 Herkimer street, Brooklyn, N. Y. This Record was kept upon small sheets of writing paper sewed together and very closely written, and age and lack of care have rendered some portions of it nearly illegible. It covers the period from April 18, 1764, to March 24, 1772. The remaining records of his pastorate are supposed to have been destroyed when the house of his daughter Eunice was burned. Copied December, 1898.

(2)

RECORD OF BIRTHS A. D. 1764.

April 18	1764	Nathaniel son to Elijah & Hannah Cook was Born
May 7	"	Nathaniel Keys & Mercy Keys Daughter was Born
June 21	"	Israel & Susannah Deweys son Born
June 27	"	John & Phebe Bates Daughter born
Aug 8	"	Stephen & Thankful Aclys son was Born
11	"	Thomas Cowdreys daughter Born
Oct 10	"	Marcus & Phebe Coles Daughter Born
	"	Robert Stiles son Nathan Born
Nov 9	"	Mary Woods Daughter born
Nov 15	"	Ebenezer and Huldah Hardings daughter Anna was Born
Nov 27	"	Mercy daughter to Lieut. Stephen Olmsted was Born
Dec 11	"	―――― Reeds son Born
13	"	Caleb and Mary Johnsons son Born Elisha
January	1765	Thomas Aclys child Born
Jany 31	"	Lemuel & Grace Shirtlief, daughter Lucy was Born
Feb 11	"	Nathan Rowleys son Born
28	"	Thomas Doolittles son Born

(3)

Mar 4	"	Israel & Mary Whitcombs Daughter Mary Born
21	"	Ruth Daughter to Elkanah & Ruth Sears born
24	"	Sarah Clarks Daughter was Born

April	21	1765	Nathaniel & Sarah Doanes son was Born
April	25	"	Ambrose Niles son Born Elihu
	29	"	Barnabas & Anne Freemans Daughter Born
May	7	"	Elisabeth Cornwell Daughter to Elisha and Anne Cornwell was Born
	29	"	Sylvanus Freemans son Born
	30	"	Othniel & Jerusha Brainerds son Born
July	5	"	Thomas Cowdreys Daughter Born
		"	Thomas Conklins Daughter Born
	7	"	Nathaniel Motts Daughter Born
	11	"	Jonathan Olmsted Gates son to Nehemiah and Anne Gates was Born
	21	"	Ephraim Norcot son to William and Bette Norcot
	24	"	Isaac & Elisabeth Baileys Daughter Born
August		"	Mary and Hannah the two Daughters of Stephen and Abigail Knowlton were born
	18	"	Daniel & Bathsheba Hills Daughter was born

(4)

Aug	30	"	Mary Niles Daughter to Barnabas & Thank'l Niles was Born
Sept	4	"	David son to Bryan & Rebecca Parmelee was Born
	5	"	Mary Arnold Daughter to Gideon & Lucy Arnold Born
	6	"	Amos & Bethiah Deweys Son was Born
	17	"	Ezra Fuller son to John & Susanna Fuller was born
Octr	7	"	Moses Freeman son to Moses and Susanna Freeman Born
Nov	20	"	Asa Tylers son Born
Nov	22	"	Eliphaz & Esther Alvords Daughter was Born Elizabeth
Dec	7	"	Elihu son to Ebenezer & Mary Hall was Born
	19	"	Joseph Smiths son Born
Jan	2	1766	Capt Abijah & Margaret Halls Daughter still Born
Feb	13	"	Calvin Hall son to Hamlin John Hall and Elisabeth Hall was born
	19	"	Jerusha daughter to Thomas & Mercy Shepard was born
	22	"	Elvira daughter to James & Asenath Bill was born

(5)

Mar	9	"	Jeremiah Woods Daughter Born
	10	"	Joshua and Anne Baileys Daughter was Born
	22	"	John & Desire Markhams Dau Abigail born
April	22	"	Lucretia Daughter to John & Azubah Hinckly was born
	29	"	Thomas Acly Junr & Sarah Aclys Son Born
May	12	"	Asa Cook Son to Zacheus & Mary Cook was born
June	14	"	Patience Bailey Daughter to Jonathan & Patience Bailey born
July	14	"	Daniel and Esther Mackall Child Born
		"	John Gernseys child born
Sept	4	"	Mane Nathaniel & Sarah Doanes Daughter Sarah Born
	16	"	Mane ——— Ebenezer & Sarah Coles Daughter Born
	20	"	Robert Stiles Daughter Born
	23	"	Moses and Elizabeth Cooks Daur Born

CONGREGATIONAL CHURCH OF EAST HAMPTON. 79

Oct	4	1766	Titus & Mercy Carriers Daughr Born
	8	"	Elijah & Hannah Cooks Daughter Born
	13	"	John & Phebe bates Daughter born
Nov	6	"	Joseph & Lydia Caswells son Born
	11	"	James & Phillis Rich son Born
	18	"	Mane Robert & Ruhamah Shattucks Daughter Mary Born
	19	"	Mane John & Edey Nortons Daughter Dorinda Born

(6)

	23	"	Dea John & Sarah Clark Son Born
	29	"	Marcus & Phebe Cole son still Born
Dec	20	"	Nathl & Mercy Keys child still Born
Dec	15	"	John Godfrey & Hannah Hopth son Born
	21	"	Ebenezer & Huldah Hardings son Amos born
Jan	16	1767	Benjamin & Prudence Goffe son Born
	18	"	Barnabas & Anne Freemans Daughter Born
	29	"	Nathan Rowleys two Daughters Born
Feby	6	"	Recompense & Dorothy Baileys son Born
	25	"	Thomas & Thankful Hills son Born
March	1	"	Thomas & Margaret Doolittle son John Born
	11	"	Barnabas Niles son Salmon Born
	23	"	Othniel Brainerds Daughter Born
April	7	"	Jonathan Shirtliefs Daughter Sarah Born
	8	"	Samuel & Elisabeth Browns Daughter Mary Born
	9	"	Caleb & Mary Johnson son Born
	25	"	Sylvanus Freemans Daughter Born
	27	"	Isaac & Elisabeth Baileys son Born
May	2	"	Samuel Hodges son Israel Born
	10	"	Israel & Mary Whitcombs son Born
		"	Jeremiah Woods child born
June	11	"	Gideon & Lucy Arnolds son Born
	15	"	John Hills Daughter Born
July	17	"	Moses & Mary White Coles Daur born
	24	"	Jabez & Mary Woods Daughter Mary Born
	29	"	Jonathan Olmsted son to Lieut Stephen and Mercy Olmsted

(7)

Aug	6	"	Amos Deweys Daughter Born
	12	"	Stephen Knowltons son Born Joshua
	29	"	Darius Gates son to Stephen and and Esther Gates Born
Sept	7	"	Wm Cornwell Goodrich son to Thomas and Esther Goodrich was born
	9	"	Joseph Freeman son to Moses and Susanna Freeman was born
Oct		"	Daniel & Esther Mackall Daughter Born
		"	William Norcot son of Wm and Bette Bette Norcot Born
Dec	26	"	Nathl & Agnis Mott son Born
Jan	4	1768	Ebenezer & Abigail Halls Daughter Born
	6	"	Mary Purples son Born
	16	"	Bryan and Rebekah Parmelee Daughter Born

CONGREGATIONAL CHURCH OF EAST HAMPTON.

Jan	17	1768	Stephen & Thankful Aclys Dar Born
			also Jared and Eunice Parmelees Daughter Born
	18	"	Esther Alvord Daughter of Eliphaz and Esther Alvord was Born
	20	"	Allen Hill son of Daniel Hill Junr and Bathsheba Hill Born
Feby	13	"	Samuel & Sarah Woods daur Born
	14	"	Lemuel & Grace Shirtlief son born
March	2	"	David & Elisabeth Caswell son was born

(8)

	7	"	Moses & Elisabeth Cooks son born
	9	"	Nathaniel Niles son Born
	25	"	Capt Abijah & Margaret Halls Daughter Born
April	16	"	John & Desire Markhams Daughter Born
April	30	"	Thomas Cowdreys child Born Jonathan
May	5	"	Nathaniel & Elizabeth Clarks Daughter Eunice Born
May	22	"	William & Elisabeth Whites child still born
July	6	"	Erastus Bill son of James and Asenath Bill was born
	8	"	Lucretia Daughter to of Thomas and Mercy Sheperd was born
July	18	"	Isaiah Cook son to Joshua and Mary Cook was Born
Aug	2	"	Ruhamah Daughter to Joseph and Lydia Caswell was Born
	13	"	Asriel son to John & Azubah Hinckley was Born
Aug	17	1768	James & Phillis Rich son Born
Sept	5	"	Andrew Fuller son to John and Susanna Fuller was Born
	6	"	Joshua Baileys son born Nathaniel
	7	"	——— Cole son to Marcus & Phebe Cole was Born

(9)

	9	"	Rachel Daughter to Elkanah and Ruth Sears was Born
	19	"	James Johnson Junr & Sarah Johnsons son Born name Amasa
	29	"	John Clark 3d & Deborah Clark, son Born
Oct	4	"	Elizabeth Sears Daughter to Ebenezer Sears Junr & Elisabeth Sears
	7	"	——— Lewis son of Nathan & Naomi Lewis was Born
Oct	19	"	——— Daughter to Samuel and Thankful Hill was Born
	25	"	Huldah Daughter to Ebenr & Huldah Harding was born
Novr		"	Jonathan Shirtliefs son Born
Dec	22	"	Hannah Daughter to Elijah & Hannah Cook Born
Jany		1769	John & Phebe Bates Daughter was Born
Feby	11	"	Lucinda Norton Daughter to John Junr & Edey Norton was Born
	17	"	Marianne Smith Daughter to Ralph and Hannah Smith was born
	26	"	Leah Freeman Daughter of Sylvanus & Leah Freeman born
Mar	11	"	Barnabas & Anne Freemans son Born
	26	"	Enos Brown son to S & El B born
April	5	"	Nathll & Mercy Keys Daughter Born
	18	"	Elijah Clarks son Born
	19	"	Isaac & Bette Baileys Daughter Born *(p 23)*

CONGREGATIONAL CHURCH OF EAST HAMPTON. 81

(10)

BAPTISMS EAST HAMPTON A. D. 1764

April 22 1764 Nathaniel Cook son to Elijah & Hannah Cook was Baptised
May   6   "   Joshua Bailey & Anne Bailey son and Daughter to Joshua & Anne Bailey were Baptised
Nov   18   "   Nathan Stiles son to Robert Stiles was Baptised & Anna Harding Daughter to Ebenezer and Huldah Harding bap
Feb   17 1765 Mercy Olmsted Daughter to Stephen & Mercy Olmsted was Baptised
Mar   10   "   Thomas Doolittle son of Thomas Doolittle was Baptised
Mar   17   "   Lucy Shirtlief Daughter to Lemuel and Grace Shirtlief was Baptised
April 14   "   Moses Rowley son to Nathan Rowley was Baptised—Mary Daughter to Israel Whitcomb and Ruth Daughter to Elkanah & Ruth Sears were Baptised
May   12   "   Elisabeth Cornwell Daughter to Elisha and Anne Cornwell Baptd
      19   "   Elisha Johnson son to Caleb and Mary Johnson Baptised
June 23   "   Anselm Brainerd son to Othniel & Jerusha Brainerd was Baptised

(11)

July 14   "   Susanna Dewey was Baptised
            "   Elisha & Enos Dewey sons to Israel Dewey Junr & Susanna Dewey were Baptised and Mercy Wood Daughter to Susanna Dewey
      28   "   Ephraim Norcot son to William & Bette Norcot was Baptised also Elihu Niles son to Ambrose & Hannah Niles was Baptised
Aug   4   "   Jonathan Olmsted Gates son to Nehemiah & Anne Gates Baptised
Sept 15   "   Mary & Hannah Knowlton Daughters to Stephen & Abigal Knowlton were Baptised also Talitha Niles Daughter to Barnabas & Thankful Niles also Mary Arnold Daughter to Gideon & Lucy Arnold Baptised
      22   "   Ezra Fuller son to John and Susanna Fuller was Baptised
Oct   13   "   David son to Bryant & Rebecca Parmelee was Baptised
Nov   3   "   Moses Freeman son to Moses and Susanna Freeman Baptised
      24   "   Elisabeth the daughter of Eliphaz & Esther Alvord Baptised

(12)

Dec   8   "   Elisha Hall son to Ebenezer and Mary Hall was baptised
Feb   23 A. D. 1766 Calvin son to Hamlin John and Elisabeth Hall was baptised & Elvira Bill Daughter to James & Asenath Bill was Baptised
Mar   23 1766 Timothy and Mary and Phebe Brainerd were Baptised Mrs Alvords Children by her 1st husband
April 27   "   Jonathan & Noah Shirtlief sons to Jonathan & Abigail Shirtlief were Baptised

May 11	1766	Jerusha Daughter to Thomas & Mercy Shepherd Abigail Daughter to John & Desire Markham & Lucretia dr to John & Azubah Hinckley were baptised
May 18	"	Asa Cook son to Zacheus & Mary Cook was baptised also Thomas & Samuel White sons to Thomas White Deceased & Susanna White but now Dewey
25	"	Samuel Sarah Nathaniel & Huldah Cowdrey sons and Daughters of Thomas Cowdrey were baptised and also Rhoda Bailey Daughter to Joshua & Ann Bailey was Baptised

(13)

July 27	"	Bathsheba Hill. Daniel Hill Junr's wife was Baptised & Patience Bailey Daughter to Jonathan and patience Bailey
Sept 28	"	Sarah Daughter to Nathl & Sarah Doane Baptised
Octr	"	Mary Daughter to Elijah & Hannah Cook Baptised
Nov 23	"	Mary Daughter to Robert & Ruhamah Shattuck baptised & Dorinda Dar to John & Edey Norton Baptised
Oct	"	Daniel son to Daniel Hill Jun and Bathsheba Hill and Elisabeth their Daughter were Baptised
Nov 30	"	Moses son to Dea John & Sarah Clark was Baptised
March 8	1767	Thomas and Margaret Doolittles son John Baptised
22	"	Amos Harding son to Ebenr & Huldah Harding Baptised also Salmon Niles son to Barnabas Niles
April 12	"	Sarah Daughter to Jonathan Shirtlief Baptised
26	"	Hannah & Mary Rowley Daughters to Nathan Rowley were Baptised
May 3	"	Abigail Brainerd Daughter to Othniel and Jerusha Brainerd was Baptised
10	"	Israel Hodge son to Samuel Hodge Baptised and Mary Brown Daughter of Samuel & Elisabeth Brown
June 21	"	Israel Whitcomb son to I & Mary Whitcomb baptised
July 5	"	Kezia Hill John Hills Daughter Baptised

(14)

26	"	Dan Arnold son to Gideon and Lucy Arnold Baptised & Mary Cole Daughter to Moses & Mary White Cole Baptised
Aug 2	"	Jonathan Olmsted Stephen & Mercy Olmsteds son Baptised also Mary Wood Daughter to Jabez & Mary Wood baptised
Sept 13	"	Joseph Freeman son to Moses & Susanna Freeman Baptised
20	"	Joshua Knowlton son to Stephen and Abigail Knowlton baptised
August	1767	Elisha Samuel & Sarah Mott sons & Daughter to Nathl & Agnis Mott were Baptised
Nov 1	"	Darius Gates son of Stephen & Esther Gates was Baptised
Jany 3	1768	William Norcot son to Willm and Bette Norcot was Baptised
10	"	William Cornwell Goodrich son to Thomas & Esther Goodrich was Baptised
Feby 21	"	Nathaniel Mott son to Nathll and Agnis Mott was Baptised

CONGREGATIONAL CHURCH OF EAST HAMPTON. 83

March 6 1768 Esther Alvord Daughter to Eliphaz & Esther Alvord Baptised
April 3 " Allen Hill son to Daniel Hill Jr & Bathsheba his wife and Lothrop Shirtlief son to Lemuel & Grace Shirtlief and Lucy Hall Daughter to Abijah & Margaret Hall were Baptised

(15)

      10 " Sarah Parmelee Daughter to Bryan & Rebecca Parmelee baptised also Eunice Hall Parmelee Daughter of Jared (& Eunice) late deceased Parmelee Baptised
May 1 " Jerusha Cole Ebener & Sarah Coles Daughter Baptised also Martha Freeman Sylvanus & Leah Freemans Daughter
    8 " Jonathan Cowdrey son of Thomas Cowdrey Bapd also Eunice Clark Daughter of Nathl & Elisabeth Clark
   22 " Sarah Acly Baptised Thomas Aclys Junr wife
   29 " Margere Markham John & Desire Markhams Daughter baptised
June 5 " James & Isaac & David Bailey the sons of Isaac & Elisabeth Bailey Baptised
   12 " Ichabod Solomon & Esther Bailey sons & Daughter to Solomon & Dorothy Bailey Baptised also Jonathan Caswell son to Joseph & Lydia Caswell
July 3 " Mary Hall Daughter to Ebenezer & Abigail Hall was Baptised
   10 " Erastus Bill son to James & Asenath Bill was Baptised
   24 " Levi Acly son to Thomas & Sarah Acly Bap
Aug 7 " Isaac Johnson son to Caleb & Mary Johnson & Ruhamah Caswell Daughter to Joseph & Lydia Caswell were Baptised
   21 " Asriel Hinckley son to John & Azubah Hinckley was Baptised
                                               (Verte to p 25)

(16)
RENEWING & COMING TO FULL COMMUNION

May 6 1764 Joshua Bailey & Anne Bailey his wife were received to full Communion
Mar 31 1765 Susanna Dewey Renewed her Covenant
April 21 " Patience Bailey and Huldah Harding were Recd to full Communion
June 9 " Sarah Clark made Confession for the sin of fornication and was accepted
July 28 " Thankful Niles was received to full Communion in this church also Ambrose & Hannah Niles Renewed their Covenant
Nov 7 " Eliphaz Alvord & Esther his wife were received to full Communion
Mar 2 1766 Mary Alvord Consert to Capt Jonathan Alvord was received into full Communion in this Church
Mar 30 " Thomas Cowdrey and —— his wife Nathaniel Doane & Sarah his wife Renewed their Covenant
April 27 " Jonathan Shirtlief & Abigail his wife Renewed their Covenant
July 27 " Bathsheba Hill was Received to full Comn
Sept 21 " John Norton Jun and Edey his wife were Recd to full Communion

84 CONGREGATIONAL CHURCH OF EAST HAMPTON.

(17)

Sept 28	1766	Othniel Brainerd recommended from the 4th Chu in Mn and receved with us to full C.
Feby 22	1767	Barnabas Niles Recommended from the Church of X at Westchester and received at this
May 3	"	John Clark Jr Recd to full Communion
June 21	"	Moses Cole Jun & Mary White Cole his wife & Mary Cunningham Recd to full Communion
July 26	"	Nathaniel & Agnes Mott Renewed their Covenant
Mar 10	1768	Jared Parmelee Renewed Covenant
April 3	"	Israel Whitcomb Recd to Covenant by a Recommendation from Marlboro
May 15	"	Joseph Caswell & Lydia his wife were Recd to full Communion
22	"	Recompense Bailey & Dorothy his wife
		Elisabeth the wife of Isaac Bailey & Thomas Acly Junr with Sarah his wife all Renewed or rather Sarah Acly entered into Covenant
June 12	"	Barnabas & Thankful Niles Recommended to the Church of X at Rumney
July 3	"	Ebenezer Hall and Abigail his wife were Recd to full Communion
Aug 14	"	James Johnson Jr & Sarah his wife & Deborah the wife of John Clark 3rd were Recd to full communion
Aug 28	"	Joshua Cook & Mary his wife were Recd to full Communion

(Verte p 29)

(18)

MARRIAGES

May 23	1764	Isaac Kneeland & Hannah Cook were married .
June 28	"	Othniel Brainerd & Jerusha Kilbourn were married
Novr 29	"	Eliphaz Alvord & Esther Hart were married
Jany 10	1765	Daniel Miller and Susanna Bevin were married
Feb 11	"	Thomas Acly and Sarah Luther were married
May 28	"	William Mihills and Sarah Stevens were married
Sept 12	"	Jonathan Bailey & Experience Wood were married
19	"	John Norton Jun and Edey Clark were married
Nov 21	"	Capt Jonathan Alvord & Mary Brainerd were married
Dec 18	"	Moses Cook & Elisabeth Cone were married
19	"	Titus Carrier & Mercy Cook were married
Feby 6	1766	Joseph Markham and Mehitabel Spencer were married
July 3	"	Joseph Caswell & Lydia Harding were married
Sept 25	"	Moses Cole & Mary White Clark were married

(19)

Oct 2	"	Thomas Hill and Thankful Goffe were married
Nov 6	"	Nathaniel Clark & Elisabeth Norton were married
13	"	Aaron Hale & Hannah Daniels were married
Mar 30	1767	Ebenezer Hall & Abigail Bailey were married
April 30	"	Samuel Wood & Sarah Clark were married

June 30	1767		Joseph White & Charity Lewis were married
July 9		"	David Bailey & Jemima Daniels were married
Augt 18		"	David Caswell & Elisabeth Green were married
Sept 24		"	Jared Parmelee & Eunice Hall married
Nov 18		"	James Johnson Junr & Sarah Clark also John Johnson & Hannah Clark also William White and Elizabeth Loveland were married
Dec 2		"	Ralph Smith & Hannah Hollister were married
3		"	Nathaniel Bosworth & Mary Smith were married also Nathan Lewis and Naomi Acly were married
Jany 28	1768		Edward Luther was married
May 11		"	Ezra Acly & Sarah West were married
Sept 8		"	Edward Purple and Mary Hodge were married

(20)
DEATHS

May 30	1764		Deceased Ellis Bailey the consort of Jonathan Bailey Etat 63 years 7 months
July 21		"	Deceased Samuel Hall son to Ebenezer & Mary Hall aged 2 years & 10 months and also Susanna Hall Daughter of Ebenezer & Mary Hall aged 4 years 11 months
July 29		"	Deceased Ruth Sears Daughter to Elkanah & Ruth Sears Et 2 y 4 mos
Augt 11		"	Thomas Cowdrey Daughter deceased aged 1 hour
Mar 17	1765		Deceased John Hale Jun Etat 30 years
April 25		"	Deceased Jabez Clark Etat 47 y 9 mos
Dec 8		"	Deceased Elihu Hall Infant son to Ebenezer & Mary Hall
Jany 2	1766		Capt Abijah & Margaret Halls Daughter still born
6		"	Deceasd Phebe Cornwell daughter to Elisha and Anne Cornwell aged 10 years 5 months
April 28		"	Deceased Isaac Baileys Daughter aged 9 months
30		"	Deceased Anne Bailey Consort to David Bailey Etat
July 6		"	Deceased Leah Freeman Daughter to Sylvanus and Leah Freeman aged 2 years & 7 months

(21)

July 14		"	Deceased Daniel & Esther Mackalls child
25		"	Deceased Jeremiah Woods child Etat 4 mos
Aug 14		"	Deceased Thomas Cunningham by falling upon an ax cut himself so yt his bowels Issued out & mortified
Oct 5		"	Deceased Elisabeth Cole Etat 25 y 7 m
11		"	Deceased Lothrop Shirtlief son to Lemuel and Grace Shirtlief Et 3 years
Nov 29		"	Marcus & Phebe Coles son still born
Dec 20		"	Nathal & Mercy Keys child still born
22		"	Deceased Joseph Whites wife Etat 63
Jany 10	1767		Deceased Mary Hall Ebeneser Halls wife in the 32 year of age
April 22		"	Deceased Philip Goffs wife

86   CONGREGATIONAL CHURCH OF EAST HAMPTON.

June	7	1767	Deceased Joseph Smiths wife Etat 45 years & 4 months
July	20	"	Deceased Moses Cole Etat 60 years
Dec	19	"	Deceased Lucretia Hinckly Etat 20 months
Jany	10	1768	Deceased Mary Arnold Etat 2 years 4 months
	20	"	Deceased Eunice Parmelee consort of Jared Parmelee Etat 17 years & 3 months
			also Deceased Mary Purples son Etat 14 days
	26	"	Deceasd Joseph Cook Junr Etat 23 yrs with Consumption

(22)

	31	"	Deceased Asa Tyler
May	5	"	Israel Dewey Deceast Etat 79 y
	21	"	William & Elisabeth Whites Child still Born
July	19	"	Deceased John Niles Etat 32 y
Augst	7	"	Deceased Moses Freeman Jr Etat 2 years & 10 months
Oct	22	"	Decesed Phebe Acly Etat 24
April	14	1769	Deceased Prince Freeman Etat 79 years 3 months
June	8	"	Deceased Gideon & Lucy Arnolds son Et 2 days
July	30	"	Nathaniel & Elisabeth Clarks Daughter still born
Nov	16	"	Deceased Selden Cook Etat 20 months
	17	"	Oliver Beuels Daughter Decd Etat 1 month
Feb	14	1770	Samuel Higgins Deceasd
Mar	13	"	Silvester Alvord son of Eliphaz and Esther Alvord Decasd Etat 20 days
May	11	"	Deceased Cybil Hall Etat 22 years
	14	"	Decased Elijah Clarks child Etat 13 months
			also Nathaniel & Elisabeth Clarks son still born
	18	"	Decd Elisabeth Clark Nathaniel Clark Consort Etat 29 years 5 months

(23)

April	28	1769	Rhoda daughter of Thomas & Margaret Doolittle Born
May	15	"	Ezra & Sarah Aclys Daughter Born
	24	"	John & Hannah Johnsons son Abner Born
	25	"	Israel & Mary Whitcomb son born Isaac
	28	"	Susanna Deweys Daughter Born
	29	"	Edward & Mary Purple son Born
June	1	"	John Hills son born n Samuel
	2	"	Jonathan & Patience Baileys son Born name Submit
	6	"	Gideon & Lucy Arnolds son born
	12	"	Caleb & Mary Johnsons son born
	24	"	Mehitable Cook Born Da' of Zac & Mary Cook
			Thomas & Thankful Hills Daughter born
	30	"	Nathl & Elisabeth Clark Daugr still born
Augt	14	"	Thomas Cowdreys Daughter Born
	15	"	Hart Gates son of Nehemiah & Anne Gates Born
	21	"	Oliver Brainerd son of Othniel and Jerusha Brainerd was born
Sept	3	"	Hiram Bosworth son of Nathaniel and Mary Bosworth was Born

CONGREGATIONAL CHURCH OF EAST HAMPTON.   87

Sept 29 1769 Jonah Gates son of Stephen and Esther Gates born
Cynthia daughter to Moses & Susanna Freeman
Oct 1 " James Cole son to Moses & Mary White Cole Born
" 7 " Oliver Beuells Daughter Born
17 " Nicholas Hosenkause son Born
Nov 17 " William & Elizabeth Whites son Born and Stephen Knowltons Daughter was Born

(24)

Dec 11 " Titus & Mercy Carriers son born
Jany 1 1770 Recompense & Dorothy Baileys son born
4 " Selden Cook son to Moses & Elisabeth Cook Born
28 " —— Cole Daughter to Ebenezer and Sarah Cole was born
Daniel Mackalls child born
Feby 18 " Benjamin & Rachel Kneelands Daughter Born
21 " Silvester son to Eliphaz & Esther Alvord was born
24 " Rowland Percivals Son Born
March " Selden Shurtlief son to Lemuel and Grace Shurtlief Born
20 " Jeremiah Woods —— Born
31 " —— Hall son to Ebenezer and Abigail Hall born
April 4 " Ebenezer Norcot son to William & Bette Norcot born
May 7 " Hannah Daughter to Jos & Lydia Caswell born
27 " Samuel & Sarah Woods son born
June 14 " David & Jemima Baileys son born
also Jonathan & Abigail Shurtliefs son born
July 4 " Norton Bill son to James & Asenath Bill Born
Aug 7 " Agnes Mott Daughter of Nathl & Agnes Mott Born
Sept 15 " —— Acly son of Stephen & Thankful Acly born

(25)
BAPTISMS

Aug 28 1768 Isiah Cook son to Joshua & Mary Cook Baptised
Oct 2 " Amasa Johnson son to James Johnson Jr & Sarah Johnson & Increase Mosely Clark son to John Clark 3d and Deborah Clark & Lucina Shepherd Daughter to Thomas & Mercy Shepherd were Baptised
9 " Rachel Sears Daughter to Elkanah and Ruth Sears & Elisabeth Sears Daughter to Ebenezer Junr & Elisabeth Sears were baptised
23 " Andrew Fuller son to John & Susanna Fuller was Baptised
30 " Susanna Rowley & Daniel Bailey son of Joshua & Anne Bailey & Huldah Harding Daughter of Ebenezer & Huldah Harding were Baptised
Jany 15 1769 Hannah Cook daughter to Elijah & Hannah Cook Baptised
Feby 12 " Lucinda Norton Daughter of John Norton Jr & Edey Norton Baptised
26 " Marianne Smith Daughter of Ralph & Hannah Smith Baptised
Mar 12 " David Shirtlief son to Jonathan & Abigail Shurtlief Baptised also Leah Freeman Daughter to Sylvanus & Leah Freeman was Baptised

88   CONGREGATIONAL CHURCH OF EAST HAMPTON.

(26)

April 30	1769	Enos Brown son to Samll & Elisabeth Brown Baptised
May 14	"	Mary & Mercy Carrier Daughters of Titus & Mercy Carrier and Selden & Lydia Cook son & Daughter to Moses & Elizabeth Cook were Baptised
June 4	"	Edward Purple son of Edward & Mary Purple Baptised
11	"	Samuel Hills son to John Hills baptised
18	"	Harris Johnson son of Caleb & Mary Johnson Baptised
22	"	Submit Bailey son to Jon Jr & Patience Bailey
July 23	"	Isaac Whitcomb son to Israel & Mary Whitcomb and Mehitable daughter to Zacs & Mary Cook & Elisabeth daughter to Isaac & Elisabeth Bailey were baptised
Augt 20	"	Hart Gates son of Nehemiah & Anne Gates Baptised
Sept 10	"	Abner Johnson son of John & Hannah Johnson & Hiram Bosworth son of Nathaniel & Mary Bosworth & Susanna Cowdrey daughter of Thomas Cowdrey were Baptised
20	"	John, Joseph, Mary, Anna, Rachel, Reliance & Lydia Smith sons and daughters of Joseph Smith Baptised
24	"	Oliver Brainerd son of Othniel and Jerusha Brainerd Baptised
Oct 1	"	Rhoda Doolittle Daughter to Thomas & Margaret Doolittle baptised
8	"	Jonah Gates son to S'ten & Esther Gates Baptised
15	"	Stephen, John, Anne and Eunice Acly sons and daughters of Stephen & Thankful Acly also James Cole son to Moses and Mary White Cole

(27)

Dec 3	"	Mercy Johnson Widow Baptised
10	"	nam Knowlton Stephn & Abigail Knowltons Daughter Baptised
17	"	Cynthia Freeman Daughter to Moses & Susanna Freeman Baptised
Jany 14	1770	Selden Cook son to Moses & Elisabeth Cook was Baptised
Feby 4	"	John Carrier son of Titus & Mercy Carrier & ——— Cole Daughter to Ebenezer & Sarah Cole was baptised
March 4	"	Elihu Bailey son of Recompense and Dorothy Bailey & Sylvester Alvord son to Eliphaz & Esther Alvd Baptised
April	"	Selden Shirtlief son to Lemuel & Grace Shirtlief Baptised also Ebenezer Norcot son to William & Bette Norcot
May 13	"	Hannah Caswell Daughter to Joseph and Lydia Caswell Baptised
May 20	"	Seth Hall son of Ebenezer & Abigail Hall Baptised
July 8	"	Hannah Wood Daughter of Jonathan and Abiah Wood Baptised
July 15	"	David Bailey son to David and Jemima Bailey was Baptised
22	"	Norton Bill son to James and Asenath Bill Baptised
29	"	Asa Shurtlief son to Jonathan & Abigail Shurtlief Baptised
Aug 12	"	Agnes Mott Daughter of Nathl & Agnes Mott Baptised

(28)

At a meeting of the sixth Church of Christ in Middletown at the house of the Revd Mr John Norton pastor of sd church

Voted 1 that this Church will Choose a committee of five Brethren to join with the Pastor to hear such grievances as may fall out in the Church between Brother and brother or any of same that may be complained of to consider whether it be Censurable and if Censurable whether it is probable that it will be proved and if so if they cant heal the difficulty then to bring it to the Church. Voted in the affirmative

2 the vote being called for the Church Chose for their Committe Deacon Isaac Smith Deacn John Clark. Elisha Cornwell Josiah Cook Capt Abijah Hall

Aug 26	1770	Timothy Parmelee son to Bryan & Rebecca Parmelee Baptised
Sept 23	"	Elijah Acly son of Sten & Th Acly Baptised
Oct 15	"	Lavinia Cook Dau of Josha & Mary Cook baptised
Nov 13	"	Isaac Hinckly son of J & A Hinckly Abihu Acly son of Thos & Sarah Acly & John Clark son of John & Deborah Clark were Baptised
Jany 3	1771	Asa Hill son to Daniel & Bathsheba Hill and Philena Freeman Daughter to Sylvanus & Leah Freeman Baptised
Mar 15	"	John Norton son to John & Edey Norton Baptised also Lois Alvord Daughter to Eliphaz and Esther Alvord Baptised
31	"	Benjamin Sears son to Elkh & Ruth Sears also Joseph Johnson son to James & Sarah Johnson were Baptised

(29)

Sept 4	1768	Jemima Bailey Recd from Middle Haddam Church & Recd in this
Oct 3	"	Jonathan Bailey & Susanna Rowley were Recd to Full Communnion
Jany 1	1769	Ralph and Hannah Smith Renewed their Covenant
April 23	"	Moses and Elisabeth Cook Edward Purple & Mary his wife Mercy wife of Titus Carrier & Mehitabel Clark were received to full Communion
June 18	"	Nathaniel & Mary Bosworth Red Covenant
Augs 13	"	Joseph Smith John Johnson and Hannah Johnson his wife & Anne Norton were Recd to full Communion
Oct 3	"	Stephen Acly & Thankful his wife renewed their Covenant
Dec 3	"	Mercy Johnson Recd to Full Communion
June	1770	Widow Dunham Recd to Full Communion
July 31	1771	Thankful Hills the wife of Samuel Hills Received to full Communion
Augst 4	"	John Hills and ——— his wife Simeon Wright & Rhoda his wife were Recd to Full Communion

90   CONGREGATIONAL CHURCH OF EAST HAMPTON.

Sept 29 1771 Isaac Kneeland & Hannah his wife Recommended from the Church in Marlborough and Received with us
Feby 6   1772 Stephen Knowlton & Joanna Strong receved to full Communion
May 3   "   ——— H E R C (Illegible)

(30)

May 4   1769 Amos Ranney and Rachel Hill married
Nov 22   "   Simeon Wright & Rhoda Cook married
Nov 30   "   Samll Higgins & Katharine Cunningham married
Jany 4   1770 Randall Shattuck and Comfort Tyler were married
Novr 2   "   William Lord & Ruth Hodge were married
     17   "   Jared Parmelee & Susanna Olmsted were married
Jany 24 1771 Nathaniel Gernsey and Damaris Alvord were married
Jany 31   "   ——— Cady & Hannah Wood were married
Feb 28   "   Lemuel West & Desire Markham were married
Mar 10   "   John Ward & Catharine Higgins were married
June 11 1771 Elizur Chapman & Dorothy Lord were married

               Samuel Hills daughter born
Sept 30 1770 Randall & Comfort Shattucks Daughter Born
Oct 10   "   Lavina Cook Daughter of Joshua & Mary Cook Born
    23   "   James & Phillis Richs daughter Born
    27   "   Simeon & Rhoda Wrights Daughter Born
Nov 4   "   Isaac Hinckley son of John & Azubah Hinckley was born
     7   "   Abihu Acly son to Thomas & Sarah Acly was born
    13   "   John Clark son of John & Deborah Clark Born
Jany 10 1771 Ebenezer & Huldah Hardings Daughter born
     24   "   Philena Freeman Daughter to Sylvanus and Leah Freeman & Asa Hill son to Daniel and Bathsheba Hill were born
Feb 18   "   Rufus Dewey Son Born
    21   "   John Clark son Born
    21   "   Elkh and Ruth Sears son born
Mar 30   "   John and Hannah Johnson son born

(1)

March 4 1771 Eliphaz & Esther Alvords Daughter Born
April 2   "   James Gates son to Nehemiah & Anne Gates was Born
April 10 "   Elijah Clarks son born
     13   "   Elijah & Hannah Cooks daughter born
     26   "   Samuel Hodges son Ichabod was born
     27   "   Nathaniel and Mary Bosworths Daughter born
     28   "   Nathan Rowleys ——— Born
     29   "   ——— & Susanna Deweys son Born
May 6   "   Israel Whitcombs ——— Born
     11   "   Isaac and Bette Baileys daughter born
June 25   "   Marcus & Phebe Coles son Born
July 5   "   Ralph and Hannah Smith Daughter Born
July 26   "   . Ezra and Sarah Aclys daughter Born

Augt 9 1771 Ebenezer and Sarah Coles daughter Born
Sept 17   "   Barnabas and Anne Freemans Daughter Born

BAPTISMS.

April 7 1771 Elizabeth Harding Daughter of Ebenezer and Huldah Harding Baptised
      21   "   Sylvester Fuller son to John and Susanna Fuller baptised
      28   "   Ichabod Hodge son to Saml Hodge and Eunice Cook Daughter to Elijah and Hannah Cook was Baptised
May 7   "   Timothy Rowley baptised
May 12   "   Mary Bosworth Daughter of Nathl & Mary B Baptised
June 7   "   James Gates son of Neh & Anne Gates Baptised
June 9 1771 Rhoda Whitcomb Daughter of Israel & M Whitcomb Baptised
June 23 "   Silena Bailey Daughter of Widow Bette Bailey baptised
July 21 "   Hannah Smith Daughter of Ralph and Hannah Smith Baptised
     31 "   Roxana and Adino daughter and son of Samuel and Thankful Hill were Baptised
Aug 4   "   Rhoda (———— baptised)?

MARRIAGES

Jany 1 1772 Job Acly & Lydia Rowley married
      9   "   Isaac Smith & Jerusha Brooks were married
     16   "   Ezra Purple and Mary Penfield were Married
          "   Joseph Lord and Ruth Purple were married
Sept 5 1771 Lemuel and Desire Wests daughter born
Oct 4   "   Aaron Hosfords son Born
Oct 30   "   Timothy Percivals child still Born
Nov 5   "   Stephen & Abigail Knowltons Da born
Nov 28   "   Elisha and Ann Cornwells son born
Dec 21   "   Thomas and Esther Goodrich son born
Dec 25   "   Hosenkause daughter born
     27 "   ———— son born

BAPTISMS

Sept 1 1771 Ira Parmelee son to Jared and Susanna Parmelee was Baptised
Nov 10   "   Tamzen Cole daughter to Ebenezer and Sarah Cole Baptised & Elisha son Elisha and Anne Cornwell was Baptised
     10 "   Nana Knowlton, Stephen Knowltons daughter was Baptised
March 2 1772 Sarah Kneeland dau of I & H Kneeland Baptised (?)
April 3 "   Moses Cook son of Moses Cook Baptised
April 19 "   Asa Bailey son to Jon & Patience Bailey Baptised
     26 "   Sarah Shurtlief daughter to Lemuel and Grace Shurtlief
Jan 7 1772 Moses Cooks son born
     21 "   Isaac & Hannah Kneelands daughter born
     30 "   John and Lois Johnsons daughter born
Mar 24   "   Jon and Patience Baileys son Born

(Last page or cover)

Dec 25 1771 Samuel Hodge and Deborah Peters were married

DEATHS

Mar 13 1770 Deceased F 15 (illegible)
Dec " Deceased Isaac & Bette Baileys daughter
Feb 18 1771 Deceased John Clark aged 91 years 7 months
Mar 15 " Deceased John Norton son to John and Edy Norton Etat 14 days
Mar 17 " Deceased David Bailey son to David and Jemima Bailey Etat 9 months
April 8 " Deceased ——— Watrous Lazarus Watrous daughter Etat
    23 " Nana Knowlton deceased etat 1 year 5 mos
    26 " Deceased ——— Hodge Samuel Hodges wife
June 9 " Deceased Nehemiah Gates Etat 37 y
July 23 " Deceased James Gates son of Widow Anne Gates
Augt 15 " Decd Jane Johnson Daughter of Ensign James & Jane Johnson Etat 9 y 9 months
Augt 21 " Lucretia Shepherd Daughter to Thomas & Mercy Shepherd Decsd etat 3 years 4 months
Oct 26 " Deceased Mercy Wood Etat 18
Dec 18 " Deceased Moses Rowleys wife aged (73 years?)
Dec 27 " Nana Knowlton Stephens Daughter Deceased

MARRIAGES

Dec 12 1771 James Acly & Hannah Spencer were married
Nov 13 " Daniel Judd & Mehetable Clark were married
Augst 28 " Dewey Hall and Hannah Kneeland were married
Sept 26 " Samuel Goff & Mary Cunningham were married
Oct 31 " John Johnson Junr & Lois Brainerd were married

BAPTISMS.

RECORD KEPT BY REV. LEMUEL PARSONS.

BAPTISMS AFTER YE REVD MR. NORTON'S DEATH BEFORE MY ORDINATION.

May 9 1779 Josiah son of Moses Cook baptised by Revd. Mr. Huntington Marlborough.
              Lucy daughter of Isaac Kneeland bapd by Mr. Huntington Marlborough.
May 17 " Israel son of Ebenezer Cole bapd by Mr. Eells Glastonbury.
Aug 23 " Cyprian son of John Hinckley bapd by Mr. Lockwood Andover.
May 24 " Lydia daughter of Ezra Ackley baptd by Mr. Little Colchester.
              Levi son of Joseph Caswell baptd by Mr. Huntington Marlborough.
April 1778 Diadama Dau. of Ralph Smith Baptd by Mr. Robbins, Westchester.

BAPTISMS AFTER MY ORDINATION.

Feby 21 1779 Elihu son of Nathaniel Mott.
       " Lucy Daughter of Gideon Arnold.
       " Susanna Daughter of John Clark Jr.
March 8 " Mercy daughter of Thomas Cowdrey.
April 18 " Abigail wife of Nathaniel White.
April 25 " Elijah son of Nathaniel White.
       " Belinda Daughter of John Norton.
May 17 " Sarah Daughter of Willm White baptd. by Mr. Parsons East Haddam.
       " Hannah Daughter of Jonathan Strowbridge baptd. by Mr. Parsons—E. H.[addam]
May 30 " Asahel son of Israel Whitcomb
June 20 " Molly Daughter of Jared Parmelee.
July 10 " Amos son of James Bill baptised by Mr. Strong Chatham
Aug 1 " Abigail daughter of Recompense Bailey
Aug 22 " Joanna Daughter of Elihu Hubbard.
Sept 6 " Ephraim son of Ephraim Harding.
       " Susanna Daughter of Moses Cook
       " Esther Daughter of Moses Cole
Octr 3 " Deborah Daughter of Nathaniel White
Oct 24 " David Allen, Adult.
       " Willm son of David Allen
       " Irana Daughter of David Allen

94   CONGREGATIONAL CHURCH OF EAST HAMPTON.

Oct 31	1779	Zuba Daughter of Hezekiah Sage of Sandisfield by Mr. Boardman.
	"	Sally Dau. of Hezh Sage of Sandisfield Bapd by Mr. Boardman.
Dec 26	"	Jonah son of Jon Trowbridge Bapd by Mr. Goodrich Durham.
Feby 13	1780	Elisha son of Oren & Hannah Alvord.
Mar 5	"	Ralph son of Ralph Smith
Mar 26	"	Martha Daughter of Ebenr Harding.
	"	Margery Daughter of Moses West Junr.
Mar 30	"	Elisha son of Dewey Hall
April 10	"	John son of Leml. & Katharine Parsons by Mr. Goodrich.
May 7	"	Eunice Daughter of Samuel Kilbourn bapt. by Mr. Boardman.
May 7	"	Deborah Daur of Samll Kilbourn bapt. by Mr. Boardman.
	"	Mary Daur of Samll Kilborn Baptd by Mr. Boardman.
May 21	"	Lucy Daur of Darius Adams.
June 25	"	Noah Son of James Rich.
July 2	"	John son of Rhuel & Hannah Alvord.
	"	Sybil Daughter of Rhuel & Hannah Alvord.
	"	Mary Daur of Rhuel & Hannah Alvord.
July 23	"	Brooks son of Isaac Smith Junr.
July 30	"	Deborah Daur of Isaac Kneeland.
	"	Lydia Daur of Joseph Caswell.
Septr 10	"	Ashbel son of Seth Alvord Junr.
Oct 15	"	Roana Daur of Ebenr Bailey
	"	Levi son of Ebenr Bailey
	"	Zilpha Daur. of Ebenr Bailey
Oct 22	"	Anna Daur of David Kneeland
Oct 29	"	Lucy Daur of Isaac Bevin Bapd by Hunn [Huntington] Marlborough.
Feb 25	1781	Elisabeth Dau of Samuel Kilbourn—Mr. Boardman
Mar 18	"	Lydia Daur of Daniel & Lydia Clark
June 1	"	Elihu son of Elihu Hubbard
July 1	"	Jabez Clark son of John Norton
	"	Chauncey son of Jared Parmelee
	"	Liva Daughter of John Johnson Junr
	"	Annis Daughter of Oren Alvord
July 22	"	Sarah Daughter of Nathaniel Mott.
	"	Elisabeth Daughter of Lemll West.
Augt 12	"	Asahel son of John Clark Jr. Bapt by Mr. Huntington Marlborough.
	"	James Hall son of Ruel & Hannah Alvord Bapt by Mr. Huntington Marlborough.
Aug 20	"	Abner son of James Bill Bapd by Mr. Gurley Exeter.
	"	Timo Kilbourn son of Joseph Johnson Baptised by Mr. Gurley Exeter.
Sept 16	"	Titus son of Titus Carrier.
Sept 23	"	Mary Daur of David Allen
Oct 16	"	Joseph son of Samll Goff.
	"	Ebenezer son of Ebenezer Bailey

Oct 16	1781	Timothy son of John Johnson.
"	"	Jabez son of John Johnson.
Nov 25	"	Gershom son of Capt Silas Dunham Bapd by Mr. Boardman.
Decr 2	"	Darius son of Ephraim Harding
Decr 9	"	Jesse son of Jesse & Lucy Kneeland.
Decr 23	"	Samll son of Lemll & Faith Parsons.
Dec 30	"	Abigail Daur of Nathaniel White.
Mar 10	1782	Lucy Daur of Moses Cole.
Mar 24	"	Hannah Daur of Dewey Hall.
	"	Hannah Daur of Ezra Ackley
April 14	"	Asahel son of Ebenr Harding.
April 28	"	Lydia Daur of Joseph Caswell.
May 26	"	Elijah son of Thos. Shephard.
	"	Ebenezer son of Willm White.
	"	Samll Shaylor son of Samll Kilbourn
June 9	"	Nathan son of Nathan Champion Lebanon.
	"	Roswell son of Benjm Harding
June 16	"	Hannah Daughter of Moses Cook Baptd by Mr. Boardman
June 30	"	Sally Daur of Ralph Smith Baptd by Mr. Boardman.
July 7	"	Matilda Daur of Ebenezer Cole.
	"	Synthia Daur of Darius Adams.
July 14	"	John son of Sylvanus & Anne Norcutt
	"	Molly Daur of Danll & Esther Parks.
	"	Clarissa Daur of Danll & Esther Parks.
Sept 1	"	Richard son of Moses West Jr.
Sept 15	"	Benjamin son of David Kneeland—Mr. Boardman.
Nov 10	"	Betsy Daur of Daniel & Lydia Clark.
Feby 2	1783	Ruth Daur of Seth Alvord Jnr.
Feby 16	"	John son of James Rich.
Feb 23	"	Nathaniel son of Ebenezer Bailey
Mar 30	"	Olive Daur of Elihu Hubbard.
May 4	"	Mercy Daur of Isaac Bevin.
July 6	"	Lydia Daur of Nathaniel & Margaret Markham.
	"	Abijah son of Nathaniel & Margaret Markham.
Aug 3	"	Josiah Son of Capt Elijah Cook.
	"	Molly Daur. of Joseph Johnson
Aug 17	"	Rubi Daur of John Clark Jur.
	"	Sage son of Danll & Esther Parks.
Sept 7	"	Susannah Daur of Ezekiel Porter of Winsted—Winchester
	"	John son of Jared & Susannah Parmelee
Oct 5	"	Jared son of John Johnson Jur.
Nov 30	"	Azuba Daur of Isaac Smith Jur.
Dec 21	"	Richard son of Widdow Gideons—Middle Haddam
Feby 8	1784	Ezeriah Spencer Son of Samll & Elisabeth Fielding
April 11	"	Roswell son of Lemuel West
	"	Enoch son of Enoch Smith Jur Middle Haddam.
April 25	"	Rachel Daur of Moses Cole.
May 23	"	Josiah Goff Adult.

May	23	1784	Bulkley son of Othniel Brainerd Jr & Grace Brainerd.
		"	Polly Daur of Samll & Anna Cowdrey.
May	30	"	Lucy Daur of Josiah & Anna Goff
June	6	"	John & Benjm, Mehitable & Susanna sons & Daughters of John & Susanna West
		"	Pheby Daur of Joseph Caswell
June	20	"	Betsy Daur of Oren & Hannah Alvord.
June	27	"	Samll son of Edward & Mary Purple.
		"	Lydia Daur of Reuben Norcutt.
		"	Rufus, Oliver, Eunice, Elijah, Lucy, Jesse & Russell sons & Daughters of Eunice Dewey & Rufus Dewey Deceased
July	11	"	Patience Daur of Dewey & Hannah Hall.
July	18	"	Livia Daur of Moses & Elisabeth Cook.
		"	Anna Daur of Amos & Anna Clark.
July	25	"	Lucy Daur of Jesse & Lucy Kneeland—Mr. Boardman.
Augt	1	"	Lucy Daur of John Gideons Middle Haddam.
Augt	15	"	Newel son of Benjm Smith Middle Haddam
Sept	5	"	Sabina Daur of Reuben Norcutt.
Sept	12	"	Phebe Daur of Ralph & Hannah Smith
		"	Lea Daur of Ebenr & Zilpha Bailey
Sept	26	"	Susanna Daur of Isaac Rich Middle Haddam
		"	Russell son of John & Lucy Parmelee
Oct	3	"	Phylena Daur of Amos & Anna Clark
		"	Elijah son of David & Jerusha Clark
Octr	10	"	Rebecca wife of Isaac Johnson, Adult.
		"	Mercy Hannah Daur of Thos. & Elisabeth Shepard
		"	Joshua son of Noadiah Taylor Middle Haddam
Octr	17	"	Molly Daur of William White.
Novr	28	"	Russell son of Isaac & Hannah Kneeland.
Jany	9	1785	Warren son of Ephraim Harding
Jany	23	"	Katharine Daur of Lemll & Faith Parsons
Mar	20	"	George Washington son of Samll & Anna Cowdrey
April	17	"	James son of David & Mercy Kneeland.
April	24	"	Thankful Patience Daur of Samll & Mary Goff
May	1	"	Moses son of Moses West Jur.
May	15	"	Rhoda Daur of Stephen & Prudence Clark
May	29	"	Ebenr Hills Adult. M. Haddam
		"	Ruth Hills Adult.
		"	Scila Daur of Ebenr & Ruth Hills.
June	5	"	Seth Croel son of Elihu Hubbard
June	19	"	Enos son of John Johnson Jr.
July	4	"	Anna Daur of John & Lucy Parmelee.
July	24	"	Selinda Daur of John & Edey Norton.
Augt	21	"	Martin son of Joseph Johnson
		"	Sarah Daur of Seth & Ruth Alvord
Augt	28	"	Rebecca Daur of Jesse & Lucy Kneeland.
Sept	11	"	Deborah Matilda Daur of Silas & Sarah Dunham
Oct	16	"	Phylena Daur of Apollos & Lucy Arnold

CONGREGATIONAL CHURCH OF EAST HAMPTON. 97

Dec	25	1785	Anna Daur of Adonijah Strong
Feb	19	1786	Sally Daur of Danll & Esther Parke
Feb	26	"	Duel son of Josiah & Anna Goff
Mar	12	"	Selden son of Ebenr & Zilpha Bailey
Mar	19	"	Mary Daur of Moses & Mary White Cole
April	16	"	Stephen son of Isaac & Sarah Bevin
April	30	"	Joseph son of Dewey & Hannah Hall
May	2	"	Aristarchus so of Capt Elijah & Lois Smith M. Haddam
June	4	"	Nathaniel son of Nathaniel & Margaret Markham
June	25	"	Selden son of Moses & Elisabeth Cook
July	2	"	Hannah Daur of Jonathan & Margery Caswell
July	9	"	Ruth Daur of Edward & Mary Purple
July	16	"	Hannah Daur of Josiah & Mary Cook M. H.
July	30	"	Oliver son of Lemuel West
July	31	"	Sally Daur of John & Azuba Haling
Sept	17	"	Grace wife of Isaac Sears Adult
		"	Alvah son of Isaac & Rebecca Johnson.
Sept	24	"	Anna Daur of Isaac & Grace Sears
		"	Lucy Daur of Isaac & Grace Sears
		"	Isaac son of Isaac & Grace Sears
Nov	5	"	Esther Daur of Jared & Susannah Parmelee
		"	Sophia Daur of Samll & Elisabeth Kilbourn
Mar	11	1787	Anna Daur of Amos & Anna Clark
		"	Nancy Daur of Samll & Anna Cowdrey
April	1	"	Bryan son of John & Lucy Parmelee
April	15	"	Anna Daur of Ebenr & Ruth Hill
April	22	"	Reuben son of Reuben Norcutt
May	20	"	James Goff Adult son of Benjmn & Prudence Goff
June	10	"	Nathaniel son of Joel & Mercy Wood
		"	John son of John & Azuba Hailing
July	1	"	Ishmael Gates son of Mary Andrews
July	15	"	Hannah Daur of William White
		"	John Huet son of Widdow Joanna Alvord
July	22	"	Nanna Woodbridge Daur of Lemll & Faith Parsons
		"	Demis Daur of Ezra Ackley
		"	Rachel Daur of David Allen
Aug	5	"	Anna Daur of Stephen & Prudence Clark
Aug	12	"	Mary Hubbard Daur of Willm & Huldah Thomas
Aug	26	"	Seth son of Seth Alvord Jr. & Ruth his wife
Sept	23	"	Alfred son of James & Mary Goff
Oct	21	"	Nancy Daur of Apollos & Lucy Arnold
Nov	11	"	Warren son of Elijah & Azubah Young
Nov	18	"	Asahel son of Widw Prudence Goff
Dec	9	"	Benjm son of Ephraim Harding
Jany	6	1788	Lovina Daur of Adonijah Strong
Feby	3	"	Polly Daur of Isaac & Grace Sears
Feby	5	"	Jabez Cyrus & Salmon sons of John & Hannah Johnson
Feby	24	"	Phylanda Daur of Oren & Hannah Alvord

98   CONGREGATIONAL CHURCH OF EAST HAMPTON.

Mar 9	1788	Lucretia Daur of Elijah & Azubah Young
"		Austin son of Jonathan & Margery Caswell
May 4	"	Hoziel son of Hoziel & Margery Smith
May 18	"	Nathan son of Moses & Mary White Cole } Mr. Selden
"		Abiel son of Isaac & Rebecca Johnson } M. Haddam
"		Rebekah Daur of Ebenr & Zilpha Bailey }
May 25	"	Hepzah, Olive & Moses son & Daurs of Phillip & Olive White
"		Deborah Daur of Edward & Mary Purple
"		Roswel son of Elihu Hubbard
June 8	"	Nathaniel Clark son of Sparrow & Eunice Smith
July 6	"	Henry & Salah sons of Salah & Anna Jackson
July 13	"	Johnson son of Daniel & Esther Parke
"		Sally Daur of Jesse & Lucy Kneeland
Octr 5	"	Lucretia, Daniel & Mary Blynn son & Daughters of Hoziel & Margery Smith
Oct 12	"	Abner son of Isaac & Sarah Bevin
Nov 16	"	Oren son of Moses & Elisabeth Cook
"		Porter son of Isaac Smith Junr
Dec 21	"	Abner Cole Adult.
Jany 4	1789	Benjm Goff Adult
Jany 11	"	Lucy Daur of Nathll & Margaret Markham
Feby 1	"	Florinda Daur of John & Edey Norton
Mar 8	"	Sabina Daur of Reuben Norcot
Mar 29	"	Azuba Daur of Elijah & Azuba Young
April 26	"	Chauncey son of David & Jerusha Clark
May 17	"	Timothy Green son of John & Lucy Parmelee
May 24	"	Sally Daur of Samll & Elisabeth Kilbourn
"		Abner son of Amos & Anna Clark
"		Phebe Ackley Daur of Abner & Lydia Cole
June 22	"	Nabby Daur of Phillip & Olive White
July 26	"	Esther Daur of Ruel & Hannah Alvord
Augt 16	"	Warren son of Lemuel West
"		Gideon son of Apollos & Lucy Arnold
Augt 30	"	Nancy Daur of Jared & Susanna Parmelee
Sept 6	"	Danll Kellogg son of Adonijah Strong
Septr 7	"	David son of Ralph & Hannah Smith
Octr 11	"	Ichabod son of Ebenr Harding Jr & Jerusha his wife
Octr 18	"	David son of David & Elisabeth Allen
Octr 25	"	Benjamin son of James & Mary Goff
Novr 8	"	Rachel Daur of Ebenr & Zilpha Bailey
April 4	1790	Anne wife of Samll Cornwell
"		Julia Daur of Samll & Anne Cornwell
May 2	"	Ruhama Daur of Joel & Mercy Wood
June 6	"	Sally Daur of Isaac & Grace Sears
July 4	"	Anna Daur of Isaac & Rebecca Johnson
July 11	"	James son of James & Sarah Markham
July 25	"	Joseph Chester son of Willm White
Augt 8	"	Ranny son of Danll & Esther Parke

RESIDENCE OF REV. JOEL WEST.
"GLIMPSES OF LAKE POCOTOPAUG."

CONGREGATIONAL CHURCH OF EAST HAMPTON.

Augt 22   1790   Abigail Daur of Jonathan & Margery Caswell
Sept 5   "   Noah son of Nathl & Margaret Markham
Dec   5   "   Gershom son of Elijah & Azubah Young Mr. Lyman Millington.

※ ※ ※

RECORD KEPT BY REV. JOEL WEST.

Nov.   4   1792   Jabez son of Reuel & Hannah Alvord
      11   "   Nabby Judd dau of Sparrow & Eunice Smith
Dec.   2   "   Charles son of Nath. & Margaret Markham
      16   "   Elijah son of Reuben & Lidia Norcut—Mr. Selden
Jany. 20   1793   Mary dau. of Elijah & Azuba Young—Mr. Huntington
Feby. 10   "   Margeree dau. of Hosial & Margeree Smith
Mar. 12   "   Zeruah Blush dau. of Libeus & Polly Hills
      17   "   Harry son of John & Lucy Parmelee
      24   "   Betsy Norton dau. of Nath. & Dolle Clark
May   5   "   Jonathan son of Ebeneezer & Zilpha Bailey
      12   "   Anne dau. of Edward & Mary Purple
June 16   "   Shaler son of Jonathan & Marjory Caswell
      19   "   David son of Wm & Elizabeth White
July 28   "   Elisha son of Daniel & Esther Parks.
Aug. 18   "   Asher Rowley child of Elizabeth Cole
Sept. 15   "   Dolle Loveman dau. of Nath. & Dolle Clark.
Oct. 27   "   Polly dau. of Appollos & Lucy Arnold.
Nov. 10   "   Horace son of Stephen & Prudence Clark
Dec.   8   "   Ira son of Nathaniel & Ruth Bailey
Mar.   9   1794   Betsy dau. of Isaac & Grace Sears
      30   "   Julia dau. of Elijah & Azubah Young
May   11   "   Dyar Clark son of Joseph & Lucy Daily.
      11   "   Erastus son of Joseph & Lucy Daily
      11   "   Joseph son of Joseph & Lucy Daily
      11   "   Clary dau. of Joseph & Lucy Daily
      11   "   Lucy dau. of Joshua & Ruth Bailey
      11   "   Timothy son of Joshua & Ruth Bailey
May   17   "   Percy an adopted dau. of John & Azuba Hinkley
June   1   "   Sophia an adopted dau. of Joseph & Hope Buel } Selden
       1   "   Sally Buel adopted dau. of Joseph & Hope Buel }
Aug. 24   "   Prudence dau. of James & Mary Goff.
      31   "   Polly dau. of Gillet & Hannah Hinkley
      31   "   Phebe dau. of Gillet & Hannah Hinkley
Nov.   2   "   Julia dau. of Joseph & Lucy Dailey
Apl.   5   1795   Amos son of Amos & Anna Clark
      26   "   Hannah dau. of Reuel & Hannah Alvord
May   24   "   Hosial son of Hosial & Margere Smith   Mr. Huntington
June   7   "   Dimis dau. of Joel & Mary Wood.
July 12   "   Lewin son of Jonathan & Margere Caswell
      26   "   Zeruah Blush dau. of Libbeus & Polly Hills
Aug. 16   "   Nathaniel Clark son of Sparrow & Eunice Smith
      23   "   Julia dau. of Isaac & Rebecca Johnson

CONGREGATIONAL CHURCH OF EAST HAMPTON.

Sept.	6	1795	Harva son of Apollos & Lucy Arnold
	6	"	Fanna dau. of Ashbel & Anna Woodbridge
Oct.	4	"	Liva dau. of Abner & Lydia Cole
	18	"	Charles son of David & Lucy Sears } Mr. Selden
	18	"	Lucy dau. of David & Lucy Sears
	25	"	Sila dau. of Benj. & Abigail Goff.
Nov.	15	"	Nancy Brockway dau. of Joel & Betsey West.
June	12	1796	Polly dau. of John & Lucy Parmele
Mar.	4	1797	Brackett son of Joel & Betsey West.
Apl.	9	"	Anna dau. of Joshua & Ruth Bailey.
	9	"	Ossmin son of Jonathan & Margere Caswell
July	2	"	Betsy Maria Sparrow dau. of Sparrow & Eunice Smith
Aug.	13	"	Artemas son of Apollos & Lucy Arnold
Oct.	8	"	Reliance dau. of Isaac & Rebecca Johnson
	8	"	Octava dau. of Lebbeus & Polly Hills
	29	"	Abner son of Abner & Lydia Cole—Mr Selden
Feby.	4	1798	Samuel son of Ashbel & Hannah Woodbridge
Apl.	29	"	Elijah son of Ebenezer Bailey
June	3	"	Julius Orlando son of John & Lucy Parmelee
	13	"	Ephraim son of Ebenezer & Phoebe Norcutt
	13	"	Manassah son of Ebenezer & Phoebe Norcutt
July	15	"	Abigail McCleave an adult
July	22	"	Anne dau. of Abigail McCleave.—Mr. Selden
	22	"	Uriah son of Abigail McCleave.—Mr. Selden
Sept.	2	"	Diodate Brockway son of Joel & Betsey West.
	2	"	Julius Norton grandson of James & Asenah Bill
Oct.	21	"	Nancy dau. of the Widow Rogers—Mr. Mills
Nov.	4	"	Otis son of Seth Jr. & Sally Alvord.
	4	"	Bulah dau. of Seth Jr. & Sally Alvord.
Aug.	25	1799	Julia dau. of Benj. & Abigail Goff
Oct.	27	"	Laura dau. of Apollos & Lucy Arnold.
Nov.	10	"	Saml. Gibson son of Lebbeus & Polly Hills
Dec.	15	"	John Cavilla Adams son of David & Hannah Strong
Apl.	20	1800	Lucy dau. of John & Lucy Parmelee—Mr. Selden
July	20	"	Evelina Orvilla dau. of Joel & Betsey West.
Aug.	25	"	Jerusha Hall dau. of David Clark.
Oct.	26	"	Joshua son of Joshua Jr. & Ruth Bailey.
May	10	1801	Amelia dau. of John & Abigail Rich.
Dec.	13	"	Lucy dau. of Apollos & Lucy Arnold.
Jany.	17	1802	Pamela dau. of Lebbeus & Polly Hills
Feby.	3	"	Danl. Butler adopted child of Moses Cook.
May	30	"	Elizabeth dau. of Seth & Sally Alvord.
Nov.	9	"	Lucy dau. of John & Lucy Parmelee.
Jany.	16	1803	Harlowe son of Ashbel & Hannah Woodbridge
May	15	"	Deborah Griffith daughter of David & Eunice Clark
Feb.	5	1804	David son of John & Lucy Parmelee.
Apr.	15	"	Chauncey Hart son of Seth & Sally Alvord.
May	13	"	Gustavus son of Lebbeus & Polly Hills.—Mr. Selden.

CONGREGATIONAL CHURCH OF EAST HAMPTON. 101

June	8	1804	Delia Elliot, daughter of Joel & Betsey West.—Mr. Selden.
	10	"	Betsy daughter of James Bores (?) of Stafford.
Apr.	28	1805	Emelia Adeline daughter of David & Eunice Clark.
	28	"	Achsah Bill daughter of Apollos & Lucy Arnold.
May	26	"	Joseph Butler son of Joseph & Abigail Rich
Apr.	20	1806	Timothy Rogers, son of Nath. & Hannah Markham.
May	11	"	Charlotte daughter of Lebbeus & Polly Hills.
June	8	"	John William son of Sparrow Smith.
	15	"	Omri son of James & Molly Goff: Mr. Gillet.
July	13	"	Abigail, daughter of Joseph & Abigail Rich
Aug.	3	"	Orpah adopted dau. of Wm. & Elizabeth White
Oct.	26	"	Betsy Emeline, daughter of Joel & Betsey West
Nov.	12	"	John, Julia, & Daniel, children of Widow Martha Ackley.
Aug.	9	1807	Nancy Emela, daughter of Joseph & Nancy Hall
Dec.	27	"	Cyrus son of James & Molly Goff.
May	1	1808	Jerusha Ann daughter of David & Eunice Clark
July	3	"	Nathaniel Austin son of Joseph & Abigail Rich
Sept.	18	"	Julius Augustus ⎱ Twin children of Lebbeus Hills
			Julia Augusta ⎰
Nov.	27	"	Brackett Mortimer son of Joel & Betsey West.
		"	Joel, adopted son of Daniel & Sarah Johnson.
Oct.	9	1809	Densy Parmelee, daughter of Timothy & Hannah Parmelee
		"	Dolly Stephens daughter of Timothy & Hannah Parmelee
		"	Jasper Ward son of Timothy & Hannah Parmelee
		"	Thomas Jefferson son of Timothy & Hannah Parmelee
		"	Pamelia, daughter of Isaac & Anna Bevin.
		"	William son of Isaac & Anna Bevin.
		"	Chauncey son of Isaac & Anna Bevin.
		"	Isaac Avery son of Isaac & Anna Bevin.
		"	Minoris son of Widow Sally Watrous.
		"	Lois Loomis daughter of Widow Sally Watrous.
June	10	1810	Joseph son of Nathan Harding Jr. & Philena, his wife.
		"	Dennis son of Nathan Harding Jr. & Philena, his wife.
		"	Abner Clark son of Nathan Harding Jr. & Philena, his wife.
		"	Philena Ann dau. of Nathan Harding Jr. & Philena, his wife.
July	22	"	Alice Amanda daughter of Joel & Betsey West.
Sept.	30	"	Abner Griswold, son of Isaac & Anna Bevin.
		1811	———
		1812	———
Mar.	14	1813	Miranda Matilda, dau. of Joel & Betsey West.
June	27	"	Amanda daughter of Nathan Jr. & Anna Harding.
July	18	"	Gurdon Ackley son of Gurdon Fowler.
		"	Samuel Kellogg son of Gurdon Fowler.
		"	Wm. Lord son of Gurdon Fowler.
		"	Sarah Ann daughter of Gurdon Fowler.
Dec.	19	"	Philo son of Isaac & Anna Bevin.
June	16	1814	Abel Shepherd son of Isaac & Sally Hinckley.
		"	Emela Smith daughter of Isaac & Sally Hinckley.

June 16	1814	Ogden Lewis son of Isaac & Sally Hinckley.
	"	Lucy Champion, daughter of Isaac & Sally Hinckley.
	"	Cleantha Eldridge daughter of Isaac & Sally Hinckley.
	"	Sarah Ann daughter of Isaac & Sally Hinckley.
	"	Oramel Jared son of Isaac & Sally Hinckley.
July 10	"	Mary Esther, daughter of David & Mehitable Clark.
Sept 25	"	Chittendon Griswold son of Joel & Betsey West.
Aug. 20	1815	Alice Stevens, daughter of Isaac & Anna Bevin.
30	"	Lucy Caswell, an adult.
July 28	1816	Diantha, daughter of W. A. & Anna Skinner.
	"	Samuel son of Warren A. & Anna Skinner.
Feb. 8	"	Samuel Wales son of Joel & Betsy West.
May 11	1817	Ruth Ann daughter of W. A. & Anna Skinner.
Aug. 10	"	Maria adopted daughter of Sally Johnson.
Sept. 5	"	Adaline daughter of Isaac & Anna Bevin.
Sept. 6	1818	Eleazer Veazey Jr. adult.
	"	Rhoda Sears, adult.
	"	Betsy Sears, adult.
Oct. 25	"	Henry Bush, adult.
	"	Lydia Bush, adult.
Nov. 1	"	Lazarus Watrous, adult.
	"	Sally Youngs, adult.
	"	Charlotte Smith, adult.
Nov. 30	"	Stiles Davenport son of Joel & Betsey West.
Jan. 3	1819	Abigail Hall, an adult.
	"	Lucy Watrous, an adult.
	"	Ansel Eber son of Benjamin & Polly Ingraham.
	"	Mary Maria daughter of Benjamin & Polly Ingraham.
	"	William White son of Benjamin & Polly Ingraham.
June 20	"	Emela daughter of Warren A. & Anna Skinner.
27	"	Mary Cook, an adult.
July 4	"	Sabrina Adaline Markham, an adult.
Sept. 5	"	Calvin Hall Jr. an adult.
	"	Emila Veazey, an adult.
Oct. 24	"	Betsy Clark daughter of Calvin Jr. & Dolly Hall.
31	"	Charles A. son of David & Lucy Buell.
	"	Mary M. daughter of David & Lucy Buell
	"	Tillson A. son of David & Lucy Buell
	"	Caroline M. daughter of David & Lucy Buell.
	"	William G. son of David & Lucy Buell.
	"	Sarah E. daughter of David & Lucy Buell.
Nov. 7	"	Eunice Sears, an adult.
	"	Azubah Smith dau. of Benj. & Polly Ingraham.
21	"	Solomon B. son of John & Rhoda Edwards.
	"	John J. son of John & Rhoda Edwards.
June 18	1820	Belinda dau. of Isaac & Anna Bevin
July 16	"	Florilla dau. of Eleazer Jun. & Elizabeth Veazey
	"	Marietta dau. of Eleazer Jun. & Elizabeth Veazey

July 16	1820	Warren son of Eleazer Jun. & Elizabeth Veazey	
"		Hiram son of Eleazer Jun. & Elizabeth Veazey	
"		John W. son of Lazarus & Anna Watrous	
"		Timothy C. son of Lazarus & Anna Watrous	
"		Abner N. son of Lazarus & Anna Watrous	
"		Fidelia A. dau. of Lazarus & Anna Watrous	
"		Harmony dau. of Lazarus & Anna Watrous	
"		Sarah E. dau. of Lazarus & Anna Watrous	
"		Elijah Morgan son of Elijah & Alice Norcutt	
"		Lydia Strickland dau of Elijah & Alice Norcutt	
Sept. 10	"	Amelia Emilissa daughter of Calvin Jr. & Dolly Hall	
May 5	1821	Achsa Tubbs an adult	
Nov. 18	"	Jaman Allen son of Philena Strong	
June 9	1822	Mary dau. of Warren A. & Anna Skinner.	
"		Lucina dau. of Warren & Talitha West.	
23	"	Joseph Chester son of Benj. & Polly Ingraham	
30	"	Lyman Harlow son of Horace & ——— Clark	
Aug. 18	"	Harriet dau. of Michael & Mary Smith.	
Nov. 3	"	Anna Mandana, dau. of Lazarus & Anna Watrous.	
Aug. 24	1823	Henry son of Warren A. & Anna Skinner	
May 2	1824	Eunice Almira dau. of E. & P. Ingraham.	
May 15	1825	Asa Day son of Warren & Talitha West.	
Sept. 11	"	John Williams son of Warren A. & Anna Skinner	
June 18	1826	Laura Ann dau. of Widow Rhoda Edwards.	
—	1827	Jane dau. of Jedediah Barstow	
—	"	Ellen Elizabeth dau. of Warren West.	
—	1828	Fredk. Mortimer son of Morris & Sabrina Baker.	

MARRIAGES.

RECORD KEPT BY REV. LEMUEL PARSONS.

Feb	11	1779	Benjm, Catharine & Sarah Goodall
April	13	"	Daniel Parks & Esther Ranny
May	4	"	Ithamar Rowley & Demis Gates
July	1	"	Jedediah Cone. E Haddam & Molly Johnson E. Hampton
Aug	11	"	Richard Cook & Mary Rowley
Sept	14	"	Gideon Knowlton E. Haddam & Lydia Smith E Hampton
Oct	19	"	Nathaniel Cone & Margery Sexton
Nov	4	"	Jonathan Bailey & Olive Welton
Mar	2	1780	John Fisk & Martha Goodrich
Mar	22	"	Willm Shattuck & Hannah Spencer.
June	7	"	Israel Lucas & Mehitable Whitcomb
Septr	21	"	Nathaniel Markham & Margaret Hall
Novr	22	"	Thomas Cornwal of Chatham & Lois Clark of East Hampton
Decr	12	"	George Gates & Phebe Peters
Dec	13	"	Lemll Parsons of Chatham & Faith Little of Colchester
Decr	19	"	Elisha Hills of Richmond & Hannah Gates of Chatham
Jany	11	1781	John Markham Jur & Asenith Smith
Jany	18	"	Capt Silas Dunham & Sarah Johnson
Mar	15	"	Enoch Niles E Haddam & Dorothy Spencer E Hampton
Mar	27	"	John Clark Esq. & Hannah Ackley
April	5	"	Thomas Shephard & Elisabeth Bailey
April	12	"	John Welch & Jemimah Morgan
July	12	"	Amos Clark & Anna Sears
July	19	"	Hoziel Smith Middle Haddam & Margery Sexton East Hampton
Sept	20	"	Noah Kellogg New Hartford & Deborah Knowlton E. H.
Oct	18	"	Jonathan Bill of Lebanon and Asenith Bill of E. H.
Dec	5	"	Israel Fox Eastbury & Abigail Hodge E. Hampton
Decr	11	"	James Bailey & Abigail Hailing
Jany	7	1782	Joel Wood & Mercy Clark
July	25	"	Othniel Brainerd Jur- E. Hampton & Grace Stocking Chatham
Sept	19	"	David Clark & Jerusha Hall
Oct	15	"	John Palmer East Haddam & Mary Percival E. H.
Oct	24	"	Aaron Tallcott Enfield & Jedidah Lord E. Hampton
Novr	27	"	Benjn Strong Haddam & Susanna Trowbridge E. H.
Jany	23	1783	Jeremiah Bettis, Pownall & Molly Castle E. Hampton
Mar	26	"	Nathaniel Freeman Jur & Livia Cornwal
May	1	"	Samll Fielding & Elisabeth Alvord 2d

CONGREGATIONAL CHURCH OF EAST HAMPTON.   105

June	22	1783	Saml Cowdrey & Anna Bailey
Augt	31	"	James Bill Jur & Hannah Goodrich
Octr	13	"	Samll Brown Jur & Polly Kellogg
Octr	16	"	Isaac Johnson & Rebecca Cole
		"	Elisha Niles Colchester & Naomi Ackley E. Hampton
Decr	4	"	Joshua Cook & Elisabeth Cary Middle Haddam
Jany	25	1784	Jonathan Bowers & Rebekah Cary Middle Haddam
Mar	4	"	Samll Skinner Bolton & Esther Brainerd E. Hampton
Mar	18	"	Elijah Hubbard Eastbury & Ruth Smith Middle Haddam
April	22	"	Thos Goodrich E. Hampton & Lydia Cornwal Chatham
April	26	"	Eliakim Stiles Munsell & Hannah Brown
June	3	"	John Goodrich & Esther Parmelee
July	1	"	John Parks & Bethiah Smith Middle Haddam
Aug	12	"	Apollos Arnold & Lucy Bill
Sept	20	"	———— Giddins & Hartland & Mercy Johnson E. H.
Sept	30	"	Jacob Brooks Haddam & Lydia Stocking M. Haddam
Oct	19	"	John Shephard Jur & Betsy Colton Chatham
Oct	20	"	Benjn Hurd & Polly Cary Middle Haddam
Oct	21	"	James Shields Chatham & Lydia Ackley E. Hampton
Novr	5	"	Joshua Bailey Jr. & Ruth Sears
Nov	21	"	Joseph Davison Pomphret & Lydia Clark E. Hampton
Dec	21	"	Abel Abel & Lucy Hubbard Middle Haddam
Decr	30	"	John Hailing & Zuba Cook
Feby	10	1785	James Risley Hartford & Hannah Bates E. H.
Mar	31	"	Samll Caswell & Anna Alvord
April	14	"	Stephen Griffith & Zilpah Clark M. Haddam
May	31	"	Lemll Smith Sandisfield & Ellis Gideons M. Haddam
		"	Stephen Taylor & Sarah Stephenson M. Haddam
June	16	"	Huet Alvord & Joanna Hill
Oct	6	"	Christian Hosenkause & Patience Bailey
Oct	11	"	William Thomas & Huldah Cook
Novr	10	"	James Markham & Sarah Cowdery
Nov	24	"	Willard Sears & Rhoda Bailey
		"	Elijah Simeon Youngs & Azuba Hinckley
Nov	29	"	Nathaniel Doane N. Hartford & Sarah Adams Middle Haddam
		"	Jonathan Caswell & Margery Markham
Decr	15	"	Abner Cole E. Hampton & Lydia Freeman M. Haddam
Decr	17	"	Phillip Francis Colchester & Lucy Cook E. Hampton
Jany	5	1786	Zachariah Hosmer & Mary Smith M. Haddam
Jany	22	"	Janna Griswold —— N. York State & Lucy Clark E Hampton
Feb	2	"	Soloman Bailey & Rhoda Mott
Febr	5	"	Benjn Goff Jur & Abigail Brainerd
Mar	9	"	Israel Hodge & Molly Stiles
Mar	16	"	Nathan Burnham E. Haddam & Mary Fuller E. Hampton
Mar	19	"	Ebenr Cole Jur & Ruth Clark
Mar	30	"	James Goff & Mary Carrier
May	31	"	Jabez Hall & Abigail Willey
Octr	19	"	Samll Skinner Colchester & Ruth Ackley Chatham

106 CONGREGATIONAL CHURCH OF EAST HAMPTON.

Novr 14	1786	Amasa Day Colchester & Elisabeth Young Chatham
Decr 28	"	Seth Hall & Hannah Hubbard
Janr 4	1787	Comfort Beeby & Lydia Cook
Jany	"	Josiah Bidwell & Lucinda Kneeland Chatham
Mar 15	"	Enos Dewey & Mercy Rich M. Haddam
April 7	"	Zephaniah Mitchel & Bethiah Scranton
	"	Elisha Thorrington & Elisabeth Mitchel
April 30	"	Abner Hubbard & Elisabeth Bates
May 3	"	Sparrow Smith & Eunice Clark
May 15	"	Abner Moses, Hartland & Anna Johnson E. Hampton
July 11	"	Asahel Matthews & Anna Harding
July 22	"	Michael Smith M. H. & Mary Hall E. H.
Aug 26	"	Joshua Goff & Hannah Barnstable
Octr 9	"	Phillip Goff Jur & Chloe Cole
Jany 3	1788	Willm McDaniel Colchester & Sarah Lucas E. H.
	"	John Lucas & Betsy Davis
Feby 5	"	Roswell Hubbard & Mehitable Cook
April 6	"	Nathaniel Ackley & Elisabeth Spencer
Novr 20	"	Willm Morgan & Abigail Wetherill
Novr 27	"	Gideon Rogers Lyme & Lucy Ackley Chatham
	"	Erastus Bill & Sarah Hall
Decr 4	"	Lemll Rich & Deborah Taylor
Decr 21	"	Samll Cornwell & Anne Rogers
Dec 23	1789	Asa Mitchell Colchester & Marcy Saxton E. Hampton
Jany 6	1790	Asa Fox Chatham & Rhoda Doolittle E. Hampton
Jany 24	"	Sanford Thomson. Blanford & Peggy Stewart Chatham
June 6	"	Thos Judd Coventry & Mary Fuller E. Hampton
July 8	"	John Trowbridge & Susanna Bates
Augt 19	"	Elisha Taylor M. Haddam & Anna Cornwell E. Hampton
Sept 23	"	Jonathan Cowdery & Deborah Toby
Octr 3	"	Ackley Lewis & Sarah Parmelee
Oct 12	"	Simeon Young & Lydia Hills
Nov 4	"	Gurdon Crocker, Colchester & Sarah Brown E. Hampton
Nov 11	"	Samll Skinner Colchester & Mary Saxton E. Hampton

* * *

RECORD KEPT BY REV. JOEL WEST.

Oct. 17	1792	Stephen Burnham (E. Htfd.) & Joanna Alvord (Chatham)
Nov. 28	"	Anson Smith & Betsy Woodworth of M. Haddam.
Jany. 6	1793	Lot Hudson & Eunice Cole E. Hampton
17	"	Elizur Skinner (Cambridge N Y.) & Elvira Bill (Chatham)
Mch. 3	"	Oliver Brainerd & Lucy Rogers E. Hampton
Sept. 5	"	Seth Alvord Jr & Sally Sears E. Hampton
26	"	Walter Chappel (Hebron) & Eunice Hall E. Hampton
Nov. 3	"	Jonathan Parmelee & Hepzibah White E. Hampton
Jany. 5	1794	Barnabas Freeman M. Haddam & Fanny Needham E. Hampton
12	"	Jonathan Peck (Hebron) & Anna Ackley (E. Hampton)

CONGREGATIONAL CHURCH OF EAST HAMPTON. 107

Mch.	2	1794	Daniel Smith (M. Haddam) & Prudence Goff (E. Hampton)
Apl.	2	"	Nath. Porter (Glastonbury) & Kerziah Hills (E. Hampton)
Aug.	5	"	John Willey Jr. & Elizabeth Sears (E. Hampton)
Sept.	11	"	Adonijah Strong & Elizabeth Cook (E. Hampton)
Oct.	5	"	Lot Hudson & Huldah Harding (E. Hampton)
Nov.	26	"	Timothy Parmelee & Hannah Smith (E. Hampton)
Jany.	8	1795	Ebenezer Norcutt & Phebe Ackley E. Hampton
	14	"	Henry Jackson & Lois Johnson E. Hampton
Feby.	26	"	John Carrier & Lucy Dailey E. Hampton
May	17	"	Jesse Penfield & Dorinda Norton Chatham
June	7	"	Rufus Shailor (Haddam) & Hannah Cole E. Hampton
July	9	"	Isaac Bailey & Polly Douile (?) E. Hampton
Sept.	6	"	Benj. Billings (Lebanon) & Mary Goff Chatham.
Nov.	4	"	Joseph Buell & Marcy Carrier E. Hampton
	8	"	Godfrey Hop & Pallinea Freeman E. Hampton
	20	"	Geo. Hall (Chatham) & Eunice Rollo (Hebron)
Dec.	7	"	John Curtis (Hebron) & Sarah Ackley (Chatham)
	31	"	Stephen Knowlton & Mary Purple E. Hampton
Jany.	20	1796	Abner Hall & Anne Griffith E. Hampton
Apl.	3	"	Jonathan Goff & Lydia Harding, E. Hampton
	12	"	Hosial Brainerd & Polly Strong Chatham
	18	"	John Patridge (Dalton) & Faith Parsons Chatham
May	1	"	John Riley & Jerusha Rich Chatham
June	1	"	Enos Brown & Anna Williams Chatham
	16	"	Samuel Hills & Polly Lewis E. Hampton
	21	"	Aseph Carter & Sabrey Billings E. Hampton
		"	Caleb Floid & Abigail Carter E. Hampton
July	24	"	David Hills & Polly Welch E. Hampton
Nov.	30	"	Timothy Fielding (Haddam) & Sarah Knowlton E. Hampton
Dec.	7	"	Nath. Markham & Polly Strong E. Hampton
Jany.	9	1797	Elijah Rowley & Sally Morgan E. Hampton
	21	"	Bulkley Davis & Lydia Alvord Chatham
Feby.	23	"	Miner Hildreth of Glastonbury & Deborah Harding of E. Hampton
Nov.	1	"	Hezekiah Smith & Belinda Norton Chatham
	15	"	Jesse Cables & Tamar Carter Chatham
Mar.	7	1798	John Norton Jr. & Lucy Johnson E. Hampton
Apl.	25	"	Ebenezer Sears & Dorcas Beebe E. Hampton
		"	Daniel Butler Newton & Susannah Cook E. Hampton
Aug.	9	"	Isaac Carrier of Marlboro & Marcy Caswell E. Hampton
Sept.	25	"	Daniel Harding & Betsey Strong E. Hampton
Oct.	17	"	Elijah Ackley & Abigail Strong E. Hampton
	25	"	John Andrus & Anna Jones Glastonbury
Nov.	11	"	Joshua Park of Tyringham & Aruna Cole of Chatham
	22	"	Noah Strickland & Lydia Norcutt Chatham
Nov.	28	"	David Wyllys & Nancy Johnson E. Hampton
	29	"	Stephen Chapman & Huldah Cone E. Hampton
Jany.	31	1799	Joseph Haling & Jerusha Penfield E. Hampton

May	7	1799	Daniel Hills & Thankful Watrous E. Hampton
	7	"	Daniel Ackley & Martha Harding E. Hampton
Dec.	3	"	William Wilson & Lucy Wright Chatham
Jany.	14	1800	Luke Osbourn of Blanford & Zilpha Bailey of E. Hampton
Mch.	27	"	Elkanah Higgins & Lydia Caswell Chatham
Apl.	2	"	Joseph Rich & Abigail McCleve Chatham
Oct.	1	"	Daniel Johnson Brookline & Sarah West E. Hampton
Nov.	13	"	Isaac Bevins & Anna Avery E. Hampton
	27	"	Israel Cole & Ruth Alvord E. Hampton
Dec.	9	"	Amaziah Archer of Hebron & Sarah Sweetland E. Hampton
	28	"	Isaac Niles of Colchester & Almira Willey E. Hampton
Jany.	29,	1801	Cyprian Hinckley & Lydia Bevins E. Hampton
Feby.	5	"	Jabez Wood & Hannah Dewey E. Hampton
Mch.	26	"	Richard Carrier & Livia Johnson E. Hampton
May	18	"	John Watrous & Sally Bevins E. Hampton
June	21	"	James Randal Providence & Betsey Veazey E. Hampton
Sept.	16	"	Edmund West & Lucy Bevins E. Hampton
	17	"	Henry Strong & Susanna Newton E. Hampton
Oct.	7	"	John Phelps of Colchester & Adosha Williams of E. Hampton
Nov.	15	"	David Clark & Eunice Griffith Chatham.
	22	"	Ezekiel Skinner of Hebron & Sarah Mott of E. Hampton
	26	"	Elisha Brown & Esther Norcutt of Chatham.
Dec.	26	"	Henry Ackley & Ruth Purple of Chatham.
Feby.	18	1802	Joseph Graham & Ruth Bailey of Chatham.
Mch.	14	"	Elisha Rowley & Polly Alvord of Chatham
	18	"	Seth Marshall of Symsbury & Rhusey Caswell of E. Hampton
Apl.	5	"	William Harrison of Munson Mass. & Esther Doane of Chatham
June	16	"	Eleazer Veazey Jr. & Elizabeth West of E. Hampton
	20	"	William Higbee of Turin N.Y. & Hannah Hop of E. Hampton
Nov.	4	"	Charles Pheps (?) & Lucy Cole E. Hampton
	23	"	Joseph Goff & Clarissa Welch
Feby.	10	1803	Enos Bigelow of Colchester & Thankful Freeman E. Hampton
Mch.	13	"	Daniel Weairs Enfield & Sarah White E. Hampton
	27	"	Samuel Brown & Sibbil Cowdrey E. Hampton
Apl.	7	"	David Buell & Lucy Arnold E. Hampton
May	22	"	Joel Crout of Glastonbury & Cata Hosencruse E. Hampton
Aug.	11	"	Nathan Harding Jr. & Filena Clark E. Hampton
Oct.	9	"	Ebenezer Rollo Hebron & Susanna Usher Chatham
Nov.	3	"	Wix Watrous, Colchester & Livia Cook E. Hampton
	20	"	Simon Smith of Waterford & Polly Burr of Chatham
Dec.	7	"	Nathaniel Markham & Hannah Rogers E. Hampton
	22	"	Jesse Dickenson of Marlboro & Anna Welch E. Hampton
Apl.	12	1804	Isaac Niles & Thankful Harding E. Hampton
	24	"	Christopher Watrous & Lucy Sears E. Hampton
May	24	"	Titus Carrier & Mehitable Watrous East Hampton
	31	"	George Sellew & Dolly Avery of Glastonbury
June	17	"	Joseph Whitmore & Electa Ackley Chatham
Aug.	2	"	Daniel Jones & Lucretia Young Middle Haddam

CONGREGATIONAL CHURCH OF EAST HAMPTON.

Sept. 23	1804		Saml. Mitchel & Mary Cone Chatham
Oct. 11		"	James Alvord & Lucy Cook E. Hampton
21		"	Thomas Rich & Susanna Freeman Chatham
Nov. 22		"	Elisha Hall & Hannah Strong E. Hampton
Dec. 2		"	Constant Welch Jr. & Patience Hall E. Hampton
Feby 3	1805		Sherwood Palmer Cambridge N.Y. & Phebe Smith E. Hampton
Mch. 3		"	Oliver Brainerd & Anna Strong E. Hampton
April 4		"	Cornelius Rich Jr. Chatham & Nancy Campbell Lyme
Apl. 16		"	Joshua Webb & Anne Welch E. Hampton
May 1		"	Dexter Parmenter PrinceTown N.Y. & Marcy Rich E. Hampton
Aug. 15		"	Josiah Carrier of Marlboro & Betsy Kellogg E. Hampton
Sept. 4		"	Wm Findly Genesee N. Y. & Betsy Alvord E. Hampton
Dec. 11		"	Timothy Abbe of Enfield & Rhoda Clark E. Hampton
Jany. 13	1806		Joseph Mitchell & Clarissa Cone Chatham
Feby. 11		"	Joseph Rogers & Eunice Smith E. Hampton
Mch. 12		"	Russell Watrous of Colchester & Anne Kellogg E. Hampton
Aug. 31		"	Joseph Hall & Nancy Arnold E. Hampton
Sept. 21		"	Chauncey Brooks & Lucy Alvord E. Hampton
Dec. 27		"	Solomon Brainard of Haddam & Lucy Bailey E. Hampton
Apl. 5	1807		Aaron Bell of Glastonbury & Prudence Swan E. H.
27		"	Abijah Markham & Cloe Freeman E. Hampton
May 17		"	Ira Brainard of Middle Haddam & Phebe Cole E. Hampton
Nov. 7		"	Selden Rogers of E. Haddam & Sally Harding E. Hampton
24		"	Geo. Welch & Celinda Niles E. Hampton
25		"	Erastus Carrier Colchester & Celinda Norton E. Hampton
Mch. 22	1808		Jesse Hubbard of Middle Haddam & Florinda Norton E. Hampton
Apl. 3		"	Austin Smith of Middletown & Hannah White E. Hampton
May 15		"	Nicholas Ames & Hannah Norcutt Chatham
Nov. 8		"	Alexander Bowls & Azubah Youngs Middle Haddam
Apl. 11	1809		Deacon Moses Cook & Widow Ede Norton E. Hampton
May 8		"	William Clark 2nd & Sophronia Post E. Hampton
30		"	Richard Cook & Susanna Brown E. Hampton
July 9		"	Bill Williams & Olive Thomas E. Hampton
Aug. 17		"	John Guller (?) of Hudson N. Y. & Dolle Freeman of M. Haddam
Sept. 4		"	Isaac Ransom of Lyme & Rachael Bailey E. Hampton
Nov. 30		"	Lazarus Watrous of Marlboro & Anna Clark E Hampton
July 4	1810		Lester Brainard of Haddam & Betsy Coe E. Hampton
Sept. 13		"	Chauncey Hills & Sally Goodrich Chatham
Oct. 13		"	Asahel Bemiss of Marlboro & Betsy Harding E. Hampton
14		"	Warren Young Chatham & Sally Dean E. Haddam
Nov. 5		"	Elijah Dickinson Glastonbury & Polly Welch E. Hampton
15		"	John Isham & Rachael Cole E. Hampton
Mch. 24	1811		Joseph Selden of Haddam & Clarissa Strong E. Hampton
July 4		"	Robert Coe & Rebecca Bailey E. Hampton
July 21		"	Daniel R. Wolcot of Bristol & Philander Alvord E. Hampton
23		"	Bliss Welch & Elizabeth Strong 2d E. Hampton
Aug. 31		"	Alvin Cook & Lucretia Smith E. Hampton

110   CONGREGATIONAL CHURCH OF EAST HAMPTON.

Sept. 23	1811	Enos Johnson & Anna Parmelee E. Hampton
Oct. 24	"	Nathaniel Pease Marlboro & Elizabeth Cole E. Hampton
Nov. 18	"	John Willey & Polly Leanon E. Hampton
24	"	Gersham Youngs & Lydia Cole E. Hampton
28	"	Nathan Champion & Mercy Bevins E. Hampton
Dec. 19	"	Stephen Bevin & Mary Brown E. Hampton
Jany. 2	1812	Josiah Bell & Lavinia Norcutt Chatham
5	"	Julius Brainard & Sylvia Ackley Chatham
20	"	Jabez S. Brainard of Haddam & Livia Cole E. Hampton
Feby. 16	"	John Ransom & Betsy Mitchell Chatham
Apl. 14	"	Joseph Dean E. Haddam & Hannah Gates E. Hampton
May 10	"	Nathaniel Gates Jr. & Nancy Smith E. Hampton
June 5	"	Allen House Eastbury & Editha Bigelow E. Hampton
Jany. 12	1813	William Holmes of Glastonbury & Abigail Ackley E. Hampton
25	"	Asaph Mitchell of Colchester & Eunice Cole Middle Haddam
Feby. 14	"	Henry Peters of Hebron & Lydia Adams of E. Hampton (black)
Mch. 7	"	Erastus Sheldon of New Marlboro Mass. & Rachael Sears E. Hampton
21	"	Guy Chappel & Susan Stills of Lyme
May 2	"	David Clark Esq. & Mehittable Hubbard of Chatham
June 22	"	Orrin Cook & Polly Parmelee E. Hampton
24	"	Vine Starr & Nancy Barton E. Hampton
Aug. 15	"	Bryan Parmelee 2d & Huldah Dean E. Hampton
22	"	Sampson Freeman & Mary Ann Joel E. Hampton
Nov. 14	"	Geo. Primus Colchester & Betsy Brister E. Hampton
25	"	Olmsted Gates & Nabby Youngs E. Hampton
Dec. 26	"	George A. Stocking & Triphena Coe Chatham
Mch. 23	1814	William Wells of Hanover Ohio & Susan Bigelow E. Hampton
Oct. 12	"	John Northam Marlboro & Rachael Kellogg E. Hampton
Nov. 2	"	John Mason Saybrook & Demis Boles Marlboro
Jany. 20	1815	Elijah Norcutt & Alice Chapman Chatham
Feby. 5	"	Erastus Mitchell & Sally Bigelow Chatham
Mar. 26	"	Giles Hall & Dolly Parmelee E. Hampton
May 9	"	Calvin Hall Jr. & Dolly Clark E. Hampton
Oct. 18	"	Nathaniel Markham Jr. & Abigail J. Smith E. H.
22	"	John Bailey & Lydia Niles E. Hampton
Dec. 24	"	Harry Roberts E. Hartford & Rhoda Bailey E. Hampton
25	"	Benjamin Sherman Norwich & Anne Johnson E. Hampton
Feby. 26	1816	Henry Bush & Lydia Strong E. Hampton
Mch. 6	"	Jared Johnson & Sally Ransom E. Hampton
May 23	"	Nathaniel C. Smith & Charlotte Strong E. Hampton
June 2	"	Aaron Brown Colchester & Laura Wilson Chatham
July 21	"	Henry Perkins & Sally Sealy Hartford
Sept. 18	"	Amos Clark Jr. & Betsy M. S. Smith E. Hampton
25	"	Harvey Russell of Marlboro & Lucretia Russel E. Hampton
Nov. 6	"	Charles Markham & Sally White E. Hampton
27	"	George Smith colored E. Haddam & Jane Dublin [slave of T. Judd] E. Hampton
28	"	Ira Lucas & Almira Barton E. Hampton

CONGREGATIONAL CHURCH OF EAST HAMPTON. 111

Dec.	4	1816	King Smith of Waterford & Mary Smith E. Hampton
Jany.	19	1817	Harry Rockwell E. Windsor & Esther Niles E. Hampton
	26	"	John P. Hauselkuse & Dency Parmelee E. Hampton
Feby.	27	"	Walter Sexton & Nancy Starr E. Hampton
July	9	"	Philo Gates & Chloe Strong E. Hampton
Oct.	21	"	Benj. A. Strong & Lucy S. Welch E. Hampton
Nov.	5	"	Hiram Markham & Laura Niles Chatham
	27	"	Philip White Jr. & Lucy Niles E. Hampton
Dec.	4	"	Russell Rich & Phebe Leonan E. Hampton
Jany.	1	1818	John Sherman Norwich & Philura Welch E. Hampton
	6	"	Arthur H. Johnson & Deborah L. Welch E. Hampton
	29	"	Wm Haling & Abigail Hall E. Hampton
Feby.	19	"	Ebenezer Hall & Laura Cole Chatham
Mch.	30	"	Erastus Buck & Eunice Wells Chatham
Apl.	16	"	Ezra Strong & Lucy Markham E. Hampton
	16	"	Leonard Selden Haddam & Ruth G. Griffith E. Hampton
June	25	"	Asa Dunham Marlboro & Mary Cole E. Hampton
Aug.	15	"	Jacob Adams & Betsy Adams E. Hampton
	30	"	Benj. Griffin Middletown & Dorcas Rich Chatham
Sept.	1	"	Harry Mosely Marlboro & Candace Beach Chatham
	10	"	James Bill Esq. & Phebe Pelton Chatham
Nov.	26	"	Dan. B. Niles & Maria A. Harrington E. Hampton
Mar.	31	1819	Moses West & Lydia Clark E. Hampton
June	24	"	Elijah Clark 2nd & Mary Hubbard Chatham
Aug.	11	"	Solomon Bailey & Anna [Mary] Leonan E. Hampton
Nov.	1	"	Geo. M. Dixon Chatham & Sally McCall Marlboro
	10	"	Wm. W. Richmond & Clarissa Bailey E. Hampton
	16	"	Elijah Staples & Nancy Brown E. Hampton
	18	"	Elijah Bailey Chatham & Harriet Bell Glastonbury
	23	"	Minorris Gladding & Emila Cole of Berlin
Dec.	1	"	Ogden Sears & Betsy Harding E. Hampton
	23	"	Lorin Cowdrey & Sarah Ackley Chatham
May	3	1820	Ezra Ayres Greenwich Mass. & Rhoda Sears E. Hampton
June	1	"	John Tubbs & Anna Leanan E. Hampton
	7	"	Willard Sears Jr. & Sally Youngs E. Hampton
Sept.	13	"	Henry Strong & Philena Arnold E. Hampton
Nov.	16	"	Isaac Haling & Julia Johnson Chatham
Dec.	14	"	Richard M. Smith & Eunice Richmond E. Hampton
Apl.	22	1821	Robert Blish & Dorothy McCall Marlboro.
May	23	"	Orimel Clark & Pamelia Bevin E. Hampton
June	10	"	Cyrus Brainard & Clarissa Barton E. Hampton
July	4	"	Lord S. Hills & Mary Cook E. Hampton
Sept.	5	"	Calvin House Glastonbury & Julia Ackley E. Hampton
	6	"	Harvey Arnold & Betsey Sears E. Hampton
Nov.	15	"	Hiram Richmond & Phebe Edwards E. Hampton
Dec.	6	"	Hubbard Barton & Deborah G. Clark E. Hampton
Jany.	1	1822	Harvey Lucas & Almira W. Niles E. Hampton
	16	"	Justin Bolles & Lydia Morgan Middle Haddam
Apl.	3	"	Joshua S. Strong & Lucy Arnold E. Hampton

May	1	1822	Diodate B. West & Nancy Rogers E. Hampton
Aug.	19	"	Roswell Brooks & Sybil Evans Chatham
Nov.	28	"	Julius Gates & Susanna Strong E. Hampton
Jany.	29	1823	Gilbert Hills & Hannah Strong E. Hampton
Apl.	13	"	Daniel Hartwell of Hartford & Betsy E. Adams Chatham
	23	"	Gilson Huxford Marlboro & Anna Billings Chatham
May	7	"	Harvey Harding & Julia Strong E. Hampton
June	22	"	Beckwith Beers Waterford & Hope Evans E. Hampton
July	20	"	Seth Alvord & Abigail Saunders E. Hampton
Sept.	25	"	Thomas Judd Chatham & Esther Carpenter Coventry
Nov.	26	"	John C. A. Strong & Deborah L. Clark Chatham
	27	"	Joseph L. Brainard & Rachael H. Rich Chatham
Dec.	11	"	Asa Grover & Susannah Trowbridge E. Hampton
Mch.	23	1824	Abner Cole Jr. & Eliza Brown E. Hampton
Sept.	26	"	Daniel W. Tower Whitestown N.Y. & Emila Hills E. Hampton
Nov.	21	"	Joseph Goff & Lucy Welch E. Hampton
Dec.	5	"	Martin Culver Manchester & Lucy Bailey Chatham
	9	"	Roderic Ackley & Marietta Spencer Chatham
Feby.	1	1825	Ephraim Parsons Glastonbury & Lydia Cole Chatham
	24	"	James Shailer of Colchester & Mehitable Chapman Chatham
Mch.	1	"	Giles Goff & Marietta Markham Chatham
	3	"	Eli. Burnham of Colchester & Eliza Ackley Chatham
	31	"	Horace Brown & Lydia Bolles Chatham
Apl.	28	"	Philo Rowley & Lucy Ann Kellogg Chatham
May	28	"	Charles Dutton Glastonbury & Harriet Grover E. Hampton
Aug.	4	"	Wm. R. Smith & Mary Ann Daniels Chatham
Sept.	4	"	Hiram Clark & Achsa B. Arnold E. Hampton
	11	"	Hiram Barton of Chatham & Lois L. Watrous Marlboro
	29	"	Horace Hinckley & Abby Ann Ackley Chatham
Nov.	21	"	Wm. A. Brown & Lydia B. Smith Chatham
	24	"	Isaac Ackley & Betsy B. Niles Chatham
	24	"	Robert U. Richmond & Caroline B. Smith Chatham
Dec.	22	"	Nehemiah Gates Jr. & Elizabeth M. Strong E. Hampton
	28	"	Jared Taylor Glastonbury & Harriet Bailey E. Hampton
Jany.	4	1826	Dr. Chas. Smith & Deborah Griffith Chatham
	5	"	Henry Flood & Flora Arnold Chatham
	12	"	Enos Adams & Rebeccah Ann Ward Chatham
Mch.	14	"	Alfred Williams Hampton & Harriet Bailey Chatham
Apl.	10	"	Gideon Brainard Haddam & Martha Ackley Chatham
	12	"	Jason Ingraham & Nancy Wells Colchester
June	10	"	Augustus Gates & Elizabeth Alvord E. Hampton
	29	"	Benj. House of Coventry & Submit West Columbia
Aug.	24	"	Walter H. Clark & Florinda N. Hinckley E. Hampton
Sept.	10	"	Minorris Watrous of Marlboro & Amelia A. Clark E. Hampton
	17	"	Barnard B. Buck & Desire Brown Chatham
	25	"	Justin Smith & Siley Cole Chatham
Oct.	12	"	Washington Smith & Cynthia Barstow E. Hampton

S. MILLS BEVIN.

THIS volume is in many ways a memorial. It records the history of this church, to keep it ever fresh in the minds of the living. The names here enrolled belong for the most part to the Church Triumphant. It is now our sorrowful task to add one more name to the list of the dead before this book is closed,—SAMUEL MILLS BEVIN, whose last labor of love was to aid in compiling and publishing these records. He joined the invisible company of just men on March 6th, 1900. And the tribute is here repeated which was given at the funeral service by his pastor, Rev. William Slade:

A TRIBUTE.

We ought at this hour to make his favorite hymn our prayer. They are the very words we need to utter, and they must have braced his spirit, too.

> " Lead, kindly Light, amid th' encircling gloom,
> Lead Thou me on!
> The night is dark, and I am far from home;
> Lead Thou me on!
> * * * * *
> So long Thy power has blest me, sure it still
> Will lead me on
> O'er moor and fen, o'er crag and torrent, till
> The night is gone,
> And with the morn those angel faces smile
> Which I have loved long since and lost awhile!"

I have permission to speak freely of his worth, who has been snatched so suddenly from our hearts. It will be a comfort to us, I trust; but I must speak simply and frankly, so that this service may be appropriate.

His was a trained life. Born of a long line of honorable ancestry, he inherited business talents and moral fibre and a large heart. These gifts were tenderly nourished in this home during his boyhood and youth. School life and college discipline developed and enlarged the resources that were in him. The life of business and responsibility, home cares and affections deepened and widened his worth.

In this age it is the trained life that is valuable. Business is national and international. Trade is swift and competition fierce. Life has many sides to-day, and it is the many-sided life—that is, the trained life—only, that can be master of all this swiftness, breadth, and depth. With steady hand and careful mind, he carried his duties in the firm where he will be sadly missed. It was his fine cultured taste that brought home the best gifts and selected and gave the beautiful mantel to our Library. He was so well equipped, that the church, the library, the school, the community claimed his counsel and his services. We overloaded him with work.

But it is his religious life that went deepest and is most precious. The religious life is the unselfish life. The religious life is the life of simple unpretending love—love of God, love of friends, love of country, and love of home and all that it holds. It is the life of good will toward men that did thrive and blossom and bear fruit abundantly in him. The workmen have *rightly* written his name in their flowers—Our Friend. He made his religious faith and feeling definite and open. He was a member and officer in the church. He gave liberally to the support of the church and to every charity and public improvement. He did everything quietly. That is a part of religion. It was his childlike temper that was so admirable.

It seemed best in publishing the records of our church anniversary that a short introduction to the book should be written, and in a note at the close I briefly spoke of our indebtedness to the faithful and arduous work of Mr. Martin L. Roberts and Mr. S. Mills Bevin in preparing what the book contains. What I had written went to the printer, and the proof came back to Mr. Bevin, and he drew his pencil through his name; then the proof came to me, and I rubbed the pencil marks away. It was his habit to efface himself. *He that loseth his life shall find it.*

His Christian life at home remains a dear and private legacy to the heart of his wife and the future knowledge of his children. Our words can add nothing to its tenderness and strength—a legacy that shall never rust nor fade.

This trained and lovable life has passed on to other tasks and finer services in the Immortal life. May his short life as a Christian and a citizen stir us all to the open and generous service of God and men.

Samuel Mills Bevin.

Born in East Hampton, Conn., March 27, 1861.
Died in Philadelphia, Pa., March 6, 1900.

He graduated from Williston Seminary in 1882, and from Princeton College in 1886. He was married in the year 1889 to Miss Julia H. Williams, of Brooklyn, N. Y. He succeeded his father, Philo Bevin, in the firm of Bevin Bros. Mfg. Co., in the fall of 1886, serving as Secretary and Assistant Treasurer until his death. He also succeeded his father as Clerk and Treasurer of the Congregational Church in 1894. At the time of his death he was President of the Board of Directors of the Chatham Public Library, a member of the School Board, Treasurer of the Chatham Hall Association, and Secretary and Treasurer of the Pocotopaug Water Power Co.

DEATHS.

RECORD KEPT BY REV. LEMUEL PARSONS.

CHILDREN STILL-BORN.

August	1779	Benjamins Strongs
Septr	1779	Edward Purples
Augst 8	1780	Edward Purples
Nov 9	"	The child of Thos Gillerey Shepherd
May 29	1782	The child of Isaac Smith Jr.
Sept 11	"	The child of Edward Purple
Aug 17	1784	The child of Ebenr Harding
Aug 31	1785	The child of Samll & Elisabeth Kilbourn
Jany 6	1786	The child of Isaac Smith Jr & Jerusha his wife
Nov 3	"	A child of Abner & Lydia Cole
April 2	1787	A child of Willard & Rhoda Sears

DEATHS AFTER MR. NORTONS DECEASE BEFORE MY ORDINATION

May 8	1778	Susanna dau. of Moses Cook aged 2 years
June 4	"	Josiah son of Moses Cook.

DEATHS AFTER MY ORDINATION.

Mch 12	1779	Died Mercy Daughter of Thos Cowdrey
July 26	"	Died Anne Johnson
Augt 25	"	Died Ebenezer son of Wm White
Aug 26	"	Susy wife of Benjm Strong
Sept 19	"	Died Lucy Daughter of Caleb Cook
Octr 27	"	Died Phillip Goff
Jany 11,	1780	Died Elisabeth Daughter of Samll Kilborn
Feby 13	"	Died Elisha son of Oren & Hannah Alvord
April 9	"	Died Katharine wife of Lemuel Parsons
May 25	"	Died Ift child of John Ward
May 31	"	Died an Infant child of Jesse Kneelands
June 26	"	Died Sarah ye wife of Deacon John Clark
July 27	"	Died Deborah ye wife of Capt Silas Dunham
Nov 9	"	Died Mercy wife of Thomas Shepherd
Jany 3,	1781	Died Lydia Daughter of Joseph Caswell
May 12	"	Elisabeth Daughter of Samll Kilbourn died.
Sept 16	"	Died Robert Patten
Octr 19	"	Died ye Widow Sarah Clark in ye 99th year of her age
Decr 25	"	Died John Hills Jur of ye Small Pox
Jany 3,	1782	Died Elijah Hills son of Samll Hills of ye Small Pox
Jany 21	"	Died John Hills of ye Small Pox

Feby 2	1782	Died an infant child of Jesse Saxtons
Feby 17	"	Died Elisha Cornwal
March 4	"	Died Asahel son of Israel Whitcomb
March 5	"	Died Annis Daur of Israel Whitcomb
March 7	"	Died an infant child of Hopkins West
April 20	"	Died Israel son of Selah Jackson
Nov 30	"	Died an infant child of John Richs
Feby	1783	Died an infant child of Jesse Saxtons
Feby 12	"	Died ye widdow Rebecca Dunham aged 99 years & 8 months
Feby 27	"	Died Ensn Stephen Gates
March 7	"	Died Willm Waterous
May 2	"	Died Esther wife of Thos Goodrich
June 4	"	Died Esther Daughter of Danll McCall
Sept 1	"	Died Hannah Sheperd Daur of Thos Shepherd aged 23 yrs.
Jany 15	1784	Died a child of Reuben Norcotts aged 16 months
Jany 16	"	Died Clement Bates
May 14	"	Died Rufus Dewey
June 21	"	Died a child of John Riches aged 3 months
June 28	"	Caleb Cook Died
Augt 27	"	Lucy Daur of Josiah & Anna Goff Died aged 2 years
Sept 21	"	Widow Hannah Cook Died aged 74 years
Sept 24	"	Josiah Carey Jr Died—Middle Haddam
Sept 28	"	Godfrey Houpt Died
Sept 30	"	An infant child of James Bills Jr & Hannah Bill Died.
Novr 17	"	Mary Daur of Moses & Mary White Cole Died aged 17 years
March 8	1785	A child of George & Phebe Gates Died aged 8 months
April 17	"	Mary wife of Deacon Isaac Smith Died aged 67 years
Sept 7	"	Charity Daur of Samll & Jemima Freeman died aged 12 months
Sept 28	"	Abigail wife of Nathan Harding died aged 69 years.
Octr 2	"	Sylvanus Higgins Died—Middle Haddam
Octr 7	"	Lydia wife of Jabez Clark Died
Novr 16	"	Jonathan Clark Died aged 96 M. Haddam
Jany 5	1786	Anna Daur of Amos & Anna Clark Died
Jany 20	"	Nicholas Hosencause Died
Jany 23	"	Sabina Daur of Reuben Norcott Died
Mar 4	"	Ruth widow of Benjmn Hunt Died M. Haddam
Mar 21	"	An infant child of Cornelius Rich Jur Died aged 1½ hours
Mar 24	"	A child of Willm & Sarah Exton Died aged 11 weeks M. H.
April 8	"	Nathaniel Cook died aged 21 years
June 7	"	Isaac son of Jesse & Molly Saxton died aged 18 Mo
July 23	"	George Carey Died
Aug 15	"	Benjm Harding Died
Oct 22	"	Elisabeth Daur of John & Elisabeth Willey Died aged 16 years
Nov 19	"	Desire wife of John Markham died
Feby 24	1787	Timo son of John & Hannah Johnson Died
April 26	"	Nathaniel son of Joel & Mercy Wood died aged 2 years
May 27	"	Huet Alvord Died aged 30 years
May 31	"	Benjm Goff Died

Augt 14	1787	Widdow Susanna Knowlton died aged 80 years
Sept 9	"	A child of Deborah Taylors Died aged ½ an hour
Nov 22	"	Capt Abijah Hall died aged 64 years
Nov 23	"	Mary Smith M. Haddam Died in her 23d year
Jany 18	1788	Salmon son of George & Martha Harding Died aged yrs.
Feb 7	"	Capt Israel Higgins M. Haddam Died aged 83 years
Mar 30	"	John Markham Died aged 80 years
May 11	"	Hoziel son of Hoziel & Margery Smith Died aged 2
June 30	"	A child of John & Asenith Markham Died aged 14 mo
July 5	"	Mary wife of Willm Bevin Died
Sept 6	"	Mary wife of Thos Cowdrey died in ye 54 year of her age
Dec 16	"	Benjm son of Benjmn & Abigail Goff Died aged 11 months
Feby 6	1789	Daniel Hill Died aged
Feb 23	"	Wid. Sarah Young Died in ye 56th year of her age
March 7	"	John Fuller Died aged 62 years
May 2	"	Lemll Tubbs child Died aged 2 weeks
June 11	"	Widow Sarah Clark Died
Augt 15	"	Samll Brown Died aged 82
Octr 13	"	David son of Ralph & Hannah Smith died aged 5 weeks
Novr 9	"	Abigail Bates Died aged
Decr 12	"	Anna wife of Jacob Goff Died aged 30
Mch 21	1790	Joshua Cook Died aged 50 years M. Haddam
Mch 29	"	Two infant children of Nehemiah & Ruth Gates died
April 10	"	Patience Daur of Ebenr & Sarah Cole Died aged 17 years
	"	Mary wife of Samll Taylor Died aged M. Haddam
April 22	"	Widow Jane Johnson Died aged
May 12	"	A child of Abijah & Anna Halls Died
June 6	"	An infant child of Edward & Mehitable Acklys Died
June 12	"	An infant child of Edward & Mehitable Acklys Died
July 4	"	A child of Stephen and Sarah Taylors died aged 5 days
Decr 12	"	Ama Daur of Stephen & Prudence Clark Died aged 3 yrs & 9 months
Decr 25	"	Isaac Bevin Died

❧ ❧ ❧

RECORD KEPT BY REV. JOEL WEST.

NOTE.—A part of the deaths recorded by the above are entered opposite their names in the List of Members.

Dec. 30	1792	Hannah Cole aged 55 years & 2 mos
Mch. 19	1793	Dolle dau. of Solomon & Rhoda Bailey age 3 y. & 7 mos.
July 12	"	An infant of Levi & Marcy Smith 3 days
Oct. 17	"	An infant of Daniel Polly age 12 days
Nov. 21	"	An infant of Solomon & Rhoda Bailey age 12 days
24	"	Eunice wife of Lot Hudson age 18 years & 11 mos.
Dec. 24	"	A child of Nehemiah & Ruth Gates age 1 year
Feby. 15	1794	A child of Abner & Elizabeth Hubbard age 10 mos.
17	"	Rhoda wife of Willard Sears age 27 y. & 11 mos.

116   CONGREGATIONAL CHURCH OF EAST HAMPTON.

Feby. 21	1794	Widow Margaret Dewey age 98 y.
April 17	"	Sally wife of Norton Bill age 20 y. 8 mo.
May 11	"	Zeruah Blush dau of Lebbeus & Polly Hills 1 year.
July 23	"	Nath. son of Sparrow & Eunice Smith 6 years 10 mo.
28	"	Laurena dau of Apollos & Lucy Arnold 2 years 10 mo.
Aug. 30	"	A child of Ashbel & Hannah Woodbridge 1 year 6 mo
Nov. 23	"	Timothy Fuller age 78 y.
Jany. 11	1795	Saml. Brown 65 y.
12	"	Nabby wife of Ichabod Lucas 30 y.
Apl. 2	"	Amasa Johnson age 26 y. & 8 mos.
June 12	"	Child of Solomon Bailey
Feb 22	1796	Polly wife of Samuel Brown
May 21	"	Margaret wife of Nath. Markham 39 y.
8	"	A child of Jos. Jr. & Marcy Buel—stillborn.
July 26	"	Lieutenant Titus Carrier 63 y.
Aug. 28	"	An infant of Geo. & Eunice Hill stillborn
Sept. 26	"	Captain Timothy Rogers.
Jany. 30	1797	An infant child Bulkley & Lydia Davis
Mch. 14	"	Asenath Rogers 31 y.
18	"	Joseph Ransom 76 y.
Apl. 28	"	Elisabeth wife of Thomas Shepherd.
July 1	"	A child of John Trowbridge
Aug. 15	"	An infant of David & Hannah Strong
Sept. 8	"	Nancy Brockway dau. of Joel & Betsey West 1 year 10 mos.
24	"	Brackett son of Joel & Betsey West 7 mos.
Dec. 17	"	William Bevin age 83 y.
Jany. 4	1798	A child of C. Chapel 9 mos.
6	"	Norton Bill age 27 y. consumption
Feby. 5	"	An infant of Ashbel & Hannah Woodbridge 2 weeks.
18	"	A child of John & Desire Filcher—Stillborn.
Mar. 16	"	Widow Hannah Cole age 88 y.
May 9	"	Thankful Goff dau. of Saml. Goff 14 y.
Apl. 16	"	Jonathan Smith died at sea of yellow fever 25 y.
July 14	"	An infant child of David & Hannah Strong
Aug. 8	"	Clark son of Nathan Harding Jr. 10 y. 7 mos.
Sept. 21	"	Festus Freeman son of Sylvanus drowned age 20 y.
21	"	Hatsel Freeman son of Sylvanus drowned age 17 y.
23	"	A child of Saml. Smith 4 mos.
Dec. 29	"	Phebe wife of Ebenezer Norcutt 29 y. 8 mos.
Feby. 26	1799	Parsons son of Duel & Phebe Rowley 2 y. 11 mos.
Mch. 27	"	Susanna Dethick age 76 y.
28	"	An infant child of John & Anna Andrus age 15 mos.
Apl. 9	"	An infant child of Caleb Chapel
June 24	"	An infant child of David Dean 3 days
28	"	Caleb Rogers age 27 y.
July 14	"	An infant child of Miner Hildreth, one week
14	"	An infant child of Roswell Wells, 3 weeks
29	"	Samuel Lucas age 80 y.

CONGREGATIONAL CHURCH OF EAST HAMPTON. 117

Aug. 12	1799	Abner Brown age 24 y.
Sept. 29	"	Widow Mary Rogers age 66 y.
Oct. 14	"	Diadama Smith age 21 y.
Nov. 2	"	Butler Newton at sea with yellow fever aged
Jany. 3	1800	Stephen Stoddard Clark age 32 y.
Feby. 22	"	Child of Lebbeus Hills age 5 y.
Mch. 11	"	Jacob Babbitt age 85 y.
17	"	Child of Lebbeus Hills age 2 y.
Apl. 30	"	Wife of Eleazer Veazey
May 30	"	Elizabeth wife of Seth Alvord age 83 y.
June 29	"	Jonathan Parmelee age 56 y.
July 8	"	Captain Lazarus Watrous age 61 y.
Oct. 23	"	Jerusha Hall infant child of David Clark, age 9 weeks.
Nov. 20	"	Aaron Clark age 79 y.
28	"	A child of ———— Grover 3 years.
5	"	John Alvord died at sea of yellow fever age 25 y.
Mar. 27	1801	Child of John Lucas age 2 y.
28	"	Widow Babbit age 83 y.
28	"	Stillborn child of Elihu Mott.
Apl. 17	"	Nathan Lewis age 58 y.
July 10	"	Child of Oliver Phelps age 9 mos.
Aug. 14	"	Child of Elisha Niles age 16 mos. Scalded to death.
27	"	Child of Asahel Matthews infant
27	"	Daughter of Elisha Niles aged 8 y.
28	"	Anna wife of Asahel Matthews aged 27 y.
Sept. 15	"	Ebenezer Harding aged 62 y.
Nov. 25	"	Lucy Hall
Dec. 26	"	Child of Solomon & Rhoda Bailey age 2 y.
Jany. 4	1802	Child of John & Lucy Parmelee age 1 y. 9 mo.
21	"	Child of Abijah & Anna Hall age 9 mos.
Feby. 2	"	Child of Isaac Bailey age 10 mos.
2	"	Child of Wm Welch infant
23	"	Child of Captain Moses & Elizabeth Cook age 3 y.
Mch. 23	"	Jemima wife of Danl. Birge age 21 y.
Apl. 24	"	Nathaniel Cowdrey age 41 y.
Sept. 25	"	Tempa Lambert
Oct. 23	"	Margaret child of Nath. Markham age 5 y.
Oct. 25	"	Polly wife of Nath. Markham age 27 y.
Nov. 9	"	Infant of John & Lucy Parmelee
Dec. 27	"	Lydia wife of Joseph Caswell age 61 y.
Feby. 24	1803	Ebenezer Hall age 71 y.
Apl. 3	"	Infant of Elisha Niles.
June 10	"	Prudence dau. of James & Mary Goff age 10 y.
July 15	"	Infant of Richard & Livia Carrier
Aug. 29	"	Dolly wife of Bryan Parmelee age 52 y.
Sept. 12	"	Elmira wife of Isaac Niles age 24 y.
Feby. 6	1804	Lucy wife of Oliver Brainerd age 36 y.
Mch. 9	"	———— wife of Gasham Watrous

Apl.	25	1804	David Hills age 18 y.
Oct.	30	"	Nath. Kyes age 70 y.
Nov.	6	"	Abner Bevin age 16 y.
Feby.	11	1805	Child of Elijah & Abigail Ackley age 5 mos.
July	28	"	Child of Ebenezer Kellogg age 7 y.
Oct.	18	"	Child of Ichabod Bailey age 8 y.
Nov.	5	"	Rowena dau. of Ebenezer Bailey age 15 y.
	27	"	Child of Geo. Gates age 2 y.
Jany.	15	1806	Widow Abigail Hall age 76 y.
	28	"	Daniel Ackley age 33 y.
Feby.	6	"	Ralph Smith age 63 y.
	24	"	Infant of Stephen Ackley Jr.
Aug.	9	"	Joseph Rogers age 39 y. Fell from stack of hay.
Sept.	19	"	Abner Andrus age 20 y. Lightning.
Oct.	26	"	A child of Elisha McCall age 1 y.
Nov.	1	"	Widow Hopkins age 78. (?)
	5	"	Elisha Hurlburt
	15	"	Jerusha Cole
Jany.	2	1807	A child of William Wilson age 5 y.
Feby.	14	"	Elijah Ackley age 37 y.
	—	"	A child of Widow Ransom
Mch.	19	"	Infant of Lemuel West.
July	7	"	Widow Lois Watrous aged 62 y.
Sept.	10	"	Widow Elizabeth Hall age 80 y.
	11	"	Widow Mary Lucas age 79 y.
Feby.	9	1808	Widow Hannah Trowbridge age 89 y.
Apl.	13	"	Molly wife of Richard Cook age 49 y.
May	26	"	Russell Whitmore age 13 y. fell down dead.
June	5	"	Esther an Indian Woman
Aug.	11	"	Betsy Clark age 18 y.
Sept.	17	"	John Watrous age 29 y.
Oct.	30	"	Christopher Comstock age 82 y.
Nov.	16	"	Anson Purple age 32 y.
Mar.	15	1809	Stephen Colley age 93 y.
Apl.	4	"	Child of Joseph of Abigail Rich age 1 y.
	17	"	Adonijah Strong Jr. drowned age 36 y.
June	6	"	Child of James & Mary Goff age 3½ y.
Apl.	27	1810	Child of Israel Coles age 4 y.
Apl.	30	"	Child of Geo. Gates age 1 y.
May	13	"	Child of Geo. Gates age 4 y.
	—	"	Amos Jackson a black man.
June	7	"	Andrew Carrier age 76 y.
	30	"	Widow Katharine Colly age 90 y.
Feby.	7	1811	Marcus Cole age 77 y.
	11	"	Saml. Smith a stranger age 57 y.
May	13	"	Hannah wife of Jabez Wood
July	21	"	Wife of Joshua Webb age 73 y.
	24	"	Infant child of Joseph Hemsted

CONGREGATIONAL CHURCH EAST HAMPTON.   119

July	27	1811	Eunice wife of David Clark age 32 y.
Sept.	11	"	A child of Noadiah Wells age 1 y.
Feb.	7	1812	Nancy a black girl age 14 y.
Apl.	19	"	Zaccheus Cook age 93 y.
Aug.	12	"	Julius Orlando son of John & Lucy Parmelee age 14 y.
Nov.	11	"	Jesse Hubbard died in the Army age 23 y.
	30	"	Abiel Johnson age 24.
June	4	1813	Jonathan Thatcher a stranger age 28 y.
Dec.	3	"	Daniel Strong age 20 y.
	22	"	Jonathan Palmer an Indian age 52 y.
	30	"	Jabin Strong age 80 y.
Apl.	8	1814	Timothy Fielding age 39 y.
	23	"	Geo. Hosford son of Geo. Evans age 12 y.
	24	"	Henry Ackley age 34 y.
May	1	"	Saml. Mott age 52 y.
	8	"	Nathaniel Gates age 50 y.
July	5	"	Infant of Marcy Exton
Sept.	25	"	Esther Ackley age 37 y.
Nov.	5	"	Chittenden Griswold son of Joel & Betsey West age 3 mos.
Mar.	19	1815	Child of Widow Sarah Fielding age 14 mos.
July	27	"	Ann Cook age 84 y.
Oct.	27	"	Widow Anna Fox of Westchester age 94 y.
Nov.	7	"	Infant of William Clark.
	13	"	Vine Starr age 30 y.
	21	"	Dorotha Goff age 61 y.
Jany.	14	1816	Captain Abner Stocking age 87 y. chilld & bruised.
Feby.	4	"	Pierce Powers an Irishman age 70 y.
Mar.	15	"	Wife of Appleton Fox age 61 y.
May	20	"	Noah Markham drowned at sea age 26 y
June	27	"	Anna wife of Dea C. Welsh age 61.
Sept.	10	"	John Haling
Oct.	28	"	Warren Goff age 21 y.
Nov.	24	"	Elkanah Sears age 82 y.
Jany.	1	1817	Bryan Parmelee Esq. age 84.
	16	"	Widow Mary Watrous age 86 y.
	20	"	Infant child of George Lee
Feby.	14	"	Child of Kellogg Strong age 17 mos.
Apl.	23	"	Infant of Young Jacob Adams
May	1	"	Benjamin Leanon age 70 y.
Sept.	1	"	Nath. Bailey age 48 y.
Oct.	12	"	Jas. Webb age 84 y.
	16	"	Widow Abigail Carrier age 87 y.
Nov.	7	"	Reliance Johnson age 20 y.
Dec.	21	"	Wife of Benajah Billings
Feby.	20	1818	Deacon Joseph Sage age 60 y.
Apl.	1	"	Infant child of Benj. Ingraham age 9 mos.
	4	"	Widow Anna Welch age 95 y.
	8	"	Timothy Parmelee age 47 y.

Apl. 20	1818	Hannah Hall age 36 y
June 28	"	John Willey age 72 y
Aug. 24	"	Lemuel Tubbs age 71 y.
Oct. 23	"	Saml. Billings age 90 y.
Dec. 4	"	Stiles Davenport son of Joel & Betsey West age 8 weeks.
Feby. 9	1819	Still born child of Eleazer Veazey Jr.
17	"	John Trowbridge age 60 y.
Mar. 2	"	Thomas Fuller age 76 y.
Apl. 24	"	Infant child of Leonard Selden of M. Haddam.
May 3	"	Rhoda wife of Solomon Bailey.
29	"	A child of Jacob Adams Jr. age 9 mos.
June 11	"	A child of Joseph Goff
Apl. 26	"	Charles Sears died in St. Jago Island of Cuba age 27 y.
Aug. 4	"	James Welch age 73 y.
Dec. 27	"	A child of Geo. Halings aged 4 y.
Jany. 19	1820	Widow Elizabeth Tubbs age 71 y.
Oct. 30	"	Widow Witherill age 84 y.
Dec. 24	"	Infant child of Geo. Haling age 4 mos.
Feby. 18	1821	Roswell Wells age 52 y.
June 10	"	Capt. Jabez Hall age 60 y.
Oct. 23	"	A child of Elijah Bailey age 13 mos.
Nov. 15	"	A child of Green Cone age 4 mos.
Dec. 11	"	Newell Goff age 18 y.
16	"	Dr. John Richmond age 54 y.
Feby. 23	1822	Joel Kellogg age 28 y.
Mch. 15	"	Infant of Joseph Goff.
Apl. 16	"	Susannah wife of Geo. Haling age 38 y.
June 5	"	David Parmelee age 18 y.
July 11	"	A child of Harvey Russell age 3 y.
Aug. 1	"	Maria Bailey age 18 y.
Nov. 6	"	A child of John & Philura Sherman age 20 mos.
16	"	Captain Enos Brown age 53 y.
30	"	Simeon Young age 53 y.
Dec. 2	"	Mary Judd age 65 y.
23	"	Dr. Richard Smith age 26 y.
Jany. 3	1823	Saml. Goff, age 98 y.
3	"	Stephen Ackley age 84 y.
5	"	Elihu Hubbard age 78 y.
11	"	Wife of Geo. Evans.
23	"	Celia wife of Horace Brown age 22 y.
Feby. 9	"	Mary wife of Adonijah Strong age 73 y.
May 8	"	Child of Amasa Daniels Jr. age 4 y.
May 16	"	Infant of Harry Roberts.
21	"	Elijah Staples found dead under a fence
Oct. 2	"	Asahel Matthews age 66 y.
23	"	Widow Phebe Cole age 87 y.
Dec. 13	"	A child of Major Nath. Markham age 19 mos.
30	"	Cornelius Rich age 80 y.

Mch. —	1824	Infant of Olmstead Gates
Apl. 7	"	Thomas Shepherd age 96 y.
May 28	"	Anna Bigelow age 67 y.
June 27	"	Clarissa wife of Joseph Goff age 41 y.
July 14	"	Widow —— Haling age 90 y.
Sept. 24	"	John Edwards age 49 y.
Apl. 1	1825	Stephen Ackley Jr. age 34 y.
11	"	Thomas Everton aged 73.
May 11	"	Olcott Adams age 20 y. black man.
17	"	Adonijah Strong age 76 y.
June 2	"	Infant of Moses & Lydia West age 8 weeks.
27	"	Nath. Cone, age 77 y.
Sept. 6	"	William W. Richardson of Munson age 27 y.
7	"	Phillis a black woman of Thomas Judds.
Sept. 13	"	Charlotte Bailey age 39 y.
Oct. 9	"	Sybol wife of Capt. Saml. Brown age 58 y.
15	"	Enos, child of Horace Brown age 3 y.
16	"	Stephen Chapman age 48 y.
26	"	Betsy Hall age 20 y.
Nov. 7	"	Dimis child of Nath. G. Cone age 9 y.
10	"	A child of Horace Brown age 4 y.
14	"	Martin Kellogg age 59 y.
28	"	David Strong age 75 y.
Dec. 8	"	Lois Chapman age 22 y.
21	"	Infant of Oramel & Parmelia Clark age 3 mos.
— —	"	Two men strangers by the name of Beckwith
Jany. 4	1826	Child of Joseph Goff age 8 y.
Feby. 16	"	Kirziah Relic of Cornelius Rich age 79 y.
22	"	Eleazer Veazey age 78 y.
Mch. 6	"	Geo. Gates age 66 y.
24	"	Calvin Barstow age 75 y.
Apl. 12	"	Jesse Clark aged 49.
15	"	Capt. Saml. Saxton age 76 y.
23	"	Jehial Judd age 63 y.
Sept. 28	"	A black infant of Enos & Rebekah Adams
Oct. 24	"	A black child of —— & Rosa Taylor

LIST OF MEMBERS.

COMPILED AND ARRANGED BY MARTIN L. ROBERTS.

THE names of some of the petitioners for the incorporation of this parish appear upon the records of the churches in East Middletown and Middle Haddam as members in full communion, and it is believed that the major portion of them with their wives were the constituent members of this church. But with the exception of the names of those who united with the church from 1764 to 1772, as per fragment of Mr. Norton's record, the names of the members for the first thirty years of its existence have not been recovered. When Mr. Parsons was ordained, February 10, 1779, he made a record of the male members in full communion at that time; but of the females, and those who had previously renewed their covenant, he made no mention. This list, however, does not pretend to be a perfect record of those who united since that time, as the records are very imperfect, and in some cases no records of either admission or dismission have been recorded. Owing to this fact, the task of compiling the list has been a difficult one, requiring a vast amount of time and patience to accomplish, and the compiler only wishes to add that he has done the best he could with it under the circumstances, and with this explanation respectfully submits it to those whom it may concern for their charitable consideration.

In the early history of the churches of New England those persons who had themselves been baptized, and who in a public manner "owned the covenant" into which their parents had entered for them, were permitted to have their children baptized, though they could not unite with the church in celebrating the Lord's Supper. This was what was called the "half-way covenant," and was practiced in this church during the first three pastorates.

REV. GUSTAVUS D. PIKE,
Acting Pastor, 1865-1867.

CONGREGATIONAL CHURCH OF EAST HAMPTON. 123

The names of those persons who "owned the covenant" during Mr. Parsons' pastorate are as follows. Those marked with a * were afterwards admitted to full communion.

NOTE.—The abbreviations used in this list are as follows: b.=born; bap.=baptized; ch.=church; d.=died; dis.=dismissed; ex.=excommunicated; E. H.=East Hampton; L.=letter; m.=married; M. H.=Middle Haddam; P.=profession; U. C.=Union Congregational; w.=wife; wid.=widow.

July	7,	1782.	Daniel Parks. Removed to New York State.
	7,	"	Esther Parks, (w. Daniel.)
May	23,	1784.	Othniel Brainerd, Jr. Removed to Winsted.
	23,	"	Grace Brainerd, (w. Othniel, Jr.)
	23,	"	Samuel Cowdrey.
	23,	"	Anna Cowdrey, (w. Samuel.)
	23,	"	Josiah Goff.
	23,	"	Anna Goff, (w. Josiah.)
June	6,	"	John West.
	27,	"	Eunice Dewey, (wid. Rufus.)
Sept.	16,	"	*David Clark.
	16,	"	Jerusha Clark, (w. David,) d. Aug. 24, 1800.
	16,	"	*John Parmelee.
	16,	"	*Lucy Parmelee (w. John.)
Oct.	10,	1784.	*Rebecca Johnson, (w. Isaac,) d. March 27, 1845.
May	29,	1785.	Ebenezer Hill, d. March 1, 1830.
	29,	"	[Ruth] Hill, (w. Ebenezer.)
Aug.	27,	1786.	Azuba Haling, (w. John.)
May	10,	1787.	James Goff, d. Feb. 8, 1849.
	10,	"	*Mary Goff, (w. James,) d. April 1, 1851.
July	15,	"	Joanna Alvord, (wid. Hewitt,) m. Stephen Burnham.
	29,	"	Huldah Thomas, (w. William.)
June	6,	1788.	*Sparrow Smith.
	8,	"	*Eunice Smith, (w. Sparrow.)
	15,	"	Hoziel Smith.
	15,	"	Margery Smith, (w. Hoziel.)
July	6,	"	*Selah Jackson.
	6,	"	*Anna Jackson, (w. Selah.)
Dec.	21,	"	Abner Cole, d. Oct. 31, 1825.
	21,	"	*Lydia Cole, (w. Abner.)
Oct.	11,	1789.	Jerusha Harding, (w. Ebenezer, Jr.,) L. from East Hartford.

Names of the male members of the church in full communion, as recorded by the Rev. Lemuel Parsons, February 10, 1779:

Seth Alvord, d. March 17, 1802, aged 87.
Gideon Arnold, d. Feb. 17, 1807, aged 72.
Ezra Ackley, dis. 1800.
Darius Adams, dis.
Joshua Bailey, d. Sept. 1, 1809, aged 78.
Othniel Brainerd, d. Dec. 9, 1815, aged 87.

Samuel Brown, d. Jan. 11, 1795, aged 65.
James Bill, d. July 25, 1823, aged 87.
Elijah Cook, d.
Joshua Cook, d.
John Clark, Jr., dis. 1809.
Moses Clark, d. Oct. 13, 1801, aged 83.
William Clark, d. Sept. 26, 1812, aged 99.
John Clark, d. Aug. 8, 1809, aged 94.
Moses Cook, d. May 15, 1818, aged 75.
Moses Cole, d. Aug. 3, 1827.
Zacheus Cook, d. April 19, 1812.
Joseph Caswell, dis.
Silas Dunham, dis.
Abijah Hall, d. Nov. 22, 1787.
Ebenezer Hall, d. Feb. 23, 1803, aged 71.
Nathan Harding, d. March 27, 1801, aged 89.
John Hinckley, d. May 24, 1811, aged 83.
Daniel Hill, d. Feb. 6, 1789.
Dewey Hall, d. May 30, 1806, aged 57.
Samuel Hodge, d. 1804.
John Johnson, d. June 28, 1842, aged 94.
Isaac Kneeland.
Stephen Knowlton, ex. Oct. 1, 1795.
Nehemiah Lord.
John Markham, d. March 30, 1788.
John Norton, d. May 15, 1808.
William Norcutt, d. March 14, 1810, aged 90.
Edward Purple, d. July 22, 1794, aged 49.
Bryan Parmelee, ex. March 1, 1803. Church of England.
James Rich.
Ebenezer Sears, d. Dec. 29, 1814, aged 92.
Isaac Smith, d. July 29, 1802.
Isaac Smith, Jr., d. Oct. 28, 1815.
William White, d. March 17, 1823, aged 80.

April	18,	1779.	Nathaniel White, p.
	18,	"	[Abigail] White, p., (w. Nathaniel.)
	23,	"	Sarah Strowbridge, L., (w. Jonathan.)
June	6,	"	Mary Bevin, L., (w. William,) d. July 5, 1788.
	20,	"	Catharine Parsons, L., (w. Rev. Lemuel,) d. April 9, 1780.
Sept.	5,	"	Elisabeth Bailey, L., dis. 1810.
Oct.	24,	"	David Allen, p.
	24,	"	[Elisabeth] Allen p., (w. David.)
Nov.	14,	"	Daniel Clark, p., dis.
Jan.	2,	1780.	Mary Andrews, p.
Mar.	5,	"	Samuel Kilbourn, p., dis.
	19,	"	Israel Whitcomb, p.
April	23,	"	Sarah Norcutt, p., (m. Eliakim Ufford,) dis.
July	2,	"	Rhuel Alvord, p., d. March 27, 1810, aged 59.

July	2,	1780.	Hannah Alvord, P., (w. Rhuel,) dis. 1825, d. Aug. 3, 1830.
Sept.	3,	"	David Kneeland, L. from Marlborough.
	3,	"	Mercy Kneeland, L. from Marlborough, (w. David.)
Oct.	8,	"	Ebenezer Bailey, P., d. June 7, 1828.
	8,	"	[Zilpha] Bailey, P., (w. Ebenezer,) d. Jan. 15, 1795.
Nov.	12,	"	Nehemiah Lord, L. from Ellington.
	12,	"	—— Lord, L. from Ellington, (w. Nehemiah.)
	26,	"	Lydia Clark, P., (w. Daniel,) dis.
Jan.	14,	1781.	Faith Parsons, P., (w. Rev. Lemuel,) dis. 1796.
May	—,	"	Abel Johnson, L.
	—,	"	—— Johnson, L., (w. Abel.)
July	1,	"	Thomas Ackley, P., d. Feb. 23, 1794, aged 53.
	1,	"	[Sarah] Ackley, P., (w. Thomas,) dis. 1795.
	1,	"	Elisabeth Ackley, P., dis. 1818.
	1,	"	Lemuel West, L. from Ellington, d. June 18, 1825, aged 78.
	1,	"	[Desire] West, L. from Ellington, (w. Lemuel,) d. Apr. 26, 1828.
Dec.	9,	"	Lucy Kneeland, L. from Marlborough, (w. Jesse,) dis. 1808.
July	7,	1782.	Benjamin Harding, P., d. Aug. 15, 1786.
	7,	"	[Olive] Harding, P., (w. Benjamin.)
	14,	"	Sylvanus Norcutt, L. from Marlborough.
	14,	"	Anna Norcutt, L. from Marlborough, (w. Sylvanus.)
June	22,	1783.	Margaret Markham, P., (w. Nathaniel,) d. May 21, 1796.
July	13,	"	George Cummings, L. from East Windsor, d. April 4, 1794, aged 62.
	13,	"	Samuel Fielding, L. from Hebron.
Sept.	7,	"	Samuel Mott, L. from Hartland, d. Feb. 26, 1801, aged 66.
	7,	"	—— Mott, L. from Hartland, (w. Samuel.)
Nov.	30,	"	Stephen Clark, P., d. Oct. 3, 1852.
June	20,	1784.	Reuben Norcutt, P., d. March 28, 1830.
July	11,	"	Amos Clark, P., d. March 20, 1843.
	11,	"	Anna Clark, P., (w. Amos,) d. July 8, 1835.
Oct.	24,	"	Jesse Kneeland, P., dis. 1808.
	24,	"	Jonathan Caswell, P.
July	17,	"	David Clark, P., d. Jan. 8, 1839.
Sept.	11,	"	Apollos Arnold, P., dis. to West Hartford, d. Nov. 10, 1842.
	11,	"	Lucy Arnold, P., (w. Apollos,) d. March 22, 1831.
June	25,	1786.	Lydia Smith, L. from Sandisfield, Mass., (w. Dea. Isaac,) d. March 24, 1799.
Aug.	20,	"	Joel Wood, L. from Cornwall, dis. 1798.
	20,	"	Mercy Wood, L. from Cornwall, (w. Joel,) dis. 1798.
Sept.	17,	"	Isaac Sears, P., dis. 1798.
	17,	"	Grace Sears, P., (w. Isaac,) dis. 1798.
Feb.	11,	1787.	Dinah Markham, P., (m. —— Alworth,) dis. 1802.
April	1,	"	Synthia Smith, P., dis. 1810.
Oct.	21,	"	Prudence Goff, P., (wid. Benjamin,) m. Daniel Smith, d. 1817.
Nov.	11,	"	Azubah Young, P., (w. Elijah,) dis. 1815.
Mar.	30,	1788.	Moses West, P., d. May 19, 1794, aged 75.
	30,	"	Olive White, P., (w. Philip,) d. April 22, 1856, aged 92.

126   CONGREGATIONAL CHURCH OF EAST HAMPTON.

Feb. 22, 1789. John Parmelee, P., ex. Jan. 28, 1818, d. June 28, 1823, aged 62.
    22, " Lucy Parmelee, P., (w. John,) d. August, 1848.
Aug. 2, " [Theda] Sexton, P., (w. Samuel,) ex. March 15, 1806, d. Jan. 22, 1831.
Jan. 3, 1790. Mary Bevin, L. from Haddam, (W. William,) d.
Mar. 7, " Joseph Buell, L. from Glastonbury, dis. 1789.
    7, " Hope Buell, L. from Glastonbury, (w. Joseph,) dis. 1789.
April 4, " Anne Cornwell, P., (w. Samuel.)
June 12, " Sarah Markham, P., (w. James,) d. 1804.
Aug. 15, " Hannah Norcutt, P., (m. Nicholas Ames,) dis. 1808.

※ ※ ※

REV. JOEL WEST, PASTOR, 1792-1826.

Names of the members of the church at the time of Mr. West's ordination not found on Mr. Parsons' records:

1792. Orrin Alvord, dis. 1811.
" Hannah Alvord, (w. Orrin,) dis. 1811.
" Lebbeus Hills, dis. 1810.
" Mary Hills, (w. Lebbeus,) dis. 1810.
" Jared Parmelee, dis. 1794.
" Susanna Parmelee, (w. Jared,) dis. 1794.
" Sarah Ackley, (w. Ezra,) dis. 1800.
" Lucy Arnold, (w. Dea. Gideon,) d. March 1, 1801, aged 63.
" Elizabeth Alvord, (w. Seth,) d. May 30, 1800, aged 83.
" Elisabeth Brown, (w. Samuel,) d. Nov. 30, 1812, aged 80.
" Asenath Bill, (w. Dea. James,) d. Jan. 2, 1810, aged 71.
" Jerusha Brainerd, (w. Othniel,) d. Aug. 11, 1806, aged 77.
" Sarah Cole, (w. Ebenezer, Jr.,) d. July 10, 1811, aged 74.
" Elisabeth Cole, (wid. Ebenezer,) d. Feb. 19, 1794, aged 85.
" Hannah Cole, (wid. Moses,) d. March 16, 1798, aged 88.
" Mary Cole, (w. Moses,) d. March 18, 1813, aged 64.
" Nabby Carrier, (wid. Andrew,) d. Oct. 11, 1817, aged 87.
" Elisabeth Cook, (w. Dea. Moses,) d. Oct. 8, 1808, aged 64.
" Mary Clark, (w. William,) d. Feb. 18, 1797, aged 76.
" Hannah Clark, (w. Dea. John,) d. 1814.
" Mary Clark, (wid. Aaron,) d. Oct. 3, 1802, aged 73.
" Mercy Carrier, (wid. Titus,) d. Aug. 5, 1819, aged 74.
" Zilpha Cunningham, (wid. Thomas,) d. Dec. 3, 1793, aged 81 years 9 months.
" Huldah Harding, (wid. Ebenezer,) d. Jan. 26, 1819, aged 78.
" Mindwell Hills, (wid. John,) d. Nov. 30, 1815, aged 83.
" Hannah Hall, (wid. Dewey,) d. Dec. 3, 1815, aged 68.
" Azuba Hinckley, (w. John,) d. Jan. 18, 1809, aged 70.
", Rebecca Knowlton, (w. Stephen,) d. Sept. 8, 1795.
" Mary Goff, (w. Samuel,) d. Dec. 23, 1823, aged 84.
" Ede Norton, (w. John,) d. Feb. 18, 1827.

CONGREGATIONAL CHURCH OF EAST HAMPTON. 127

		1792.	Eunice Norton, (wid. Rev. John,) d. May 27, 1796, aged 83.
		"	Betsey Norcutt, (w. William,) d. June 13, 1828.
		"	Mary Purple, (w. Edward,) (m. Stephen Knowlton,) d.
		"	Sarah Parmelee, (wid. Jonathan,) d. Feb. 14, 1794, aged 86.
		"	Jerusha Smith, (w. Dea. Isaac, Jr.,) d. July 11, 1836, aged 91.
		"	Elisabeth Sears, (w. Ebenezer,) d. July 4, 1797, aged 63.
		"	Ruth Sears, (w. Elkanah,) d. May 7, 1823, aged 90.
		"	Elizabeth White, (w. William,) d. 1814.
		"	Bethia Smith, (w. Ezra,) d. April 22, 1793.
Dec.	7,	1792.	Eunice Norton, P., d. Oct. 12, 1845.
Jan.	27,	1793.	Nathaniel Clark, P., d. Jan. 13, 1814, aged 70.
	27,	"	Dolle Clark, P., (w. Nathaniel,) d. March 11, 1838, aged 87.
Mar.	17,	"	Selah Jackson, P., dis. 1795.
	17,	"	Anna Jackson, P., (w. Selah,) dis. 1795.
	17,	"	Polly Arnold, P., d. April 18, 1793, aged 20.
Aug.	18,	"	Hannah Strong, L. from Marlborough, (w. David,) d. Jan. 24, 1808.
	18,	"	Elisabeth Cole, P., (m. Nathaniel Pease,) dis. 1813.
Sept.	29,	"	Nathaniel Mott, P., d. June 1, 1808, aged 76.
	29,	"	Agnes Mott, P., (w. Nathaniel,) dis. 1809.
	29,	"	Lydia Cole, P., (w. Abner,) d. Dec. 9, 1804, aged 44.
Mar.	9,	1794.	Joshua Bailey, Jr., P., dis. 1807.
	9,	"	Ruth Bailey, P., (w. Joshua, Jr.,) dis. 1807.
May	4,	"	Lucy Daily, P., (w. Joseph,) dis. 1798.
July	6,	"	Clarissa Bill, P., (m. Oliver Bill), dis. 1798.
	6,	"	Achsa Bill, P., d. May 3, 1812, aged 35.
Aug.	17,	"	Gillett Hinckley, P., dis. 1797.
	17,	"	Hannah Hinckley, P., (w. Gillett,) dis. 1797.
	17,	"	Ashbel Woodbridge, L. from East Windsor, dis. 1805.
	17,	"	Hannah Woodbridge, L. from East Windsor, (w. Ashbel,) dis. 1805.
Oct.	4,	1795.	David Sears, P., d. April 29, 1842.
	4,	"	Lucy Sears, P., (w. David,) d. 1829.
May	20,	1798.	Phebe Norcutt, P., (w. Ebenezer,) d. Dec. 29, 1798, aged 29 years 8 months
July	15,	"	Abigail McCleve, P., (m. Joseph Rich.)
Oct.	14,	"	Ann Shepherd, L. from Chatham, (w. Thomas,) dis. 1808.
	14,	"	Sally Alvord, P., (w. Seth, Jr.,) d. Feb. 2, 1819, aged 58.
	14,	"	Hannah Rogers, P., (wid. Timothy,) (m. Nathaniel Markham,) d. Nov. 29, 1853.
Aug.	13,	1799.	Deborah Hodge, P., (w. Samuel,) d. Sept. 16, 1799, aged 73.
July	20,	1800.	Betsey West, P., (w. Rev. Joel,) d. Sept. 26, 1853.
June	25,	1801.	Thankful Ackley, P., (w. Stephen,) d. Sept. 9, 1813, aged 76.
June	3,	1803.	Amasa West, P., d. in Wisconsin.
June	30,	1805.	Azuba Smith, P., (m. Benj. Cobb,) d. May 18, 1865, aged 81.
Aug.	18,	"	Betsey Alvord, P., (m. William Finley,) dis. 1805.
Oct.	27,	"	Joseph Hall, P., dis. 1808.
Dec.	1,	"	Lucy Alvord, P., (w. James H.,) dis. 1808, d. Sept. 11, 1850.

Dec.	1,	1805.	Nancy Arnold, P., (m. Joseph Hall,) dis. 1808.
	1,	"	Nancy Rogers, P., (m. Diodate B. West,) d. July 5, 1855.
Sept.	28,	1806.	Martha Ackley, P., (wid. Daniel,) (m. Gideon Brainerd,) d. Aug. 16, 1866.
Oct.	26,	"	Martha Richmond, L., from Brookfield, Mass., d. 1814.
April	15,	1808.	Daniel Johnson, L. from Jamestown, ex. Feb. 5, 1813. Baptist.
	15,	"	Sally Johnson, L. from Jamestown, (w. Daniel,) d. Sept. 9, 1834.
July	17,	"	Joshua Root, L. from Gilead, dis. 1809.
	17,	"	Sarah Root, L. from Gilead, (w. Joshua,) dis. 1809.
April	16,	1809.	Philanda Alvord, P., (m. Daniel R. Wolcott,) dis. 1811.
May	7,	"	Annis Alvord, L. from 1st ch. Middletown, dis. 1811.
Oct.	1,	"	Hannah Parmelee, P., (w. Timothy,) d. April 5, 1814, aged 43.
	1,	"	Anna Bevin, P., (w. Isaac,) d. June 19, 1850.
	1,	"	Sally Watrous, P., (wid. John,) d. Jan. 3, 1866.
May	20,	1810.	Hannah Strong, (w. David,) L. from Lyme, d. Nov. 11, 1835.
	20,	"	Susanna Strong, P., (w. Henry,) d. April 15, 1820, aged 40.
June	3,	"	Philena Harding, P., (w. Nathan, Jr.,) dis. 1814.
July	1,	"	Stephen Knowlton, restored to membership, d. Jan. 29, 1814.
Nov.	17,	1811.	Gurdon Fowler, P., dis. 1814.
	17,	"	Anna Fowler, P., (w. Gurdon,) dis. 1814.
	17,	"	Ruth Gates, P., (w. Nehemiah,) d. Aug. 18, 1844.
June	28,	1812.	Mary Mitchell, L. from Westchester, d.
Oct.	30,	1813.	Isaac Hinckley, P., dis. 1815.
	30,	"	Sally Hinckley, P., (w. Isaac,) dis. 1815.
Sept.	25,	1814.	Joseph Sage, L. from Middletown, d. Feb. 20, 1818.
	25,	"	——— Sage, (w. Joseph,) L. from Middletown, d.
Aug.	30,	1815.	Lucy Caswell, P., (w. Joseph.) Removed to Exeter, N. Y.
Sept.	17,	"	Artemas Arnold, P., d.
Oct.	22,	"	Philena Arnold, P., (m. Henry Strong,) d. March 8, 1868.
	22,	"	Polly Arnold, P.
June	30,	1816.	Warren A. Skinner, L. from Westchester, d. Jan. 4, 1862.
	30,	"	Anna Skinner, (w. Warren A.,) L. from Westchester, d. Sept. 18, 1879.
May	3,	1818.	Abigail Welsh, P., (w. Constant,) d. Jan. 31, 1834, aged 64.
July	5,	"	Sparrow Smith, P., d. July 14, 1842.
	5,	"	Eunice Smith, P., (w. Sparrow,) d. Feb. 11, 1850.
	5,	"	Mehitable Clark, P., (w. David,) d. Nov. 26, 1854.
	5,	"	Lydia Beebe, P., (wid. Comfort,) d.
Sept.	6,	"	Eleazer Veazey, Jr., P., d. March 6, 1855.
	6,	"	Elisabeth Veazey, P., (w. Eleazer, Jr.,) d. Jan. 6, 1861.
	6,	"	Selden Cook, P., ex. Dec. 11, 1823. Methodist.
	6,	"	Sally Cook, P., (w. Selden,) ex. Dec. 11, 1823. Methodist.
	6,	"	Hannah Alvord, P., dis. 1825, d. Aug. 17, 1832. Winsted.
	6,	"	Betsey Sears, P., (m. Harvey Arnold,) d. Jan. 23, 1849.
	6,	"	Rhoda Sears, P., (m. Ezra Ayres, Greenwich, Mass.,) dis.
Oct.	25,	"	Henry Bush, P., ex. Jan. 1, 1841.
	25,	"	Lydia Bush, P., (w. Henry,) d. Oct. 16, 1844.
Nov.	1,	"	Willard Sears, P., d. Aug. 23, 1838.
	1,	"	Betsey Sears, P., (w. Willard,) d. Jan. 9, 1831.

CONGREGATIONAL CHURCH OF EAST HAMPTON.   129

Nov. 1, 1818. Benjamin Ingraham, P. Removed to Ohio.
1, " Polly Ingraham, P., (w. Benjamin.) Removed to Ohio.
1, " Rachel Bailey, P., (wid. Nathaniel,) d. Sept. 19, 1850.
1, " Titus Carrier, P., ex. Dec. 11, 1823. Methodist.
1, " Mehitable Carrier, P., (w. Titus,) ex. Dec. 11, 1823. Methodist.
1, " David Buell, P., dis. Sept. 5, 1856, U. C., d. April 5, 1858.
1, " Lucy Buell, P., (w. David,) d. May 18, 1853.
1, " Mary Goff, P., (w. James,) dis. April, 1840, to ch. in Burton, O.
1, " Abigail Niles, P., (w. Daniel,) d. Jan. 4, 1853.
1, " Lazarus Watrous, P., d. March 14, 1850.
1, " Anna Watrous, P., (w. Lazarus,) d. Oct. 7, 1874.
1, " Sally Youngs, P., (w. Demas,) dis. 1820.
1, " Eleanor Higgins, P., (w. Ornan,) dis. 1823.
1, " Nathaniel C. Smith, P., dis. Sept. 5, 1856, U. C., d. Aug. 25, 1888.
1, " Charlotte Smith, P., (w. Nathaniel C.,) dis. Sept. 5, 1856, U. C., d. July 12, 1862.
1, " Esther Alvord, P., dis. 1825, d. Aug. 28, 1835. Winsted.
1, " Beulah Alvord, P., (m. George Clark,) dis. April 22, 1844. Granby.
Jan. 3, 1819. Abigail Hall, P., (w. Jabez,) ex. Aug. 30, 1823.
3, " Prudence Richmond, P., (w. Dr. John,) d. March 11, 1822.
3, " Lucy Watrous, P., dis. Sept. 28, 1856, U. C., d. Feb. 16, 1874.
Mar. 7, " Sarah Fielding, P., (wid. Timothy.)
7, " Rhoda Edwards, P., (w. John,) d. March 23, 1856, aged 69.
April 25, " Phebe Caswell, P., d. 1822.
June 27, " Mary Cook, P., (m. Lord S. Hills,) d.
July 4, " Horace Clark, P., dis. Sept. 5, 1856, U. C., d. Nov. 13, 1879.
4, " * Diodate B. West, P., d. June 14, 1881.
4, " Lucy Arnold, 2d, P., (m. Joshua Strong,) dis. 1822.
4, " Sabrina Adeline Markham, P., (m. Morris P. Baker,) dis.
Sept. 5, " Rebecca Johnson, P., (w. Isaac,) d. March 27, 1845.
5, " Calvin Hall, Jr., P., dis. Sept. 5, 1856, U. C., d. Jan. 23, 1881.
5, " Dolly L. Hall, P., (w. Calvin, Jr.,) dis. Sept. 5, 1856, U. C., d. July 13, 1880.
5, " Elijah Norcutt, P., dis., Sept. 5, 1856, U. C., d. Dec. 25, 1871.
5, " Emilia Veazey, P., (m. Stephen G. Sears,) dis. Sept. 5, 1856, U. C., d. April 3, 1879.
Oct. 3, " Evelina O. West, P., dis. Sept. 5, 1856, U. C., d. April 20, 1889.
Nov. 7, " Eunice Sears, P., (m. Henry Snow,) dis. March 8, 1835.
7, " Elisabeth Alvord, P., (m. Augustus Gates,) dis.
5, 1820. Mary Smith, P., (w. Michael,) d. Nov. 20, 1843.
May 6, 1821. Achsa Tubbs, P., (m. David Hodge.) Removed to Vermont.
Nov. 4, " Talitha West, L. from Westchester, (w. Warren,) dis. Oct. 2, 1836.

* Diodate B. West was one of the petitioners for the formation of the Union Congregational Church, Sept. 5, 1856, but failing to comply with their requirements at the time of its organization, he maintained an irregular standing with this church for some years, when at his request, by a vote of the church, so much of the petition as related to him was rescinded, and he was restored to full membership.

130   CONGREGATIONAL CHURCH OF EAST HAMPTON.

May 1,	1822.	Elkanah Ingraham, L. from North Lyme.
1,	"	Mary Ingraham, L. from North Lyme, (w. Elkanah,) d. June 17, 1823.
Dec. 14,	1823.	Orren Bowers, P., dis. Sept. 5, 1856, U. C., d. Jan. 9, 1879.
Mar. 7,	1824.	Esther Judd, L. from Coventry, (w. Thomas,) d. Jan. 10, 1846.
Sept. 5,	"	John C. Robertson, P., dis. March 3, 1833.
Oct. 4,	"	Charles Smith, L. from N. S. (?), dis. 1826.
May 7,	1826.	Elisabeth Barstow, L. from Jewett City, dis. April, 1853.
July 1,	1827.	Warren West, P., dis. Oct. 2, 1836.
1,	"	Lucy Strong, P., (wid. Ezra,) d. Dec. 26, 1859.
1,	"	Sarah Clark, P., (m. Ephraim Meech,) dis. 1850, d. April 7, 1877.
1,	"	Jerusha Kellogg, L., (w. Alfred,) d. Nov. 6, 1828.
1,	"	Anna Brown, P., (wid. Enos,) d. March 6, 1871.

✤ ✤ ✤

REV. TIMOTHY STONE, PASTOR.

Aug. —,	1828.	Julia Haling, P., (w. Isaac,) d. July 29, 1838.
July 5,	1829.	Henry Bailey, P., dis.
5,	"	Nabby Markham, P., (wid. Nathaniel,) d. Aug. 6, 1880.
5,	"	Betsey West, P., (m. Justin Dickinson,) dis.
26,	"	John Hall, P., d. Aug. 19, 1829.
Sept. 20,	"	Isaac Bevin, P., d. May 8, 1870.
20,	"	Jedediah Barstow, P., d. April 5, 1846.
20,	"	Cyprian Hinckley, P., dis. Sept. 5, 1856, U. C., d. Oct. 13, 1864, aged 86.
20,	"	Lydia Hinckley, P., (w. Cyprian,) d. Sept. 19, 1844.
20,	"	Augustus Adams, P., dis. June 9, 1834.
20,	"	Amos Clark, Jr., P., d. March 26, 1885.
April 4,	1830.	Samuel Kilbourn, L., d. Nov. 13, 1834.
4,	"	Elisabeth Kilbourn, L., (w. Samuel,) d. April 19, 1833.
4,	"	Lydia Young, P., (wid. Simeon,) d. March 16, 1839.
4,	"	Jerusha Smith, P., d. May 18, 1860.
Sept. 5,	"	Augustus Gates, P., dis., d. Feb. 9, 1845.

✤ ✤ ✤

REV. SAMUEL IVES CURTIS, PASTOR.

Jan. 1,	1833.	John C. A. Strong, P., d. Sept. 26, 1870.
1,	"	Deborah L. Strong, P., (w. John C. A.,) dis. 1870, d. Aug. 29, 1885.
1,	"	Alice S. Bevin, P., (m. 1st Constant Welsh, 2d Samuel B. Childs.)
Mar. 3,	"	Rebecca T. Curtis, (w. Rev. Samuel I.,) L., d. March 25, 1842.
3,	"	Silas Smith, L., d. Sept. 30, 1839.
Sept. 15,	"	Ephraim T. Barstow, P., dis.
Nov. 3,	"	Stephen G. Sears, P., dis. Sept. 5, 1856, U. C., d, Oct. 12, 1874.
3,	"	Betsey M. S. Clark, P., (w. Amos, Jr.,) d. Aug. 6, 1887.

ABNER G. BEVIN,
1810 1896.

PHILO BEVIN,
1813-1893.

AMIEL ABELL,
1808-1888.

HIRAM VEAZEY,
1816-1889.

CONGREGATIONAL CHURCH OF EAST HAMPTON.   131

Nov. 3, 1833. Harriet Markham, P., (w. Timothy R.,) dis. Sept. 5, 1856, U.C.
    3, " Sarah S. Bevin, P., (w. William,) dis. Sept. 5, 1856, U. C.
    3, " John W. B. Smith, P.
    3, " Delia E. Smith, P., (w. John W. B.,) d. Feb. 13, 1867.
    3, " Amiel Abell, P., d. Oct. 6, 1888.
    3, " Mariette Abell, P., (w. Amiel,) d. Oct. 4, 1888.
    3, " Warren Veazey, P., dis. Sept. 5, 1836, U. C., d. Dec. 10, 1880.
    3, " Betsey L. Veazey, P., (w. Warren,) dis. Sept. 5, 1856, U. C.
    3, " Samuel Skinner, P., d. Oct. 16, 1895.
    3, " Titus C. Goff, P., dis. June 9, 1834, to Ohio.
    3, " Allen C. Clark, P., dis. May, 1849, to Bolton, Conn.
    3, " Elisabeth Wheeler, P., dis.
    3, " Laura Wheeler, P., dis. May, 1852, Portland.
    3, " Anzolette D. Smith, P., (m. Philo S. Parsons,) dis. Sept. 5, 1856, U. C., d.
    3, " Charlotte A. Bush, P., (m. Zamon Cady,) name stricken from roll, Feb. 28, 1851.
    3, " Catharine C. Markham, P., (m. Abner G. Bevin,) d. Sept. 11, 1845.
    3, " Ruth Ann Skinner, P., (m. Ambrose N. Markham,) d. July 22, 1892.
    3, " Adeline Bevin, P., (m. Samuel B. Childs,) d. April 2, 1876.
May 3, 1835. Alfred Williams, L., ex. Aug. 15, 1855.
    3, " Silas Hills, L., d. April 27, 1864.
Mar. 6, 1836. Dorcas Shipman, P., (wid. Beriah N.,) dis. Oct. 19, 1856, U. C., d. July 16, 1872.
    6, " Sabrina A. Baker, L., (w. Morris P.,) dis. Sept. 18, 1856, U. C., d. Feb. 21, 1887, aged 84.
Jan. 1, 1837. Abner G. Bevin, P., d. July 25, 1896.
    1, " Edward M. Simpson, P., dis. March, 1848.
    1, " Rhoda Roberts, P., (w. Harry,) dis. Jan., 1855.
    1, " Harriet Williams, P., (w. Alfred,) d. June 15, 1844.
    1, " Mary Hills, P., (w. Silas,) d. April 16, 1884.
    1, " Electa M. Shipman, P., (m. Tillson A. Buell,) dis. Sept. 5, 1856, U. C.
    1, " Cordelia A. Shipman, P., (m. Alphonzo B. Cone,) d.
    1, " Matilda M. West, P., (m. Erastus Day,) dis. Jan. 3, 1847.
    1, " Alice A. West, P., d. Oct. 29, 1841.
    1, " Amelia Ann Clark, P., (m. Chauncey Bevin,) d. April 16, 1885.
Nov. 5, " Esther Scoville, L. from Old Lyme, (w. Isaac,) dis. June, 1853.

REV. RUFUS SMITH, PASTOR.

Mar. —, 1839. Cyrus Goff, P., d. April 15, 1839.
    —, " Laura Goff, P., (w. Cyrus,) dis. Aug., 1842, (m. William R. Carpenter.)
    —, " Lois Barton, P., (w. Hiram,) d. Jan. 23, 1887.
June —, " Abigail Hall, (w. Jabez,) restored, d. April 12, 1843.

132   CONGREGATIONAL CHURCH OF EAST HAMPTON.

Oct. —,	1839.	Morris P. Baker, P., d. May 2, 1855.
Mar. 8,	1840.	Florilla Goff, P., (w. Joseph N.,) d. Nov. 8, 1878.
April —,	"	Augustus Adams, L. from Westchester, d. Dec. 30, 1880.
—,	"	Rufus Smith, Jr., L., dis. Jan., 1843, Yale College, d. Oct. 14, 1847.
—,	"	Clarissa Smith, L., (w. Rev. Rufus,) dis. April, 1847.
—,	"	Mary Smith, L., d. April 14, 1847.
July 4,	1841.	Timothy R. Markham, P., dis. Sept. 5, 1856, U. C., d. Oct. 30, 1883.
4,	"	Mary Ann West, P., dis. Sept. 5, 1856, U. C.
Sept. —,	"	Deborah Haling, L. from Gilead, (m. Aaron Washburn, Stillwater, N. Y.)
—,	1842.	David Watson Watrous, P.
—,	"	Richard S. S. Clark, P., dis. April, 1851.
—,	"	Laura Ann Skinner, P., (w. Samuel.)
—,	"	Sarah E. Watrous, P., (m. Alex. N. Niles,) d. May 25, 1897.
Nov. —,	"	Philo Bevin, P., d. Sept. 5, 1893.
—,	"	Fidelia A. Bevin, P., (w. Philo,) d. May 14, 1861.
Mar. —,	1843.	Alphonso B. Cone, P., d. Aug., 1859.
—,	"	Maria Niles, P., (w. Dan. B.,) d. Aug. 7, 1890, aged 89.
July —,	1844.	Betsey E. Sears, L., dis. March, 1855, to Marlborough, d.
July —,	1845.	Frances M. Clark, L. from East Haddam, (w. Allen C.,) dis. May, 1849.

*** *** ***

REV. WILLIAM RUSSELL, PASTOR.

Jan. 4,	1846.	Elizabeth Gates, L. from New London, (wid. Augustus,) (m. Orrin H. Lee,) dis. to Granby, Nov. 4, 1853.
May 3,	"	Noah S. Markham, P., dis. June 23, 1861, to Glastonbury.
3,	"	Hiram Veazey, P., d. Nov. 23, 1889.
3,	"	Belinda Veazey, P., (w. Hiram,) d. March 7, 1899.
3,	"	Amy Clark, P., dis. Sept. 5, 1856, U. C., d. Jan. 1, 1881.
3,	"	Julia Ann Clark, P., (m. 1st James F. Jones, 2d Simeon P. Hurlbut,) dis.
3,	"	Amanda M. Clark, P., (w. Alonzo.)
3,	"	Amelia Melissa Hall, P., dis. Sept. 5, 1856, U. C.
3,	"	Emeline M. Hall, P., (m. O. C. West,) dis. Sept. 5, 1856, U. C.
July 5,	"	Minories Watrous, P., d. Jan. 22, 1882.
5,	"	Emilia A. Watrous, P., (w. Minories.)
5,	"	Gurdon W. Goodrich, P.
5,	"	Roxanna M. Goodrich, P., (w. Gurdon W.)
5,	"	Harriet R. Richmond, P., dis. Aug., 1855.
5,	"	Jane E. Niles, P., d. Jan. 29, 1851.
5,	"	Julianne B. West, P.
5,	"	Ann Alvord, P., (m. Noah S. Markham,) dis. June 23, 1861, to Glastonbury.
5,	"	Rosepha Ann West, P., (m. Henry B. Doane,) dis. Sept. 5, 1856.
5,	"	Cornelia N. Smith, P., (m. D. Watson Watrous,) d. June 13, 1866.

CONGREGATIONAL CHURCH OF EAST HAMPTON. 133

July 5, 1846. Jane E. Barstow, P., dis. April, 1853.
Sept. 27, " Annette Watrous, P., (m. Wm. E. Barton,) d. Mar. 11, 1863.
 27, " Rosanna Skinner, P., (m. Horatio D. Chapman), dis. 1854.
Oct. 30, " Eleanor Wells, L., (w. Asa,) d. Jan., 1849.
Nov. 1, " Mary Adeline Williams, P., (w. Alfred,) dis. Jan. 17, 1864.
 1, " Mary Elisabeth Norton Clark, P., (m. Reuben Payne,) dis. June, 1853.
April 30, 1847. Sarah E. Russell, L., (w. Rev. William,) dis. Aug. 3, 1856.
May 2, " Charles F. Rich, L., dis. Jan., 1855.
 2, " Julia A. Rich, L., (w. Charles F.,) dis. Jan., 1855.
Sept. —, 1848. Agnes Wier, L., (w. ———,) dis. May, 1850.
 —, " Dorothy Purple, L., (w. Nathaniel,) d. Sept. 20, 1879.
Jan. 28, 1849. Laura Bevin, L. from Westchester, (w. Abner G.,) d. Sept. 11, 1898.
July 1, " Alonzo Clark, P., d. Dec. 16, 1896.
May —, 1850. Joseph Russell, L., dis. Aug., 1855.
May 4, 1851. Elijah Ransom, L. from Colchester, dis. April 1, 1852. Colchester.
 4, " Sophia E. Ransom, L. from Colchester, (w. Elijah,) dis. April 1, 1852. Colchester.
 4, " Mary E. Sears, P., dis. Sept. 5, 1856, U. C.
July 6, " Helen M. Smith, P., (w. Henry S.,) d. Aug. 14, 1896.
 6, " Eliza C. Staplins, P., dis. April 1, 1852. Colchester.
Oct. 3, 1852. John W. Skinner, L. from East Haddam, dis.
 3, " Hannah A. Skinner, L. from East Haddam, (w. John W.,) dis.
Sept. 1, 1853. Frances A. Strong, (w. David,) L. from Middle Haddam, d. March 22, 1856.
Nov. 4, " Richard S. S. Clark, L. from North Ch., New Haven, dis. Sept. 6, 1874, to Mt. Carmel.
 4, " Elisabeth Strong Clark, (w. Richard S. S.,) L. from Bolton, dis. Sept. 6, 1874, to Mt. Carmel.
Jan. 5, 1855. Allen C. Clark, L. from Bolton.
 5, " Frances M. Clark, (w. Allen C.,) L. from Bolton, d. April 5, 1897.
— —, " (?) Rachel Holbrook, (wid. Chester,) L. from Bolton, dis. May 4, 1876, to Mt. Carmel.
July 2, " Clarine A. Skinner, P., (w. Henry.)
 2, " Rebecca A. Clark, P., d. Feb. 7, 1893.
 2, " Alice A. West, P., (m. Don Carlos Carpenter.)
 2, " Mary Matilda Sears, P., (m. 1st ——— Gold, 2d John Hanchett,) d. Dec. 22, 1875.

* * *

REV. L. H. PEASE, ACTING PASTOR.

Feb. 24, 1856. Isaac A. Bevin, L. from East Haddam, d. Sept. 28, 1883.
 24, " Huldah Ann Bevin, L. from East Haddam, (w. Isaac A.,) d. May 9, 1877.
Dec. 7, " Chauncey Bevin, P., d. Aug. 10, 1884.

Dec. 7, 1856. David Strong, P., dis. July 12, 1868. Winsted.
7, " Henry Emerson Niles, P.
7, " Lyman F. Skinner, P., dis. Dec. 25, 1870. Meriden.
7, " Diantha Carpenter, L. from M. E. Ch., (wid. Anson,) d. Nov. 9, 1873.
July 19, 1857. Festus E. Adams, P., d. Oct. 30, 1890.
19, " Eunice G. Adams, P., (w. Festus E.)
19, " Alexander N. Niles, P.
19, " William E. Barton, P., d. Feb. 9, 1895.
19, " Warren Skinner, P., d. Aug. 17, 1872.
19, " James M. Moore, P., dis. June 23, 1861. Broad Brook.
19, " Joel West Smith, P.
19, " Irvin H. Abell, P.
19, " Mary J. Watrous, P.
19, " Mary Purple, P., dis. to Middle Haddam, April 23, 1882, d. Oct. 18, 1888.
19, " Catharine Rich, P., (w. Denison A.)
19, " Josephine Barton, P., (w. Henry V.)
19, " Marion M. Markham, P., (m. John P. Purple,) d. Dec. 18, 1863.
19, " Anna Rich, P.
19, " Jane Bevin, P.
19, " Lavinia Bevin, P., (m. 1st J. B. White, 2d D. C. Norcutt.)
19, " Lavinia Snow, P., (m. Rufus D. Clark,) d. May 6, 1863.
19. " Charity Adams, P., (w. Augustus,) d. Dec, 27, 1877.
19, " Louisa M. Adams, P., d. Aug. 27, 1893.
Sept. 6, " Timothy D. Goff, P., d. June 12, 1886.
6, " Evelina M. Goff, P., (w. Timothy D.,) d. May 6, 1887.
6, " Sarah E. Goff, P.
6, " Lucy A. Goff, P.
6, " Mandana Moore, P., (w. James M.,) dis. June 23, 1861.
6, " Philanda E. Markham, P.
6, " Sophia Bailey, P., d. Dec. 20, 1879.
6, " Mary Emeline Hills, P., (m. Albert Parks.)
6, " Eleanor Melissa Hills, P., (m. Legrand S. Carpenter.)
— —, —, (?) William Dickson, L. from Glasgow, Scotland, d. Dec. 13, 1885.
— —, —, (?) Jane Dickson, L. from Glasgow, Scotland, (w. William,) d. Feb. 18, 1883.
— —, —, (?) Ellen Dickson, L. from Glasgow, Scotland, dis. March 20, 1859, to Middletown.
Jan. 3, 1858. Jerome L. Alvord, P., d. July 14, 1871.
3, " Emily V. Alvord, P., (w. Jerome L.)
3, " Sarah Skinner, P., (w. Warren.)
3, " Hannah Markham, P., (w. Alexander H.,) d. Jan. 9, 1881.
July —, " Jared C. Kellogg, L. from Hebron, d. Nov. 4, 1891.
—, " Frances M. Kellogg, L. from Hebron, (w. Jared C.,) d. Dec. 25, 1891.

CONGREGATIONAL CHURCH OF EAST HAMPTON. 135

REV. H. A. RUSSELL, PASTOR.

May	6,	1860.	Lorenzo Dow Rich, P.
	6,	"	Don Carlos Carpenter, P., d. Dec. 5, 1880.
	6,	"	Abner A. Bevin, P.
	6,	"	Leander A. Bevin, P.
	6,	"	Lucius H. Goff, P.
	6,	"	Clark O. Sears, P., d. Jan. 31, 1891.
	6,	"	Charlotte Josephine Sears, P., (w. Clark O.,) d. July 10, 1899.
	6,	"	Rufus D. Clark, P., d. March 22, 1869.
	6,	"	Henry Snow, P.
	6,	"	Legrand S. Carpenter, P.
	6,	"	Lavina A. Ackly, P., d. Jan. 30, 1881.
	6,	"	Ann Augusta Markham, P., (m. John M. Starr.)
	6,	"	Jane Elizabeth Calef, P., d.
	6,	"	Martha Geraldine Roberts, P.
	6,	"	Hattie West (Barton), P., (m. Henry T. A. Freeman,) dis. Dec. 29, 1867.
	6,	"	Caroline Tilden Carpenter, P., (m. 1st William P. Waite, 2d George F. Jones.)
	6,	"	Eunice Snow, L. from Wyoming, N. Y., (wid. Henry,) d. Jan. 9, 1875.
	6,	"	Sarah S. Russell, L. from Falls Village, (w. Rev. Henry A.,) dis. Aug. 1, 1865.
July	1,	"	William Henry Bevin, P.
	1,	"	Herman Elijah Rich. P.
	1,	"	Maria G. Strong, P., (w. David,) d. Feb. 2, 1865.
	1,	"	Martha Rich, P., (wid. Amos.)
	1,	"	Agnes Dickson, P., (m. Aaron F. Beebe.)
	1,	"	Ann Eliza Strong, P., (w. Nathaniel.)
Nov.	4,	"	John Watrous Barton, P., d. Oct. 9, 1867.
	4,	"	Victoria Gates Barton, P., (w. John W.,) (m. Geo. H. Buckland,) dis. Jan. 3, 1868.
	4,	"	Leverett Samuel Sexton, P., d. Feb. 2, 1865.
	4,	"	Matilda A. Sexton, P., (w. Leverett S.,) d. July 2, 1885.
Aug.	18,	1861.	Amy Fuller, L. from M. E. Ch., Haddam Neck, (wid. Sylvester,) dis. Oct. 7, 1866.
Feb.	2,	1862.	Louise D. Root, L. from Marlborough, (m. Prentice B. Skinner,) d Nov. 3, 1876.
July	20,	"	John C. Shepard, L. from Westchester, d. Nov. 27, 1897.
	20,	"	Mary A. Shepard, L. from Westchester, (w. John C.)
Jan.	4,	1863.	Cushman A. Sears, M. D., P., dis. July 21, 1867. Portland.
	4,	"	Evelyn H. (Lay) Sears, (w. Cushman A.,) L. from Old Lyme, dis. July 21, 1867. Portland.
June	14,	"	Clark Strong, L. from Fulton, Mo., dis. May 5, 1867. Winsted.
	14,	"	Juliette Strong, L. from Fulton, Mo., (w. Clark,) dis. May 5, 1867. Winsted.
Jan.	4,	1864.	Abby L. Markham, P., (w. F. George,) dis. June 14, 1867.
	4,	"	Nancy M. Skinner, P., (w. Lyman F.,) d. Nov. 16, 1864.
May	15,	"	Jane C. Bevin, L. from Westchester, (w. Philo.)

136   CONGREGATIONAL CHURCH OF EAST HAMPTON.

REV. G. D. PIKE, ACTING PASTOR.

— —, 1865. Mary Elizabeth Purple, L. from E. Haddam, (w. John P.,) dis. April 23, 1882, to M. Haddam.
— —, 1866. Eleanor Niles, P., (w. Henry E.,) d. March 9, 1895.
— —, " Celena Rose, P., (m. Henry Snow.)
— —, " Helen Dickson, L., dis. to Cromwell.
— —, " Catharine Dickson, L., dis. Nov. 4, 1866, to Glasgow, Scotland.
May 6, " Samuel B. Childs. P., d. April 13, 1892.
6, " Nelson Flood, P., d. May 11, 1877.
6, " Henry Skinner, P., d. April 14, 1892.
6, " Henry S. Smith, P.
6, " Hubert E. Carpenter, P.
6, " Anna Carpenter, P., (w. Hubert E.)
6, " Josephine W. Abell, P., (w. Irvin H.)
6, " Stella Niles Smith, P., (m. John W. Leslie.)
6, " Ella Kellogg, P., (m. 1st William H. Keney, 2d Charles H. Bullard,) dis. Jan. 9, 1887.
6, " Louisa L. Kellogg, P., (m. Frederick A. Lillie.)
6, " Dan. B. Niles, P., d. April 26, 1878.
6, " Mary E. Morgan, P., d. June 14, 1888.
6, " Ruth A. Carpenter, P., (m. Martin L. Roberts,) dis. June 9, 1878, to Howard Ave. Ch., New Haven.
6, " Alexander E. Ingraham, P., dis. to Guilford, July 12, 1868.
6, " Ozmer C. Hills, P., dis. to Colorado Springs, Col., Aug., 1880.
July 1, " Abby T. Shepard, P., (m. James Dickson.)
1, " Abby J. Morgan, P., (m. Waldo J. Gates,) dis. to Higganum.
1, " Maggie Dickson, P., (m. Nelson Flood,) d. Aug. 8, 1881.
1, " Maria L. Morgan, P., (m. Norman W. Spencer,) dis. June 18, 1876. Haddam.
1, " Mary F. Goff, P., (w. Lucius H.)
1, " D. Hawley Skinner, P., d. June 2, 1888.
1, " Gwinnett Carpenter, P.
1, " Henry T. Sellew, P.
1, " Gertrude A. Smith, P., (m. Alfred I. Kellogg,) dis. Oct. 16, 1870. Chippewa Falls, Wis.
1, " S. Jane Strong, P., (w. James H.)
1, " Amelia C. Demay, P., (w. Stephen R.,) dis. April 16, 1876. Cromwell.
1, " Julia B. Starr, P., (m. Asa Brooks,) dis. Dec. 25, 1870. E. Haddam.
1, " Chauncey G. Bevin, P.
Sept. 1, " Horatio D. Chapman, L. from East Haddam.
1, " Rosanna Chapman, L. from East Haddam, (w. Horatio D.,) d. Sept. 24, 1899.
May 5, 1867. Eliza Dutton, P., (m. Andrew Flood.)

CONGREGATIONAL CHURCH OF EAST HAMPTON. 137

REV. G. W. ANDREWS, PASTOR.

May 3, 1868. George W. Goff, P.
    3, " Stephen R. Demay, P., dis. April 16, 1876. Cromwell.
    3, " M. Adelaide Day, P., (w. Roderic,) d. May 10, 1897.
    3, " Lavina M. Markham, P., (w. E. Erskine,) dis.
    3, " Emma N. Payne, P., (m. Demas W. Cornwell,) dis. Feb. 29, 1876. Portland.
    3, " Florence A. Smith, P., (m. Newman E. Sears,) dis. Jan. 18, 1885.
    3, " Ida V. Shepard, P., (m. Lewis H. Markham,) dis. Feb. 17, 1895. Natick, Mass.
    3, " Nettie A. Watrous, P., (m. George M. Starr,) d. July 31, 1883.
    3, " Mary E. Riley, P.
    3, " Rev. George W. Andrews, L., from Bloomfield, Ohio, dis. Nov. 3, 1872. Montgomery, Ala.
    3, " Harriet W. Andrews, (w. Rev. George W.,) L. from Bloomfield, Ohio, dis. Nov. 3, 1872. Montgomery, Ala.
Nov. 1, " Alfred I. Kellogg, P., dis. Oct. 16, 1870. Chippewa Falls, Wis.
    1, " Jane C. A. Rich, P., (w. Lorenzo D.)
    1, " Mary Ann Cone, L. from Colchester, (w. D. Porter.)
Feb. —, " E. Morgan Norcutt, L. from U. C., dis. to Coventry.
May 2, " Jane M. Watrous, L. from 1st Ch., E. Haddam, (w. D. Watson.)
June —, " Bartlett S. Daniels, L. from M. H., d. April 25, 1878.
    —, " Florilla Daniels, L. from M. H., (w. Bartlett S.,) d. Aug. 2, 1880.
July —, " Laura P. Noetling, P., (w. William F. G., M. D.)
    —, " Jennette C. Trowbridge, P., (w. John G.,) dis. Westchester.

✦ ✦ ✦

REV. B. A. SMITH, ACTING PASTOR.

Dec. 25, 1870. Walter C. Clark, L. from Ottawa, Ont., dis. Jan. 20, 1878. M. E. Ch.
    25, " Eliza M. Clark, (w. Walter C.,) L. from Ottawa, Ont., d. Dec. 23, 1877.
Nov. 5, 1871. Rev. Burritt A. Smith, L., dis. June 16, 1876, d. June 16, 1899.
    5, " Ellen M. R. Smith, L., (w. Rev. Burritt A.,) dis. June 16, 1676. Worcester, Mass.
    5, " Anna M. C. Smith, L., (m. Fredk. P. Barnard,) dis. April 24, 1881.

✦ ✦ ✦

REV. JOEL S. IVES, PASTOR.

July 12, 1874. John M. Starr, P.
    12, " Howard N. Smith, P., dis. Dec. 20, 1886.
    12, " Kate L. Rich, P., (w. Herman E.)
    12, " Elisabeth B. Sellew, P., (w. Henry T.)

138   CONGREGATIONAL CHURCH OF EAST HAMPTON.

July 12, 1874. Lucy C. Strong, P., (m. Chauncey G. Bevin.)
    12,   "   Salome G. Strong, P.
    12,   "   Anna M. Barton, P.
    12,   "   Grace M. Smith, P.
    12,   "   Kate J. Dickson, P., (m. Amasa R. Darling.)
    12,   "   Elizabeth C. Chapman, P., (m. Thomas S. Brown.)
    12,   "   Anna S. Chapman, P., (m. Ferdinand W. Allis,) dis. Feb. 15, 1889.
    12,   "   Nellie M. Day, P., (m. James A. Forbes.)
    12,   "   Lizzie Jane Niles, P.,(m. Eugene T. Goodrich,) d. May 7, 1883.
    12,   "   Anna M. Bevin. P., (m. Henry C. Wadsworth.)
    12,   "   Anna J. Johnson, P., dis. June 13, 1880. Davisville, Cal.
    12,   "   Marilla C. West, P.
    12,   "   Maria L. Jackson, P., dis. Nov. 20, 1885. Savannah, Ga.
    12,   "   Irene M. Skinner, P.
    12,   "   Meda A. Lewis, P., (m. Abbott W. Arnold,) d. May 5, 1896.
    12,   "   Sophia B. Cone, P., (m. Hiram V. Childs.)
    12,   "   Imogene C. Skinner, L. from Glastonbury, (w. D. Hawley.)
Jan. 3, 1875. Rev. Joel Stone Ives, L. from Castine, Me., dis. Dec. 9, 1883.
    3,   "   Emma S. Ives, (w. Rev. Joel S.,) L. from Meriden, dis. Dec. 9, 1883.
Nov. 7, " Samuel T. Rodman, L. from Baptist Ch., Moosup.
    7,   "   Jennie C. Rodman, P., (w. Samuel T.)
    7,   "   Jennie A. Andrews, L. from South Glastonbury, (wid. Arthur,) (m. Amasa D. Kellogg,) dis. Nov. 6, 1878, to Cobalt.
May 7, 1876. Julia E. Haling, P., (m. 1st Lorin F. Morgan, 2d Charles Barber.)
    7,   "   Mary Jane Haling, P.
    7,   "   Annie E. Strong, P., (m. Judson J. Meigs,) dis. Dec. 14, 1890.
Mar. 4, 1877. Martin L. Roberts, P., dis. June 9, 1878, to Howard Ave. Ch., New Haven.
    4,   "   Samuel Kirby, P., dis. Dec. 23, 1887, to Middletown.
    4,   "   Mary L. Parks, P., (m. Edwin P. Kneeland,) dis. March 5, 1882, to Exeter.
    4,   "   Mary C. Buell, P., dis. Dec. 4, 1881, to Bap. Ch., Plantsville.
    4,   "   Belle Sellew, P., (m. Dan. B. Niles,) dis. Feb. 15, 1889, to 4th Ch., Hartford.
Jan. 6, 1878. George Royal, M. D., P., dis. April 16, 1882, to Rockville.
    6,   "   Albert W. Sexton, P.
    6,   "   Clayton L. Smith, P.
    6,   "   Wilbur F. Starr, P.
    6,   "   Gertrude E. Barton, P., d. Oct. 27, 1881.
    6,   "   Annette Barton, P., (m. Newton N. Hills.)
    6,   "   Mary Grace Markham, P.
    6,   "   Mary E. Sears, P., (m. Clayton L. Smith.)
    6,   "   Emily H. Skinner, P., (m. George B. Lord.)
Mar. 3, " Annie Davis Kirby, (w. Samuel,) L., dis. Dec. 23, 1887.
June 9, " Ellen M. Starr, (w. Wilbur F.,) L. from New Haven.

CONGREGATIONAL CHURCH OF EAST HAMPTON. 139

July	7,	1878.	Anna M. Bevin, P., (w. C. Clark.)
May	4,	1879.	Chauncey Clark Bevin, P.
	4,	"	Mary O. Markham, P., (w. Daniel N.)
	4,	"	Harriet E. Markham, P., (m. George Peck.)
	4,	"	Sarah E. Markham, P.
	4,	"	Ida Josephine Sears, P., d. Nov. 15, 1892.
	4,	"	Lizzie Adelaide Sears, P., d. June 28, 1886.
	4,	"	Hattie Rose Skinner, P., (m. Arthur M. Parks.)
	4,	"	Edith Delia Smith, P., (m. Geo. S. Stanton,) dis. Feb. 24, 1895.
	4,	"	Laura A. A. Chapman, P., (m. Jonathan W. Williams,) dis. Mar. 25, 1892. Colchester.
	4,	"	Carrie Veazey Sears, P., (m. Wm. B. Hills,) dis. Dec. 29, 1892.
	4,	"	Frank G. Steadman, L. from U. C.
	4,	"	Dolly Steadman, P., (w. Frank G.)
	4,	"	Julia C. Smith, (wid. William E.,) L. from Bridgeport, d. Oct. 8, 1886.
Feb.	8,	1880.	Sarah O. Sellew, P., b. Jan. 20, 1801, d. June 4, 1880.
Mar.	7,	"	Mary E. Arthur, L. from Episcopal Ch., M. H., (m. William N. Markham.)
July	4,	"	John S. Hall, L. from M. E. Ch., (Marysville, Mo.,) 1899.
Oct.	29,	"	Chauncey B. West, L. from Marlborough, d. Aug. 28, 1893.
	29,	"	Mahala West, (w. Chauncey B.,) L. from Marlborough.
	29,	"	Euphrasia West, (wid. Edmund,) L. from Marlborough.
May	7,	1882.	Daniel Brooks, L. from U. C., d. March 24, 1888, aged 90.
	7,	"	Clarissa Brooks, (w. Daniel,) L. from U. C., d. Oct. 18, 1899.
	7,	"	William I. Brooks, L. from U. C.
	7,	"	Cornelia W. Brooks, L. from U. C., (w. William I.)
	7,	"	Leon Sudley Tracy, P., dis. July 27, 1890. *New Haven.
	7,	"	Flora Eveline Rich, P., (m. Newell M. Goslee,) dis. June 20, 1895. Buckingham.
	7,	"	Eva Varina Rich, P.
	7,	"	Nellie Marie Banning, P.
	7,	"	Susie Diantha Carpenter, P., (m. Williard Kline,) Siebert, Ind.
Oct.	29,	"	Edward F. Bigelow, L. from Colchester, dis. Jan. 15, 1884. Portland.
Jan.	7,	1883.	George Bevin, L. from Northfield, d. July 9, 1892.
	7,	"	Amelia A. Bevin, (w. George,) L. from Northfield, dis. May 2, 1895. Leverett, Mass.
	7,	"	Robert H. Hall, L. from U. C.
	7,	"	Elisabeth A. Hall, (w. Robert H.,) L. from Columbia.
May	6,	"	Lorin F. Wood, M. D., P., dis. April 17, 1887, to Westerly, R. I.
	6,	"	Abbie E. Wood, P., (w. Lorin F.,) dis. April 17, 1887, to Westerly, R. I.
	6,	"	John W. Conant, P.
	6,	"	Alice Conant, P., (w. John W.)
	6,	"	Elisabeth C. Goff, P., (w. Harmanus W.,) d. Sept. 4, 1883.
	6,	"	Arthur M. Parks, P.

140   CONGREGATIONAL CHURCH OF EAST HAMPTON.

May 6,	1883.	Irving S. Brooks, P.
6,	"	Dora B. Baker, P., (m. W. W. B. Markham.)
6,	"	Eudosia S. Baker, P.
6,	"	Flora L. Baker, P., (m. Newton H. Markham.)
6,	"	Adeline E. Ackley, P.
6,	"	Maud E. Barton, P.
6,	"	Grace E. Conklin, P., (m. Frank W. Bevin.)
6,	"	Desdemona Reed, P.
July 1,	"	Charles H. Johnson, L. from New Britain, dis.
1,	"	Caroline C. Johnson, (w. Chas. H.,) L. from New Britain, dis.
1,	"	Fanny E. Hills, (w. Alphonso A.,) L. from U. C.
1,	"	Viola G. Hills, P., (m. Burton Brewer.) E. Hartford.
1,	"	Frances L. Skinner, P., (m. Charles D. Crosby.)
Sept. 2,	"	Mahala A. Hale, P., (w. Amos M.)
Oct. 28,	"	Josephine R. West, P., (w. Luman M.,) d. Aug. 15, 1884.

✦ ✦ ✦

REV. EDWARD P. ROOT, PASTOR.

May 24,	1885.	Margery Abell, P.
24,	"	Lois Josephine Barton, P.
24,	"	Angelina Hayes Beebe, P.
24,	"	Abbie Lay Chapman, P.
24,	"	Herbert Glover Clark, P.
24,	"	Clara Adeline Cone, P., (m. Arthur Willey.)
24,	"	Isadora Imogene Dickson, P.
24,	"	Ellen Augusta Flint, P., (m. Malcolm Brooks.)
24,	"	Houston Flint, P.
24,	"	Cornelia Elisabeth Goff, P., (m. Harry W. Strong.)
24,	"	Eugene Bulkley Goff, P.
24,	"	Jane Annette Goff, P.
24,	"	Lucy Bell Goff, P., (m. Sanford Chapman.)
24,	"	Frank L. Griffith, P., d. July 7, 1895.
24,	"	Clara Antoinette Griffith, P., (w. Frank L.,) (m. Daniel Burns.)
24,	"	Martha Maria Rich, P., (m. Norman B. Hurd,) dis. Oct. 6, 1893. New Britain.
24,	"	Pearl P. Shepard, P., (m. Halsey Mead, Jr.)
24,	"	Emma Maria Smith, P., (w. Burdette.)
24,	"	Lavina Louise Snow, P.
24,	"	Minnie Rose Snow, P.
24,	"	Laura F. Van Benthuysen, P.
24,	"	Ralph Carpenter Waite, P.
24,	"	Frederic Eugene Watrous, P., dis. 1892. Meriden.
24,	"	Josie Bell West, P., (m. William Demay,) dis. Nov. 4, 1897. Derby.
24,	"	Emma D. Goff, (w. George W.,) L. from Preston.
24,	"	Mary Bryant, (wid. Ira,) L. from New Haven, d. Oct. 28, 1887.

REV. EDWARD P. ROOT,
Pastor, 1884-1892.

CONGREGATIONAL CHURCH OF EAST HAMPTON. 141

May 24,	1885.	Rev. Edward P. Root, L. from Hampden, Mass., dis. Dec. 29, 1892.
24,	"	Fannie B. Root, (w. Edward P.,) L. from Hampden, Mass., dis. Dec. 29, 1892. .
July 5,	"	Winfield Veazey Abell, P., dis. Dec. 28, 1893. Columbia, S.C.
5,	"	Levi Dingwell Butler, P., d. July 3, 1894.
5,	"	Mary Ann Butler, P., (w. Levi D.)
Nov. 5,	"	Mary Annette Banning, P., (w. William W.,) d. May 7, 1889.
6,	1887.	George H. Mead, L. from Brooklyn, N. Y.
6,	"	Rebecca A. Mead, (w. George H.,) L. from Brooklyn, N. Y.
6,	"	Carrie Bell Mead, L. from Brooklyn, N. Y., (m. Wm. E. Hale, Jr.,) dis. Feb. 19, 1893, to Middletown.
6,	"	Halsey Mead, L. from Brooklyn, N. Y.
6,	"	Jennie A. Mead, (w. Halsey,) L. from Brooklyn, N. Y.
6,	"	Millie H. Mead, L. from Brooklyn, N. Y.
Dec. 30,	"	Elijah C. Barton, L. from U. C.
30,	"	Helen M. Barton, (w. Elijah C.,) L. from U. C.
30,	"	Henry Glover Clark, L. from U. C.
30,	"	Frances A. Clark, (w. Henry G.,) L. from U. C.
30,	"	Lyman H. Clark, L. from U. C.
30,	"	Julia E. Clark, (w. Lyman H.,) L. from U. C.
30,	"	Cynthia Chapman, (w. H. Ellsworth,) L. from U. C.
30,	"	Mary E. Gillett, (wid. Bennett,) L. from U. C.
30,	"	Margaret Haling, L. from U. C.
30,	"	Amelia M. Hall, L. from U. C., d. April 23, 1892.
30,	"	Mary E. Markham, L. from U. C., d. May 12, 1895.
30,	"	Carrie D. Sears, L. from U. C.
30,	"	William Utley, L. from U. C., d. Dec. 12, 1893.
30,	"	Emeline R. Utley, L. from U. C.
30,	"	Betsey L. Veazey, (wid. Warren,) L. from U. C., d. Jan. 21, 1897.
30,	"	John Watrous, L. from U. C.
30,	"	Leonora A. Watrous, (w. John), L. from U. C., d. Nov. 6, 1899.
30,	"	Elnora A. Watrous, L. from U. C.
30,	"	Laura Jane Wells, (w. Lyman O.,) L. from U. C.
30,	"	George H. White, L. from U. C., d. April 18, 1891.
30,	"	Ellen A. White, (w. George H.,) L. from U. C.
Jan. 1,	1888.	Walter C. Clark, L. from M. E. Ch.
1,	"	Hester Ann Clark, (w. Walter C.,) L. from M. E. Ch., d. June 12, 1895.
1,	"	Ann E. Mead, (wid. Halsey B.,) L. from Brooklyn, N. Y.
1,	"	Annie E. Mead, L. from Brooklyn, N. Y., d. Jan. 10, 1896.
1,	"	Catharine Mead, L. from Brooklyn, N. Y.
Aug. 31,	"	Clark M. Watrous, L. from Union.
31,	"	Mary Watrous, (w. Clark M.,) L. from Union.
Mar. 4,	1890.	Edwin D. Barton, L. from U. C.
4,	"	Marion L. Barton, (w. Edwin D.,) L. from U. C.

142   CONGREGATIONAL CHURCH OF EAST HAMPTON.

Mar. 4, 1890. Elisabeth Welch Bevin, (w. William H.,) L. from Bap. Ch., Bristol.
  4, " S. Mills Bevin, P.
  4, " Julia H. Bevin, (w. S. Mills,) L. from Brooklyn, N. Y.
  4, " Mary R. Goodrich, (w. Eugene T.,) L. from Westchester, dis. Sept. 5, 1895.
  4, " Lucy Deborah Barton, P.
  4, " Charles Davis Brooks, P.
  4, " Carrie May Brooks, P.
  4, " Crayton F. Carpenter, P.
  4, " Gertrude P. Clark, P., (m. James Evelyn Rich.)
  4, " Almira Elisabeth Sellew, P.
  4, " Emma Viola Sellew, P., (m. Crayton F. Carpenter.)
  4, " Ann Eulalie Strong, P., (w. Charles H.)
July 3, " Mary Watrous, L. from M. E. Ch., Bristol, (w. William M.,) dis. March 2, 1899, to M. E. Ch., Bristol.
Mar. 1, 1891. George Watrous, L. from Bap. Ch., Bristol, dis. 1892. Bristol.

※ ※ ※

REV. HENRY HOLMES, ACTING PASTOR.

June 23, 1891. Harriet J. Beckwith, L. from St. Paul's Ch., Willimantic, (w. Robert A.)
July 12, " Carl O. Johnson, P.
  12, " Dagoma Johnson, P., (w. Carl O.)
Sept. 16, " Rev. Henry Holmes, L. from St. Paul, Minn., dis. Oct. 8, 1893. Wis.
Nov. 8, " Amy Elva Carpenter, P., (m. Alfred J. Vingo.)
  8, " Carrie L. Clark, P.
  8, " Richard Flood, P.
  8, " Clifford C. Barton, P.
Dec. 26, " Lucy Whittemore Holmes, (w. Rev. Henry,) L. from Glenwood, Minn., dis. Oct. 8, 1893. Wis.
Jan. 10, 1892. Emma D. Alvord, P.
— —, " (?) Mary Wippert, P., dis. Sept. 9, 1897. Hartford.
Mar. 13, " Robert A. Beckwith, P.
May 8, " Frederic W. Arthur, P.
  8, " Catharine Arthur, (w. Frederick W.,) L. from Bap. Ch., Brooklyn, N. Y.
  8, " Sarah S. Smith, (wid. Nathaniel C.,) L. from U. C., d. March 12, 1896.
  8, " Sarah E. A. Chapman, L. from U. C.
  8, " Maude E. Chapman, P., (m. Irving H. West.)
July 3, " Annie Brainerd, (w. Harris R.,) L. from Colchester, d. Dec. 23, 1893.
  3, " Bessie C. Starr, (w. Vine B.,) L. from Middlefield.
  3, " H. Welton Porter, L. from Hebron.

REV. HENRY HOLMES,
Acting Pastor, 1891-1893.

CONGREGATIONAL CHURCH OF EAST HAMPTON. 143

July	3,	1892.	Kate Estelle Porter, (w. H. Welton,) L. from Hebron, d. May 26, 1895.
	3,	"	Milton Legrand Carpenter, P.
	3,	"	Ambrose Markham Starr, P.
	3,	"	George Henry Sellew, P.
	3,	"	William M. Watrous, P.
Sept.	11,	"	Peter Feld, P.
	11,	"	Lena Feld, P., (w. Peter.)
	11,	"	Jennie Marietta Rich, P.
	11,	"	Ola Maria Goff, P., (m. Albert J. West.)
	11,	"	Kirby Selden Carpenter, P.
Nov.	6,	"	Julia Gertrude Bevin, P.
	6,	"	Minnie Bolles Clark, P.
	6,	"	James Evelyn Rich, P.
Jan.	1,	1893.	Edith Niles Graham, P., (m. Frank E. Stearns.)
Mar.	5,	"	Marie Emma White, P., (m. Fred. F. Gates.)
	5,	"	Mabel Adeline Barton, P.

* * *

REV. C. W. COLLIER, ACTING PASTOR.

Mar.	4,	1894.	Louisa E. Brainerd, P., (wid. Oliver.)
	4,	"	Harris R. Brainerd, P.
	4,	"	Cassie Bell Brainerd, P.
Nov.	4,	"	Flora Holden, L. from Cobalt.
Jan.	4,	1895.	Rev. Christopher W. Collier, L. from White Oaks, Mass., dis. June 5, 1899. Orange, Mass.
	4,	"	Jennie Wheeler Collier, (w. Rev. C. W.,) L. from White Oaks, Mass., dis. June 5, 1899. Orange, Mass.
	4,	"	Ralph Eugene Carpenter, P.
	4,	"	Eva B. Carpenter, (w. Ralph E.,) L. from Marlborough.
Jan.	5,	1896.	Lola Marion Barton, P.
Nov.	1,	"	Lizzie Stevens, (w. Henry L.,) L. from Westbrook.
	1,	"	Jonathan W. Williams, L. from Colchester.
	1,	"	Laura A. A. Williams, (w. Jonathan W.,) L. from Colchester.
Jan.	3,	1897.	Lelia Alberta Field, P.
Mar.	7,	"	Irving H. West, P.
May	2,	"	James H. Anderson, L. from Colchester, dis. Dec. 15, 1899, Hope Presbyterian Ch., Philadelphia.
July	4,	"	Hayden L. Clark, L. from U. C.
	4,	"	Leonora N. Clark, (w. Hayden L.,) L. from U. C.
Sept.	5,	"	William Hoskins, P.
	5,	"	Lewellyn Lewis Rodman, P.
	5,	"	Lyman Horatio Clark, P.
	5,	"	Chester Benjamin Steadman, P., d. Oct. 19, 1897.
Oct.	3,	"	Lucy S. Smith, (w. Edward M.,) L. from Norwich Town.

REV. WILLIAM SLADE, ACTING PASTOR.

Nov.	6,	1898.	Marshall Bevin, P.
	6,	"	Bertha White, P.
	6,	"	Winfield Veazey Abell, L. from Columbia, S. C.
Mar.	4,	1899.	Olie Blanche Goodrich, P., (m. William Hoskins.)
	4,	"	Charles Kuhner, P., dis. Dec. 14, 1899, 3d Ch., Torrington.
July	2,	"	Leon S. Tracy, L. from Davenport Ch., New Haven.
	2,	"	Clara L. Tracy, (w. Leon S.,) L. from Davenport Ch., New Haven.
	2,	"	Gettine L. Purple, (w. Mayo S.,) L. from M. E. Ch., Haddam Neck.
	2,	"	Ida M. Sexton, (w. Albert W.,) L. from M. E. Ch.
Nov.	5,	"	Rev. William Slade, L. from 1st Congl. Ch., Williamstown, Mass.
	5,	"	Mary B. Slade, (w. Rev. William,) L. from 1st Congl. Ch., Williamstown, Mass.

List of Members, 1900.

Alice S. Childs, P., (wid. Samuel B.,) - - - - - - - - 1833.
John W. B. Smith, P., - - - - - - - - - - - - "
David W. Watrous, P., - - - - - - - - - - - 1842.
Laura A. Skinner, P., (wid. Samuel,) - - - - - - - - "
Amanda M. Clark, P., (wid. Alonzo,) - - - - - - - - 1846.
Emilia A. Watrous, P., (wid. Minories,) - - - - - - "
Gordon W. Goodrich, P. (Columbus, O.,) - - - ʹ - - - "
Roxanna M. Goodrich, P., (w. Gordon W.) (Columbus, O.,) - - "
Julianna B. West, P., - - - - - - - - - - - "
Allen C. Clark, L., - - - - - - - - - - - 1855.
Clarine A. Skinner, P., (wid. Henry,) - - - - - - - "
Alice A. Carpenter, P., (wid. Don Carlos,) - - - - - - "
Henry E. Niles, P. (Albany, N. Y.,) - - - - - - - 1856.
Eunice G. Adams, P., (wid. Festus E.,) - - - - - - 1857.
Alexander N. Niles, P. (Cottage City, Mass.,) - - - - - "
Joel W. Smith, P., - - - - - - - - - - - "
Irvin H. Abell, P., - - - - - - - - - - - "
Mary J. Watrous, P., - - - - - - - - - - - "
Catharine Rich, P., (w. Denison A.,) - - - - - - - "
Josephine Barton, P., (w. Henry V.,) - - - - - - - "
Anna Rich, P., - - - - - - - - - - - - "
Jane Bevin, P., - - - - - - - - - - - - "
Lavina Norcutt, P., (w. Dewitt C.,) - - - - - - - "
Sarah E. Goff, P., - - - - - - - - - - - "
Lucy A. Goff, P., - - - - - - - - - - - "
Philanda E. Markham, P. (Enfield, Conn.,) - - - - - "
Mary E. Parks, P., (w. Albert.) (Hebron, Conn.,) - - - - "
Eleanor M. Carpenter, P., (w. Legrand S.,) - - - - - "
Emily V. Alvord, P., (wid. Jerome L.,) - - - - - - 1858.
Sarah Skinner, P., (wid. Warren,) - - - - - - - "
Lorenzo D. Rich, P., - - - - - - - - - - 1860.
Abner A. Bevin, P., - - - - - - - - - - - "
Leander A. Bevin, P. (New York,) - - - - - - - "
Lucius H. Goff, P., - - - - - - - - - - - "
Henry Snow, P., - - - - - - - - - - - - "
Legrand S. Carpenter, P., - - - - - - - - - "
Ann Augusta Starr, P., (w. John M.,) - - - - - - - "
Martha G. Roberts, P., - - - - - - - - - - "
Caroline T. Jones, P., (w. George F.,) - - - - - - "
William H. Bevin, P., - - - - - - - - - - "

146   CONGREGATIONAL CHURCH OF EAST HAMPTON.

Herman E. Rich, P., - - - - - - - - - 1860.
Martha Rich, P., (wid. Amos,) - - - - - - - "
Agnes Beebe, P., (wid. Aaron F.,) - - - - - - "
Ann Eliza Strong, P., (wid. Nathaniel,) - - - - - "
Mary A. Shepard, L., (wid. John C.,) - - - - - - 1862.
Jane C. Bevin, L., (wid. Philo,) - - - - - - - 1864.
Celena Snow, P., (w. Henry,) - - - - - - - 1866.
Henry S. Smith, P., - - - - - - - - - "
Hubert E. Carpenter, P., - - - - - - - - "
Anna Carpenter, P., (w. Hubert E.,) - - - - - - "
Josephine W. Abell, P., (w. Irvin H.,) - - - - - "
Stella N. Leslie, P., (w. John W.) (Chippewa Falls, Wis.,) - - "
Louisa L. Lillie, P., (w. Frederick A.) (Manchester, Conn.,) - - "
Abby T. Dickson, P., (wid. James,) - - - - - - "
Mary F. Goff, P., (w. Lucius H.,) - - - - - - "
Gwinnett Carpenter, P., - - - - - - - - "
Henry T. Sellew, P., - - - - - - - - - "
S. Jane Strong, P., (wid. James H.,) - - - - - "
Chauncey G. Bevin, P., - - - - - - - - "
Horatio D. Chapman, L., - - - - - - - - "
Eliza Flood, P., (w. Andrew,) - - - - - - - 1867.
George W. Goff, P., - - - - - - - - - 1868.
Mary E. Riley, P. (Boston, Mass.,) - - - - - - "
Jane C. A. Rich, P., (w. Lorenzo D.,) - - - - - "
Mary Ann Cone, L., (wid. D. Porter,) - - - - - "
Jane M. Watrous, L., (w. D. Watson,) - - - - - 1869.
Laura P. Noetling, P., (w. William F. G.,) - - - - "
John M. Starr, P., - - - - - - - - - 1874.
Kate L. Rich, P., (w. Herman E.,) - - - - - - "
Elizabeth B. Sellew, P., (w. Henry T.,) - - - - - "
Lucy C. Bevin, P., (w. Chauncey G.,) - - - - - "
Salome G. Strong, P., - - - - - - - - "
Anna M. Barton, P., - - - - - - - - - "
Grace M. Smith, P., - - - - - - - - - "
Kate G. Darling, P., (w. Amasa R.,) - - - - - "
Elizabeth C. Brown, P., (w. Thomas S.,) - - - - "
Nellie M. Forbes, P., (w. James A.,) - - - - - "
Anna M. Wadsworth, P., (w. Henry C.) (Hartford, Conn.,) - - "
Marilla C. West, P., - - - - - - - - - "
Irene M. Skinner, P., - - - - - - - - "
Sophia B. Childs, P., (w. Hiram V.,) - - - - - "
Imogene C. Skinner, L., (wid. D. Hawley,) - - - - "
Samuel T. Rodman, L. (Hillstown, Conn.,) - - - - 1875.
Jennie C. Rodman, P., (w. Samuel T.) (Hillstown, Conn.,) - - "
Julia E. Barber, P., (w. Charles F.) (Terryville, Conn.,) - - - 1876.
Mary J. Haling, P., - - - - - - - - - "
Albert W. Sexton, P., - - - - - - - - - 1878.
Clayton L. Smith, P. (Bridgeport, Conn.,) - - - - - "

CONGREGATIONAL CHURCH OF EAST HAMPTON. 147

Wilbur F. Starr, P., - - - - - - - - - 1878.
Annette Hills, P., (w. Newton N.,) - - - - - - "
Mary Grace Markham, P. (Providence, R. I.,) - - - - "
Mary E. Smith, P., (w. Clayton L.) (Bridgeport, Conn.,) - - - "
Emily H. Lord, P., (w. George B.,) - - - - - - "
Ellen M. Starr, L., (w. Wilbur F.,) - - - - - - "
Anna M. Bevin, P., (w. C. Clark,) - - - - - - "
C. Clark Bevin, P., - - - - - - - - - 1879.
Mary O. Markham, P., (w. Daniel N.,) - - - - - "
Sarah E. Markham, P., - - - - - - - - "
Harriet E. Peck, P., (w. George.) (Westchester, Conn.,) - - "
Hattie R. Parks, P., (w. Arthur M.,) - - - - - - "
Frank G. Steadman, L., - - - - - - - - "
Dolly Steadman, P., (w. Frank G.,) - - - - - - "
Mary Markham, L., (w. William N.,) - - - - - - 1880.
John S. Hall, L. (Marysville, Mo.,) - - - - - - "
Mahala West, L., (wid. Chauncey B.,) - - - - - "
Euphrasia West, L., (wid. Edmund,) - - - - - - "
William I. Brooks, L., - - - - - - - - 1882.
Cornelia W. Brooks, L., (w. William I.,) - - - - "
Eva V. Rich, P., - - - - - - - - - "
Nellie M. Banning, P., - - - - - - - - "
Susie D. Kline, P., (w. Willard.) (Siebert, Ind.,) - - - "
Robert H. Hall, L., - - - - - - - - 1883.
Elisabeth A. Hall, L., (w. Robert H.,) - - - - - "
John W. Conant, P. (Mystic, Conn.,) - - - - - "
Alice Conant, P., (w. John.) (Mystic, Conn.,) - - - - "
Arthur M. Parks, P., - - - - - - - - "
Irving S. Brooks, P., - - - - - - - - "
Dora B. Markham, P., (w. William W. B.,) - - - - "
Eudosia S. Baker, P., - - - - - - - - "
Flora L. Markham, P., (w. Newton H.,) - - - - - "
Adeline E. Ackley, P., - - - - - - - - "
Maud E. Barton, P., - - - - - - - - "
Grace E. Bevin, P., (w. Frank W.,) - - - - - - "
Desdemona Reed, P. (Unknown,) - - - - - - "
Fanny E. Hills, L., (w. Alphonso A.,) - - - - - "
Viola G. Brewer, P., (w. Burton.) (East Hartford, Conn.,) - - "
Frances L. Crosby, P., (w. Charles H.,) - - - - - "
Mahala A. Hale, P., (w. Amos M.,) - - - - - - "
Margery Abell, P., - - - - - - - - 1885.
Lois J. Barton, P.. - - - - - - - - "
Angelina H. Beebe, P., - - - - - - - - "
Abbie Lay Chapman, P., - - - - - - - - "
Herbert G. Clark, P., - - - - - - - - "
Clara A. Willey, P., (w. Arthur,) - - - - - - "
Isadora I. Dickson, P., - - - - - - - - "
Ellen A. Brooks, P., (w. Malcolm,) - - - - - - "

148   CONGREGATIONAL CHURCH OF EAST HAMPTON.

Houston Flint, P.,   -   -   -   -   -   -   -   -   -   -   -   1885.
Cornelia E. Strong, P., (w. Harry W.,)   -   -   -   -   -   "
Eugene B. Goff, P.,   -   -   -   -   -   -   -   -   -   -   "
Jane A. Goff, P.,   -   -   -   -   -   -   -   -   -   -   "
Lucy B. Chapman, P., (w. Sanford,)   -   -   -   -   -   "
Clara A. Burns, P., (w. Daniel,)   -   -   -   -   -   -   "
Pearl P. Mead, P., (w. Halsey, Jr.,)   -   -   -   -   -   "
Emma M. Smith, P., (w. Burdett,)   -   -   -   -   -   "
Lavina L. Snow, P.,   -   -   -   -   -   -   -   -   -   "
Minnie R. Snow, P.,   -   -   -   -   -   -   -   -   -   "
Laura F. Van Benthuysen, P.,   -   -   -   -   -   -   "
Ralph C. Waite. P.   (New Haven,)   -   -   -   -   -   "
Emma D. Goff, L., (w. George W.,)   -   -   -   -   -   "
Mary A. Butler, P., (wid. Levi D.,)   -   -   -   -   -   "
George H. Mead, L.,   -   -   -   -   -   -   -   -   -   1887.
Rebecca A. Mead, L., (w. George,)   -   -   -   -   -   "
Halsey Mead, L.,   -   -   -   -   -   -   -   -   -   "
Jennie A. Mead, L., (w. Halsey,)   -   -   -   -   -   "
Millie H. Mead, L.,   -   -   -   -   -   -   -   -   -   "
Elijah C. Barton, L.,   -   -   -   -   -   -   -   -   "
Helen M. Barton, L., (w. Elijah C.,)   -   -   -   -   -   "
Henry G. Clark, L.,   -   -   -   -   -   -   -   -   -   "
Frances A. Clark, L., (w. Henry G.,)   -   -   -   -   -   "
Lyman H. Clark, L.,   -   -   -   -   -   -   -   -   -   "
Julia E. Clark, L., (w. Lyman H.,)   -   -   -   -   -   "
Cynthia Chapman, L., (w. Horace E.,)   -   -   -   -   -   "
Mary E. Gillett, L., (wid. Bennett,)   -   -   -   -   -   "
Margaret Haling, L.,   -   -   -   -   -   -   -   -   -   "
Carrie D. Sears, L.,   -   -   -   -   -   -   -   -   -   "
Emeline R. Utley, L.,   -   -   -   -   -   -   -   -   "
John Watrous, L.,   -   -   -   -   -   -   -   -   -   "
Elnora A. Watrous, L.,   -   -   -   -   -   -   -   -   "
Laura Jane Wells, L., (w. Lyman O.,)   -   -   -   -   -   "
Ellen A. White, L., (wid. George H.,)   -   -   -   -   -   "
Walter C. Clark, L.,   -   -   -   -   -   -   -   -   -   1888.
Ann E. Mead, L., (wid. Halsey B.,)   -   -   -   -   -   "
Catharine Mead, L.,   -   -   -   -   -   -   -   -   -   "
Clark M. Watrous, L.,   -   -   -   -   -   -   -   -   "
Mary Watrous, L., (w. Clark M.,)   -   -   -   -   -   "
Edwin D. Barton, L.,   -   -   -   -   -   -   -   -   -   1890.
Marion L. Barton, L., (w. Edwin D.,)   -   -   -   -   -   "
Elisabeth W. Bevin, L., (w. William H.,)   -   -   -   -   -   "
S. Mills Bevin, P.,   -   -   -   -   -   -   -   -   -   "
Julia H. Bevin, L., (w. S. Mills,)   -   -   -   -   -   "
Lucy D. Barton, P.,   -   -   -   -   -   -   -   -   -   "
Charles D. Brooks, P.,   -   -   -   -   -   -   -   -   "
Carrie M. Brooks, P.,   -   -   -   -   -   -   -   -   "
Crayton F. Carpenter, P.   (Waterbury,)   -   -   -   -   -   "

CONGREGATIONAL CHURCH OF EAST HAMPTON. 149

Gertrude P. Rich, P., (w. J. Evelyn,) - - - - - - - 1890.
Almira E. Sellew, P., - - - - - - - - - "
Emma V. Carpenter, P., (w. Crayton F.) (Waterbury,) - - "
Ann E. Strong, P., (w. Charles H.,) - - - - - - ¢ "
Harriet J. Beckwith, L., (w. Robert A.,) - - - - - 1891.
Carl O. Johnson, P., - - - - - - - - - "
Dagoma Johnson, P., (w. Carl O.,) - - - - - - "
Amy E. Vingo, P., (w. Alfred J.,) - - - - - - "
Carrie L. Clark, P., - - - - - - - - - "
Richard Flood, P., - - - - - - - - - "
Clifford C. Barton, P., - - - - - - - - "
Emma D. Alvord, P., - - - - - - - - - 1892.
Robert A. Beckwith, P., - - - - - - - - "
Frederic W. Arthur, P., - - - - - - - - "
Catharine Arthur, L., (w. Frederic W.,) - - - - - "
Sarah E. A. Chapman, L., - - - - - - - "
Maude E. West, P., (w. Irving H.,) - - - - - - "
Bessie C. Starr, L., (w. Vine B.,) - - - - - - "
H. Welton Porter, L., - - - - - - - - "
Milton L. Carpenter, P., - - - - - - - - "
Ambrose M. Starr, P., - - - - - - - - "
George H. Sellew, P. (New Haven,) - - - - - "
William M. Watrous, P. (Bristol, Conn.,) - - - - "
Peter Feld, P., - - - - - - - - - "
Lena Feld, P., (w. Peter,) - - - - - - - "
Jennie M. Rich, P., - - - - - - - - "
Ola M. West, P., (w. Albert J.,) - - - - - - "
Kirby S. Carpenter, P., - - - - - - - - "
Julia G. Bevin, P., - - - - - - - - "
Minnie B. Clark, P., - - - - - - - - "
James E. Rich, P., - - - - - - - - "
Edith N. Stearns, P., (w. Frank E.,) - - - - - - 1893.
Marie E. Gates, P., (w. Fred F.,) - - - - - - "
Mabel A. Barton, P., - - - - - - - - "
Louisa E. Brainerd, P., (wid. Oliver,) - - - - - 1894.
Harris R. Brainerd, P., - - - - - - - - "
Cassie B. Brainerd, P., - - - - - - - - "
Flora Holden, L., - - - - - - - - "
Ralph E. Carpenter, P., - - - - - - - - 1895.
Eva B. Carpenter, L., (w. Ralph E.,) - - - - - "
Lola M. Barton, P., - - - - - - - - 1896.
Lizzie Stevens, L., (w. Henry F.,) - - - - - - "
Jonathan W. Williams, L., - - - - - - - "
Laura A. A. Williams, L., (w. Jonathan W.,) - - - - "
Lelia A. Field, P., - - - - - - - - - 1897.
Irving H. West, P., - - - - - - - - "
Hayden L. Clark, L., - - - - - - - - "
Leonora N. Clark, L., (w. Hayden L.,) - - - - - "

150   CONGREGATIONAL CHURCH OF EAST HAMPTON.

William Hoskins, P., - - - - - - - - - 1897.
Lewellyn L. Rodman, P.   (Hillstown, Conn.,) - - - - "
Lyman H. Clark, P., - - - - - - - - - "
Lucy S. Smith, L., (w. Edward M.,) - - - - - - "
Marshall Bevin, P., - - - - - - - - - 1898.
Bertha White, P., - - - - - - - - - "
Winfield V. Abell, L., - - - - - - - - - "
Olie B. Hoskins, P., (w. William), - - - - - - 1899.
Leon S. Tracy, L., - - - - - - - - - "
Clara L. Tracy, L., (w. Leon S.,) - - - - - - "
Gettine L. Purple, L., (w. Mayo S.,) - - - - - "
Ida M. Sexton, L., (w. Albert W.,) - - - - - - "
Rev. William Slade, L., - - - - - - - - "
Mary B. Slade, L., (w. Rev. William,) - - - - - - "

www.ingramcontent.com/pod-product-compliance
Lightning Source LLC
Chambersburg PA
CBHW020245170426
43202CB00008B/229